STUDIES
IN THE
DEEPER LIFE

Advanced Bible Course

STUDIES
IN THE
DEEPER LIFE

A Scriptural Study of Great Christian Truths

E. W. KENYON

WHITAKER
HOUSE

Unless otherwise indicated, all Scripture quotations are taken from the American Standard Edition of the Revised Version of the Holy Bible. Scripture quotations marked (MOFFATT) are taken from *The Bible: James Moffatt Translation,* © 1922, 1924, 1925, 1926, 1935 by HarperCollins San Francisco; © 1950, 1952, 1953, 1954 by James A. R. Moffatt. Scripture quotations marked (KJV) are taken from the King James Version of the Holy Bible. Scripture quotations marked (WEYMOUTH) are taken from *The New Testament in Modern Speech: An Idiomatic Translation into Everyday English from the Text of "The Resultant Greek Testament"* by R. F. (Richard Francis) Weymouth. Scripture quotations marked (TWENTIETH) are taken from The Twentieth Century New Testament. Scripture quotations marked (ROTHERHAM) are taken from *Rotherham's Emphasized Bible,* 1901.

Bible translations by William John Conybeare (CONEYBEARE) are taken from *The Life and Epistles of St. Paul,* Scribner, 1858. Bible translations by Arthur S. Way (WAY) are taken from *The Letters of St. Paul to Severn Churches and Three Friends,* MacMillan and Co., 1906.

The forms LORD and GOD (in small caps) in Bible quotations represent the Hebrew name for God, *Yahweh* (Jehovah), while *Lord* and *God* normally represent the name *Adonai,* in accordance with the Bible version used.

Boldface type in the Scripture quotations indicates the author's emphasis.

STUDIES IN THE DEEPER LIFE:
Advanced Bible Course

Edited and compiled by Ruth Kenyon Housworth

Kenyon's Gospel Publishing Society
P.O. Box 973
Lynnwood, WA 98046-0973
www.kenyons.org

ISBN: 978-1-64123-405-4
Printed in the United States of America
© 2011, 2020 by Kenyon's Gospel Publishing Society

Whitaker House
1030 Hunt Valley Circle
New Kensington, PA 15068
www.whitakerhouse.com

1 2 3 4 5 6 7 8 9 10 11 ᜊᜈ 27 26 25 24 23 22 21 20

ABOUT PHOTOCOPYING THIS BOOK

CONTENTS

Lesson 1
THE INTEGRITY OF THE WORD

The Word is God speaking to you.

"Thus saith Jehovah" is repeated over two thousand times from Exodus to Deuteronomy.

God and His Word are one. The Word is always now.

> *The Logos of God is a living thing, active and more cutting than any sword with double edge, penetrating to the very division of soul and spirit, joints and marrow—scrutinizing the very thoughts and conceptions of the heart.* (Hebrews 4:12 MOFFATT)

And now, notice carefully the next verse:

> *And no created thing is hidden from him; all things lie open and exposed before the eyes of him with whom we have to reckon.* (verse 13 MOFFATT)

The Word is called the Logos. Jesus is the Logos, and the Logos is a living thing—not in the book, not on the written page, but in the lips of the believer.

There is no created thing hidden from Him, this living Word.

The Word searches us out, finds us.

This paragraph should be studied carefully.

THE WORD IS OUR CONTACT WITH GOD

- The Word is our contact with God the Father.
- It is His contact with us.
- John 16:8 reads, *"He…will convict the world in respect of sin, and of righteousness, and of judgment."*

WE ARE CONVICTED BY THE WORD

- This conviction can come from no other source than the Word. It is a threefold conviction:
  1. First, He convicts of our union with Satan: *"…of judgment, because the prince of this world hath been judged,"* (John 16:11) that the natural man is judged in Satan, is a child of Satan. (See John 8:44–45; 1 John 3:10.)
  2. Second, He convicts of righteousness, showing that although we are children of the devil, righteousness is available and belongs to us.
  3. Third, He convicts of sin because we believe not on *Him*. There is only one sin for which the sinner will be judged: that is the rejection of Jesus Christ.

WE ARE RECREATED BY THE WORD

- *"Of his own will he brought us forth by the word of truth, that we should be a kind of first-fruits of his creatures"* (James 1:18). (See also John 3:3–8.)
- *"Having been begotten again, not of corruptible seed, but of incorruptible, through the word of God, which liveth"* (1 Peter 1:23).

- The Word imparts to us eternal life. Were it not for the Word, we would not know that there was a redemption or a substitution or a new creation.
- Write out 2 Corinthians 5:17–18:

_____

_____

_____

OUR MINDS ARE RENEWED BY THE WORD

> *And be not fashioned according to this world: but be ye transformed [transfigured] by the renewing of your mind, that ye may prove what is the good and acceptable and perfect will of God.* (Romans 12:2)

> *And have put on the new man, that is being renewed unto knowledge after the image of him that created him.* (Colossians 3:10)

- The mind is renewed by studying the Word and by acting upon it. One may study the Word for years, but if he does not act it, live it, is not a doer, the mind is not renewed.
- James gives us the secret in James 1:22: *"But be ye doers of the word, and not hearers only, deluding your own selves."*
- Many Bible students are deceiving themselves because they are not acting, living, doing the Word.

WE ARE INDWELT BY THE WORD

- *"Let the word of Christ dwell in you richly; in all wisdom teaching and admonishing one another"* (Colossians 3:16). What does Paul mean by letting the Word dwell in us richly? This is one of the most striking sentences in this epistle.
- *"If ye abide in me, and my words abide in you, ask whatsoever ye will, and it shall be done unto you"* (John 15:7). The Word here is dwelling in us, producing prayer fruit. Read verse 8 carefully: *"Herein is my Father glorified, that ye bear much fruit; and so shall ye be my disciples."*
- It is prayer fruit. It is the Word bringing forth its own kind in the believer's life.
- It is not only committing the Word to memory, which is valuable, but it is letting that Word become an integral part of our beings. It lives in us.
- *"That Christ may dwell in your hearts through faith; to the end that ye, being rooted and grounded in love"* (Ephesians 3:17). Christ and the Word are one. It is the Word dwelling in you which is equivalent to Christ personally being in you.
- Letting the Word have right-of-way in your life is letting Christ have right-of-way. The Word dominating you is the Lordship of Christ in you.

WE ARE BUILT UP WITH THE WORD

> *And now I commend you to God, and to the word of his grace, which is able to build you up, and to give you the inheritance among all them that are sanctified.* (Acts 20:32)

- He commends us to the Word of His grace. This Word builds the Christ nature and the love nature of the Father into the individual. In other words, God is building Himself into us, making Himself a part of us as the Word dominates, rules, and satisfies our spirit nature.

- You cannot build one up spiritually on philosophies or theories about the Word, or on the history of the Word. We are only made spiritual by living in the Word and by the Word living in us.

WE ARE HEALED BY THE WORD

- *"He sent his word, and healed them"* (Psalm 107:20 KJV). How few of us have realized that it is the Word that heals us.

- We talk about faith in the Word—nothing wrong in that—but it is when Isaiah 53:4 becomes a reality in our spirit—*"Surely he hath borne our griefs, and carried our diseases* [marginal rendering]; *yet we did esteem him stricken, smitten of God, and afflicted"*—that it operates in our physical bodies.

- He was stricken and smitten with our diseases and sins.

- And then the Word declares, *"…with his stripes we are healed"* (verse 5).

- We read it and meditate upon it, and we know that it is true. *"I watch over my word to perform it"* (Jeremiah 1:12).

- We know that the Father watches over His Word, and that He will make that Word good in us.

- He said, *"Surely he hath borne our griefs, and carried our diseases."* Then we do not need to carry them. They cannot be a part of us because He put our diseases and sins on Jesus—*"Him who knew no sin he made to be sin on our behalf; that we might become the righteousness of God in him"* (2 Corinthians 5:21).

- The righteousness of God cannot be sick then and cannot be ruled by sin. Satan has no dominion over the righteousness of God unless we give it to Him.

- It is the Word that has made us know this. It is the Word that has saved us, recreated us, and it is the Word that heals us now. It is the Word that makes us masters of Satan.

- Mark 16:17: *"In my name shall they cast out demons."*

- It is the Word that has taught us the value of the name, the authority of the name, and our legal right to the use of the name. So it is the Word in reality that has healed us.

WE KNOW THE FATHER THROUGH THE WORD

For the Father himself loveth you, because ye have loved me, and have believed that I came forth from the Father.
(John 16:27)

That the world may know that thou didst send me, and lovedst them, even as thou lovedst me.
(John 17:23)

If a man love me, he will keep my word: and my Father will love him, and we will come unto him, and make our abode with him.
(John 14:23)

- These three Scriptures prove beyond the shadow of a doubt that the Father loves His children, these new creation folks, as much as He loved Jesus, and that it is a joy to make His home with them.

- What would it mean to have the Father and Jesus both living in your home? It would ensure the rent, the taxes, and all the bills, because the Father would pay His way and enable you to meet every obligation. How intimate He wishes to become with us. (See Matthew 6:31–33.)

FAITH COMES THROUGH THE WORD

> *The word of faith, which we preach.* (Romans 10:8)

> *Looking unto Jesus the author and perfecter of our faith.* (Hebrews 12:2)

- I used to wonder how we could look unto Jesus. Then, when I found that the Word and Jesus were one, I knew that by looking into the Word and acting on it, I brought Jesus on the scene instantly. And when I knew how faith is perfected by our acting on the Word, letting the Word loose in us, to live in us, dominate us, rule us, I had found the secret.
- *"They shall lay hands on the sick, and they shall recover"* (Mark 16:18). This means nothing until we act on it.
- *"In my name shall they cast out demons"* (verse 17). This Scripture means nothing until we act on it.
- *"That whatsoever ye shall ask of the Father in my name, he may give it you"* (John 15:16). This Scripture is useless, dead, until we act on it. It is acting on the Word that builds faith in the believer. You may have all the promises; you may have the mighty Spirit dwelling in you; but if you do not act on the Word, God is impotent in you. Acting on the Word makes Jesus vitally real to the believer. (See 2 Corinthians 5:7.)

THE WORD ON OUR LIPS

> *Because if thou shalt confess with thy mouth Jesus as Lord…with the mouth confession is made unto salvation.* (Romans 10:9, 10)

- It is the Word in my lips that counts. The Word becomes a living thing in the lips of the believer; it brings the unsaved man under conviction; it gives him faith to act on the Word; it causes the believer to *"trust in the LORD with all [his] heart"* (Proverbs 3:5 KJV).
- Your word becomes God's Word, and your lips become God's ambassador. God's Word in your mouth, fresh from the love in your heart, burns in the heart of the hearer.

FEEDING ON THE WORD

- Matthew 4:4: *"Man shall not live by bread alone, but by every word that proceedeth out of the mouth of God."*
- Jeremiah 15:16: *"Thy words were found, and I did eat them; and thy words were unto me a joy and the rejoicing of my heart: for I am called by thy name, O Jehovah, God of hosts."*
- Psalm 78:24–25: *"And he rained down manna upon them to eat, and gave them food from heaven. Man did eat the bread of the mighty."*
- Job 23:12: *"I have not gone back from the commandment of his lips; I have treasured up the words of his mouth more than my necessary food."*

HOW MUCH DO YOU REMEMBER?

1. What is the Word of God doing?
2. Give the three convictions by the Word.
3. Why is it necessary to hear the Word in order to be saved?
4. What is a renewed mind?
5. Discuss the difference between memorizing the Word and having the Word indwell you.
6. Quote the Scripture that shows we receive our inheritance through the Word.
7. Discuss how the Word brings healing.
8. What does it mean for you to act on the Scriptures that tell you that God is your Father?
9. How does the Word become effective in your lips?
10. Give Scriptures that show the need of feeding on the Word.

LESSON 1 NOTES

Lesson 2
THE PREVAILING WORD

The Word takes the place of the unseen Christ. Meditation in the Word is a visit with Him. The Word becomes a part of one by meditation. The Word living in us gets into our blood.

Acts 19:20 (KJV): *"So mightily grew the Word of the Lord and prevailed."*

A revival in Ephesus was shaking the nation. It was not Paul's preaching; it was not his logic or philosophy; it was the Word of God.

Acts 12:24 (KJV): *"But the Word of God grew and multiplied."*

It grew in the minds of the people. It gained the supremacy over them.

FAITH MAKES THE WORD PREVAIL

- Faith comes when the Word prevails over the thinking processes.
- In Matthew 8:23–27, we see the Word prevailing in Jesus's lips over the laws of nature. You remember that He said, *"Oh ye of little faith"* (verse 26).
- *"Then He arose, and rebuked the winds and the sea; and there was a great calm. And the men marvelled, saying, What manner of man is this, that even the winds and the sea obey him?"* (verse 26).
- The Word prevailed in Matthew 8:5–12. The Word in Jesus's lips prevailed over the disease in the Centurion's servant.
- In Matthew 14:13–21, the Word in Jesus's lips ruled the law of supply and demand. Five loaves and two fishes multiplied until five thousand people were fed and twelve baskets of fragments were left over.
- John 1:1–3: *"In the beginning was the Word, and the Word was with God, and the Word was God. The same was in the beginning with God. All things were made through him; and without him was not anything made that hath been made."*

JESUS AND THE WORD ARE ONE

- God honors the human language by calling Jesus the Word. The whole universe was brought into being by words. A Spirit spoke in Genesis 1:14–19. *"Let them be for lights in the firmament of the heaven to give light upon the earth"* (verse 15).
- The Word of God, a Spirit, creates material things, proving that the spirit is greater than the material.
- John 1:14: *"And the Word became flesh, and dwelt among us."*
- You see, we have the spoken Word in the lips of Jesus; then we have the Word made flesh dwelling in our midst; then we have the spoken Word in the lips of the apostles before the Pauline Revelation came.
- First Thessalonians 2:13 (MOFFATT): *"Wherefore, we also give continual thanks to God because when you heard from me the spoken Word, you received it not as the word of man but as it is in truth, the Word of God, Who Himself works effectually in you that believe."*
- While Paul was in Thessalonica it was the spoken Word, but his Epistles are the written Word, the life-giving Word.
- Psalm 107:20: *"He sendeth his word and healeth them."*

- And that Word was manifested in the flesh, as the spoken Word through the lips of Jesus, as the spoken Word through the apostles, and finally was put upon paper in the language of men so that we might have a permanent record of this living Word.

THE WORD PREVAILS OVER THE SENSES

- Romans 4:17–19 gives us a graphic picture of the Word prevailing over the fear and hope and sense knowledge in the mind of Abraham. God's Word was spoken through an angel to this man, and it declared: "(...A father of many nations have I made thee) before him whom he believed, even God, who giveth life to the dead, and calleth the things that are not, as though they were" (verse 17).
- And notice carefully the next sentence: "Who in hope believed against hope, to the end that he might become a father of many nations" (verse 18).
- Hope and faith were in combat. Faith won and made hope a reality.
- You remember Hebrews 11:1: "Faith is assurance of things hoped for."
- Hope is always in the future; it is a dream, it is never real.
- Faith reaches up and grasps hope and brings it into the realm of the present.
- Romans 4:19: "And without being weakened in faith he considered his own body now as good as dead (he being about a hundred years old), and the deadness of Sarah's womb."
- That man had hoped for a child. Now faith has changed the hope into reality.
- "Yet looking unto the promise of God [spoken through an angel], he wavered not through unbelief, but waxed strong through faith, giving glory to God, and being fully assured that what he had promised, he was able also to perform [would become a reality]" (verses 20-21).
- And so Abraham's faith was reckoned to him as righteousness. This righteousness gave the man a standing with God, the standing of a friend with God.

THE WORD IN OUR LIPS

- Acts 6:7 tells us that the Word of God increased as they preached and practiced what they had heard from the Master's lips. The Word began to develop and grow until it became a mighty force in the hearts of men and women. It was the prevailing Word.
- In my ministry, the Word has been a living, growing force. The Word is eternal. Like God, it is ever young, it is ever new.
- Matthew 24:35: "Heaven and earth shall pass away, but my words shall not pass away."
- It is a part of God…it is what God *is*.
- John 14:8, Philip has asked Jesus, "Show us the Father, and it sufficeth us." Jesus said, "Have I been so long time with you, and dost thou not know me, Philip? He that hath seen me hath seen the Father" (verse 9). Jesus and the Father were one. Jesus and the Word, the Logos, are one.
- In John 12:49–50, Jesus said,

    For I spake not from myself; but the Father that sent me, he hath given me a commandment, what I should say, and what I should speak. And I know that his commandment is life eternal; the things therefore which I speak, even as the Father hath said unto me, so I speak.

- You can see Jesus's fearlessness in the presence of disease and of demons. He was using the Father's Words and He knew that they could not fail.
- Second Timothy 4:2: "Preach the word; be urgent in season, out of season; reprove, rebuke, exhort, with all longsuffering and teaching."

- Jesus preached the Word and it healed the sick; it broke the power of demons over men.
- The apostles preached the Word, and the sick were healed, the dead were raised, and the multitudes were recreated.
- To preach the Word means to preach Christ, because Christ is the Word. To preach the gospel means to preach the Word, the good news.

THE WORD MAKES US LOVE

- Until the Word prevails, John 13:34–35 will never be known in the world: *"A new commandment I give unto you, that ye love one another; even as I have loved you, that ye also love one another. By this shall all men know that ye are my disciples if ye have love one to another."*
- Love was the prevailing power, that unseen something that governed the early church.
- First John 4:7–8: *"Beloved, let us love one another; for love is of God; and every one that loveth is begotten of God, and knoweth God. He that loveth not knoweth not God; for God is love."*
- Love here is proof of the new birth. Only the lovers have evidence that they have passed out of death into life, because they love the brethren. *"He that loveth not [his brother] abideth in death."* (1 John 3:14)
- He has never received eternal life, the nature of God. Only as the Word prevails in the heart do we actually know the reality of these divine things. The Word makes us love.
- First John 2:10: *"He that loveth his brother abideth in light, and there is no occasion of stumbling in him."*
- The Word of love prevailing in heart takes a man out of the realm of weakness and failure, where his words will cause offense, and his actions will lead others to do wrong.

THE WORD MAKES US CONQUER

- If he hates his brother, he is living in darkness. The Word has not prevailed in his life. He is walking as a common man.
- First Corinthians 3:3: *"For ye are yet carnal [ruled by the senses]: for whereas there is among you jealousy and strife, are ye not carnal, and do ye not walk after the manner of [common] men?"*
- How many believers, because the Word does not prevail in them, live as common men? Disease and sickness prevail over them because they do not walk in the light of the Word.
- In John 8:12, Jesus said, *"I am the light of the world: he that followeth me shall not walk in the darkness, but shall have the light of life."*
- As long as sickness prevails over you, you are walking in darkness. You mentally assent to the Word, but you do not act upon it. As long as you walk in poverty, and your testimony is of your needs and your lack, the Word has not prevailed in your life.
- Philippians 4:19 has no place in the life that is not dominated by the Word: *"And my God shall supply every need of yours according to his riches in glory in Christ Jesus."*
- When the Word prevails, you have plenty for yourself and for others.
- Philippians 4:13 has not yet gained the ascendancy in the unfruitful life: *"I can do all things in him that strengtheneth me."*
- A faltering, stumbling confession is present when the Word has not prevailed over your reasoning faculties, and when Christ and the Word have not become a reality.
- Romans 10:8: *"But what saith it? The word is nigh thee, in they mouth, and in thy heart: that is, the word of faith, which we preach."*

- My heart never recognized the secret of faith until I saw this truth: that the Word must prevail over my mind. When the Word became as real to me as the word of a friend or a banker, then faith ceased to be a problem.

- I no longer thought of faith or the need of it. You see, Jesus never intimated a need of faith. Why? Because He had the Father's Words. Did God say it? Yes! THEN IT IS!

- Psalm 27:1: *"Jehovah is my light and my salvation; whom shall I fear; Jehovah is the strength of my life; of whom shall I be afraid?"* Did He say that He is the strength of my life? Then He IS. I have all the strength I need for any emergency or any need.

- Do I lack wisdom? (Most of us do.) Well, 1 Corinthians 1:30 says that God made Jesus to be wisdom unto us. That means that we shall have ability to use the knowledge that is given to us in the Word, that we are no longer to walk in darkness, for we have the light of life.

- Colossians 1:13–14 has become a reality: *"Who delivered us out of the power of darkness, and translated us into the kingdom of the Son of his love; in whom we have our redemption."*

- Delivered out of weakness, out of spiritual blindness, delivered out of the old mental state of inability, we can now do all things in Him because He has become our ability.

- Second Corinthians 3:5–6 has become our very own: *"Not that we are sufficient of ourselves, to account anything as from ourselves; but our sufficiency is from God; who also made us sufficient as ministers of a new covenant."*

- The Word at last prevails. We are what He says we are. We can do what He says we can do. He is what He said He is, and no Word from Him is void of ability to make good in us.

HOW MUCH DO YOU REMEMBER?

1. Give examples of the prevailing Word in the four Gospels.

2. What makes the Word prevail?

3. Give three forms in which the Word exists.

4. What does Paul say about hope in Romans 4:17–19?

5. What does it mean to have the Word in our lips?

6. Can we walk in love if the Word does not prevail? Give scriptural proof.

7. How do we walk in the light?

8. What does walking in darkness mean?

9. What is the relationship between the Word and a victorious walk?

LESSON 2 NOTES

_____

_____

_____

_____

_____

_____

_____

_____

_____

_____

_____

_____

_____

_____

_____

_____

_____

_____

_____

_____

_____

_____

_____

Lesson 3
ACTING ON THE WORD

Believing demands action, creates action.

Mental assent admires, admits, but does not act.

Acting on the Word is letting Christ act through you. Acting on the Word, then, gives God an opportunity.

Giving the Word its place is giving Christ His position of Lordship.

The problem of believing is made simple when we know that it is acting on what God has spoken.

> *Everyone therefore that heareth these words of mine, and doeth them, shall be likened unto a wise man, who built his house upon the rock; and the rain descended, and the floods came, and the winds blew, and beat upon that house; and it fell not; for it was founded upon the rock.* (Matthew 7:24–25)

"Everyone who hears these teachings and acts upon them will be found to resemble a wise man who built his house upon the rock" (verse 26 WEYMOUTH). (The *"rock"* is "doing the Word." He that does not do that Word never builds upon a solid foundation.)

"And everyone that heareth these words and doeth them not, shall be likened unto a foolish man who built his house upon the sand."

The hearer must become a **doer**, or else the entire structure that he builds will be destroyed.

Jesus illustrates that. He made us know what acting on the Word really means.

The wise man is the **doer** of the Word. The other hears but does not act upon it. He is a sense-knowledge hearer. He is a mental assenter. He may be a vague, indefinite hoper, but he is not a **doer**. He responds to reason instead of the Word. His spiritual life is built on sand.

If he has faith in anything, it is in man, what man has done…science, works, organization, etc.

You can tell whether a man is building on the sand or on the rock, by noticing whether he is practicing or not, whether he is acting on the Word.

James 1:22–25:

> *But be ye doers of the word, and not hearers only, deluding your own selves. For if any one is a hearer of the word and not a doer, he is like unto a man beholding his natural face in a mirror: for he beholdeth himself, and goeth away, and straightway forgetteth what manner of man he was. But he that looketh into the perfect law, the law of liberty, and so continueth, being not a hearer that forgetteth but a **doer** that worketh, this man shall be blessed in his doing.*

THE SELF-DELUDED

+   The one who thinks that knowledge is all that is necessary will fail.
+   It is the doer of the Word, the man who practices it, lives it, walks in it, that builds it into his own life, whom God honors.

- There is grave danger of deluding our own selves.
- We know the Word. We may be familiar with the original Greek or Hebrew. We may know the history of the Word, but that is all wasted energy if we do not live in the Word, **practice it.**
- When you come to a hard place, and need money, you resolutely turn to the Lord, because you know that *"My God shall supply every need of yours"* (Philippians 4:19). You have taken your place. You act the part of a real believer. Instead of turning to the beggarly elements of the world, you turn to the Father.
- Or, if a loved one is sick, instead of being frightened, you remember the Word. Write out Isaiah 53:4:

_____

_____

_____

- We know it now. We act on that Word. We do not fear, we are not disturbed, because we know that the Word says that with His stripes we are healed.
- Or if some calamity has come, some rumor, the adversary has stirred things to our detriment, we know that the Word tells us, in Isaiah 54:17, *"No weapon that is formed against thee shall prosper; and every tongue that shall rise against thee in judgment thou shalt condemn. This is the heritage of the servants of Jehovah, and their **righteousness** which is of me."*
- You see, you can trust Him. You bank on Him. Your expectations are from Him. You do not turn to the beggarly help of sense-knowledge.
- We do the Word, we live the Word, we act the Word, we trust implicitly in the Word, and we know that God and His throne are back of every word. That gives us a quiet, restful confidence.
- John 15:9: *"Abide ye in my love."*
- You remember that He loves you and that you are born of that new kind of love. You remember 1 John 4:8: *"God is love."* And you remember that you are a partaker of His nature. (See 2 Peter 1:4.)
- And so, with a quiet confidence, you live love, you practice love. You are a doer of love. You are not a hearer only. You are not only an admirer of love, but you are an actual **doer.** You live in the love realm. You speak love, you walk in love, you live in that love.
- John 13:34: *"A new commandment I give unto you, that ye love one another, even as I have loved you."* You face that squarely and you decide it definitely in your own life, that you are going to love men *"even as."* That means that you are going to practice it.
- Men may not understand you. They may think that you are unwise. But you live this love life. You are taking Jesus's place, acting as Jesus would act. You are one that loves as Jesus loved, and you are not deluding yourself now; for in John 8:12, Jesus said, *"I am the light of the world. He that followeth me* [or practices what I teach]*…shall have the light of life."* You are going to prove to the world that you have the light.
- They that walk in human reason are walking in darkness, and they know not whither they go. They have deluded themselves. The great teachings are mere doctrines to them, a part of their creed. They will assent that it is true, but they dissent when you ask them to practice it.
- The one who loves as Jesus loved will not delude anyone else.
- There are Word-hearers, mere listeners—good talkers, but not **doers.**

- John 15:5: *"I am the vine; ye are the branches. He that abideth in me and I in him, the same beareth much fruit."* What kind of fruit is it? It is love fruit; it is faith fruit; it is prayer fruit. It is the same kind of fruit that Jesus bore. It will be doing what Jesus did.

- *"If ye abide in me and my words abide in you; ask whatever ye will, and it shall be done unto you"* (verse 7). The doer abides in Christ, and His words are living in him in the measure that he lives them, does them, practices them. All his decisions are made by the Word. He is living in the realm of the living Christ. Notice this eighth verse: *"Herein is my Father glorified, that ye bear much fruit; and so shall ye be my disciples."* What kind of fruit is it? It is the fruit that comes from doing the Word.

- The hearer may show many blossoms of promise, but it is the doer that delivers the ripened fruit. The Word lives in him; he lives in the Word. He is the fruit-bearing branch—a real doer. Prayer is a reality. He is not talking off into space. He is in the throne room in the presence of the Father. Here the name of Jesus is always honored. He receives that for which he asks.

- Did you notice, *"If ye abide in me and my words abide in you"*? That is the real doing of the Word, not just doctrine, but God speaking and God living in His own Word in us.

THE REAL DOER

- James 2:20 (MOFFATT): *"Faith without deeds is barren."* It is mere empty words—lovely, beautiful—but they are never crystallized or made real. Weymouth says, *"Without corresponding actions."*

- Unless you are a doer of the Word, you are not a believer of the Word. You have nothing but a mental assent without action, a mere empty profession of religion of words. Jesus would call them a sand foundation, just a sand house made by idle hands on the seashore to be destroyed by the next incoming tide.

- What a danger is a religion of words if there is no corresponding action. If one is not a **doer** of the Word, he is a foolish builder on the sand of the senses.

- First John 3:17–18: *"But whoso hath this world's goods and beholdeth his brother in need, and shutteth up his compassion from him, how doth the love of God abide in him? My little children, let us not love in word, neither with the tongue, but in deed and truth."*

- How does the love of God function in a man that only loves with words—empty words, idle words? He studies the Word, he knows all about the Word. He hears, he knows, but he does not **do**.

- Let us act love; let us do love. We are love's product, the sons and daughters of love. Love brought us into being, but we must let love do its perfect work in us. We must let love loose in us. Love bears the light. Then let love lead. Follow in the light of love. (See 1 John 1:5–6.)

- First John 3:19–23:

    Hereby shall we know that we are of the truth, and shall assure our heart before him: because if our heart condemn us, God is greater than our heart, and knoweth all things. Beloved, if our heart condemn us not, we have boldness toward God; and whatsoever we ask we receive of him, because we keep his commandments and do the things that are pleasing in his sight. And this is his commandment, that we should believe in the name of his Son Jesus Christ, and love one another, even as he gave us commandment.

- This is heart searching. When you can say, "God, you know that I am walking in the light of love, I am doing your Word;" then you persuade your heart. As you go into His presence for intercession, your heart is not fearful; your heart does not condemn you. Your heart is in perfect fellowship with this living Word and you have boldness in His presence, conscious that you are welcome. You make your petition in the name of Jesus, and you know that the Father hears you and that you have the petition of your heart. You are a **doer** of the Word. The Word is living in your lips. It is just as though the Master spoke it Himself.

+ That man gets what he prays for. We do the things that are pleasing to Him. In other words, we are taking Jesus's place. We are Father-pleasers just as Jesus was. (See John 8:29.)

+ It is a doer of the Word that receives things from God. Idle words may entertain men, but they do not reach God.

+ Ephesians 3:20: *"Now unto him that is able to **do** exceeding abundantly above all that we ask or think, according to the power that worketh in us."* Note the word **do**. We are doers of the Word. But you say, "How can I do it? I have not the ability to live this life." Well, He said that He is able to do exceeding abundantly above all that you ask or think, and it is going to be according to the ability of God that is at work within you.

+ Matthew 28:20: *"Lo I am with you always, even unto the end of the world."* He is with you in the living Word. He is with you in the presence of the mighty Spirit that lives in us. He hasn't left us alone, and He will not leave us alone. His ability is our ability; His strength is our strength.

+ As we begin to do the Word, He begins to do in us and through us. How it thrills us as we realize that 1 John 4:4 is absolutely true: *"Ye are of God, my little children, and have overcome them: because greater is he that is in you than he that is in the world."*

+ You are not of this world, even as Jesus is not of the world. You are here, but you are energized by Him. You have Him as your wisdom. 1 Corinthians 1:30 is absolutely true in your case. God has made Him to be wisdom unto you. He is your redemption as well. A redemption from your weakness and failure and lack of ability and ignorance. You are redeemed out of the fear of that.

+ Colossians 1:9 tells us that we have exact knowledge, complete knowledge, perfect knowledge. That knowledge is in the Word, when illuminated by the Spirit. This mighty One that is in us is taking out of the Word all that you need and bringing it into you as you study it.

+ Your walk now will be the fruitage of that Word. How it thrills us to be laboring together with Him. (See 2 Corinthians 6:1.) You are not working alone. Romans 8:31, *"If God is for us, who is against us?"*

(CONTINUED IN LESSON 4)

NOTE TO STUDENTS:

As we are limited in space, many of the Scripture references are not written out. We ask you, however, to look up these Scriptures and to study them carefully.

HOW MUCH DO YOU REMEMBER?

1. Describe the difference between mental assent and faith.
2. What illustration does Jesus use to teach that in order for a man's structure to stand, he must become a "doer" of the Word?
3. What does it mean to delude ourselves?
4. Why is it necessary for us to act on the Word?
5. What are the fruits of acting on the Word?
6. Show the relationship between walking in fellowship and a successful prayer life.
7. How does acting on the Word bring us the ability of the Father?
8. How can we act on Romans 8:31?
9. How can we walk in love? Explain.

LESSON 3 NOTES

_____

_____

_____

_____

_____

_____

_____

_____

_____

_____

_____

_____

_____

_____

_____

_____

_____

_____

_____

Lesson 4
WHAT THE CHURCH HAS FAILED TO SEE

God knew what He must do to redeem man. He knew the hopelessness of man under Satan's dominion.

Ephesians 2:12: *"That ye were at the time separate from Christ, alienated from the commonwealth of Israel, strangers from the covenants of promise, having no hope and without God in the world."*

First, the Gentile world was separated from Christ and Christ alone had eternal life. They were alienation from the commonwealth of Israel, did not have any share in the Abrahamic Covenant, and were strangers from the covenants of promise. They have no part in the common lot of Israel—*"Having no hope and without God."*

And yet, they were eternal beings.

That Scripture ought to make evangelists of every believer.

SATAN WAS CONQUERED BY JESUS

+ Hebrews 9:12: *"Nor yet through the blood of goats and calves, but through his own blood, entered in once for all into the holy place, having obtained eternal redemption."*

+ What God has said about our redemption has meant nothing to the multitudes in the church. To the teachers it is a theological fact, but it is not vital.

+ Ephesians 1:7: *"In whom we have our redemption through his blood, the forgiveness of our trespasses according to the riches of his grace."*

THREE MIGHTY FACTS

+ Here are three mighty facts: In Christ we have our redemption from Satan's dominion. It is an eternal redemption. It is operative now.

+ We have the remission of our trespasses. The word *"forgiveness,"* is not properly translated. It comes from the Greek word, *aphesis.* It should always be translated "remission." Remission means to wipe out everything we have ever done up to the time we come to Christ. No matter how much Satan has enwrapped us in his snares, the minute we are born again we stand before God new creations without the smell of our past life upon our spirits. The instant we are born again, we become the righteousness of God in Christ. (See 2 Corinthians 5:21.)

+ The instant that we become the righteousness of God, Satan's dominion over us is broken. Instead of being slaves of the adversary, we become masters of the adversary. Instead of circumstances lording it over us, we become the masters of circumstances.

+ Philippians 4:11 (Twentieth): *"Not that I speak in respect to want, for I have learned that in whatsoever state I am, therein to be independent of circumstances."*

+ Revelation 1:17–18: *"I am the first and the last and the Living one; and I was dead, and behold, I am alive for evermore, and I have the keys of death and of Hades."*

+ This One who has the keys of death and Hades is the Head and Lord of the new creation. Colossians 1:18: *"And he is the head of the body, the church: who is the beginning, the firstborn from the dead; that in all things he might have the preeminence."*

+ He is sitting upon the throne at the right hand of the majesty of heaven. Ephesians 2:6 declares that we are legally sitting with Him in heaven.

+ We were dead in our trespasses. He made us alive with Christ and raised us up with Him and He made us sit with Him in the heavenlies in Christ. That is our legal standing with God today, and the foundation of our legal rights.

+ The Holy Spirit through the Word can make our present vital right in redemption a reality. The days of weakness and failure are ended for the man who knows the Word and dares to act upon it.

THE REALITY OF THE NEW CREATION

+ This is not only a theological fact but a living reality.

+ Second Corinthians 5:17–18: *"Wherefore if any man is in Christ, he is a new creature: the old things are passed away; behold, they are become new. But all things are of God, who reconciled us to himself through Christ."* Now note it carefully, *"If any man is in Christ."* When we accept Christ as our Savior and confess Him as our Lord, we become a branch of the Vine. *"I am the Vine and ye are the branches"* (John 15:5). We become utterly one with Christ.

+ Second Peter 1:4 tells us that we become partakers of the divine nature and have escaped the corruption that came into the world through Adam's transgression. That corruption is spiritual death. The escape is eternal life.

+ *"I came that they might have life, and may have it abundantly"* (John 10:10). That word "life" is from the Greek word *zoe.* It means God's divine nature.

+ John 6:47: *"He that believeth hath eternal life."*

+ You see, the Spirit would have us know this fact: that believing is possessing. The instant that you believe, you have. You may mentally assent and never have. You may hope, and never have; but the instant you believe it is yours.

+ First John 5:13 is a reality in the new creation. *"These things have I written unto you that ye may know that ye have eternal life, even to you that believe on the name of the Son of God."*

+ The instant you believe you become a possessor of the Father's nature. You become as much a child of God as Jesus was in His earth walk. You may not have developed; you may not have taken advantage of your privileges as a son; but you are a son, an heir of God and a joint heir with Christ. Until we recognize that we are new creations, the very sons and daughters of God, we will never take our place.

+ *"Wherefore if any man is in Christ, he is a new creature."* In the mind of God, the old man has stopped being. A new man has taken his place, and Ephesians 4:23–24 has become a living, thrilling reality.

THE AUTHORITY OF HIS NAME

+ The church has never recognized the authority that has been given the name of Jesus. When God planned our redemption, He knew the measure of the ability of our enemy. He knew that Jesus had paralyzed the death-dealing power of the enemy. He knew that He must give us ability to dominate Satan and all his works; for if He did not, the new creation would fall prey to the adversary as the first creation had.

+ Second Corinthians 2:11: *"That no advantage may be gained over [you] by Satan, for we are not ignorant of his devices."*

+ The Scripture describes the adversary, tells us much about him. But it tells us more of what we are in Christ; and as we come to know our place in Christ, our rights and privileges, we become very conscious of any division in our walk. We know the moment we step out of love, we step into No-Man's-Land where the adversary gains the ascendancy.

- In 2 Corinthians 11:3, Paul says, *"But I fear, lest by any means as the serpent beguiled Eve in his craftiness, your minds might be corrupted from the simplicity and the purity that is toward Christ."*

- And so, when He left us, He gave us the sword of the Spirit—the Word.

- Ephesians 6:17 (KJV): *"And take the helmet of salvation and the sword of the Spirit, which is the word of God".*

- The sword of the Spirit is never used to wound or to slay men, but it is used against the adversary; for our combat is not against flesh and blood, but against principalities and powers, against the rulers of this world's powers. You see, we have come out of darkness into light, out of the kingdom of Satan into the kingdom of the Son of His love, and our combat is against the forces of darkness that surround us. For we are in the light and we walk in the light as He is in the light. That light is the Word. That light is love. That light gives us a fellowship, companionship with the Father and with Jesus.

- In 1 John 3:8, that Spirit tells us about Jesus. Write out the verse:

  _____

  _____

  _____

- But He is now sitting at the right hand of the Father. He is with us in the Word. His ability and wisdom have been given to us. But He is giving us one weapon besides the sword of the Spirit that Satan cannot withstand.

- You remember John 14:12–13 where Jesus said, *"He that believeth on me, the works that I do shall he do also; and greater works than these shall he do; because I go unto my Father. And whatsoever ye shall ask in my name, that I will do"* (KJV).

- You remember in John 16:23: *"In that day ye shall ask me no question."* So this does not mean prayer, but this is the use of Jesus's name in another form, in combat with the enemy and with the enemy's works. Jesus came to destroy the works of the adversary.

- Well, we are to take Jesus's place now and use His name just as Peter and John did in Acts 3:4. That impotent man held out his hand to Peter, sitting as he did at the Beautiful Gate of the temple. And Peter said, *"Look on us"* (KJV). And he gave heed, expecting to receive something from them. In the name of Jesus Christ of Nazareth, Peter raised him up and immediately his ankle bones received strength. And leaping up, he began to walk and entered into the temple with them walking and leaping and praising God. A miracle had happened, a startling manifestation of the living Christ.

- A crowd gathered about them and Peter said, *"And his name through faith in his name hath made this man strong, whom ye see and know"* (Acts 3:16 KJV).

- The disciples were arrested for this—locked up; but the next morning they were brought before the Sanhedrin, the same company of men who had judged Jesus and insisted upon His crucifixion. When they had brought the apostles, they said, *"By what power, or in what name, have ye done this?"* (Acts 4:7). And Peter said,

  > *If we this day are examined concerning a good deed done do an impotent man by what means he is made whole; be it known unto you all, that in the name of Jesus of Nazareth, whom ye crucified, whom God raised from the dead, even in him doth this man stand here before you whole.*
  > (Acts 4:9–10)

- Read carefully now the whole story in the fourth and fifth chapters and see how the name of Jesus conquered the Sanhedrin, defeated them thoroughly. They said, *"But that it spread no further among the people"* (Acts 4:17). They scourged them and sent them out and forbade their speaking that name. But the name had begun to do its mighty work. Multitudes were healed. Thousands upon thousands flocked into the city from the surrounding towns and were healed.

- The disciples were arrested again. Acts 5:19–20: *"But an angel of the Lord by night opened the prison doors, and brought them out, and said, Go ye, and stand and speak in the temple to the people all the words of this Life."*

- The Sanhedrin gathered in the morning. They sent officers to the jail to bring the disciples. When they came to the jail, they found the keepers standing at the doors, but when they opened the prison, the disciples could not be found. Then consternation filled the hearts of the Sanhedrin. They sent for the men who were preaching in the temple and brought them without violence.

- The high priest said, *"We strictly charged you not to teach in this name, and behold, you have filled Jerusalem with this teaching and attempt to bring this man's blood upon us"* (Acts 5:28).

- Peter answered, *"We must obey God rather than men. The God of our fathers raised up Jesus, whom ye slew, hanging him on a tree. Him did God exalt with his right hand to be a Prince and a Savior, to give repentance to Israel, and remission of sins"* (Acts 5:29–31).

- They were cut to the heart. They were staggered. A man named Gamaliel, a teacher of the law who had the honor of the people, commanded to put the men from them and said that a noble miracle had been done. He admonished them not to take further action for they might find themselves fighting against God. Then they called the apostles and charged them not to speak in the name of Jesus, and let them go.

- You notice that they did not object to the teaching of the resurrection, but they were afraid of the authority that that name held.

- Has that name lost any of its authority? The church has never used it. You hear them pray to Jesus and for Jesus's sake, but we hear almost no one pray intelligently to the Father in this name.

THE POWER OF ATTORNEY

- You see, Jesus gave us the power of attorney to use His name. John 15:16: *"Whatsoever ye shall ask of the Father in my name, he may give it you"* (KJV).

- And in John 16:23–24 we read, *"And in that day ye shall ask me no question. Verily, verily, I say unto you, if ye shall ask anything of the Father, he will give it you in my name…ask, and ye shall receive, that your joy may be made full."*

- Also, in Mark 16:17, we read in the Great Commission: *"And these signs shall accompany them that believe."*

- Then we find, *"And they went forth, and preached every where, the Lord working with them, and confirming the word with signs following"* (Mark 16:20 KJV).

HOW MUCH DO YOU REMEMBER?

1. What was the spiritual condition of the Gentile world before Christ came?
2. What three great things has redemption brought to us?
3. What is the meaning of the word *remission*?
4. Explain the secret of the new creation truth. What is the characteristic of the new creation?
5. How are we to use the sword of the Spirit?
6. What other great weapon has the Father given to us to use to combat the powers of darkness?

LESSON 4 NOTES

_____

_____

_____

_____

_____

_____

_____

_____

_____

_____

_____

_____

_____

_____

_____

_____

_____

_____

_____

_____

_____

_____

_____

_____

Lesson 5
THE WORD LIVING IN US

ENTERING INTO THE FAMILY OF GOD

+ One comes into the family of God by confessing the Lordship of Jesus over his life.
+ Romans 10:9–10:

  > If thou shalt confess with thy mouth the Lord Jesus, and shalt believe in thine heart that God hath raised him from the dead, thou shalt be saved. For with the heart man believeth unto righteousness; and with the mouth confession is made unto salvation.　(KJV)

+ And then in the eleventh verse, He climaxes it by saying, "*Whosever believeth on Him shall not be ashamed.*"
+ You see, the recognition of the Lordship of Jesus is the condition on which we receive eternal life.
+ Faith is not a creation of the intellect but of the human spirit; and when He says, "*Believe in thine heart,*" He means that our spirits act upon the Word.
+ So, with the heart man believes that Jesus is his righteousness, and then he makes a confession of his salvation, of the Lordship of Jesus over his life. "Lordship" really means "the bread provider," the one who sustains, protects, and cares for us. So, in the very beginning of the divine life, Jesus assumes the responsibility of our caretaker. We have Matthew 6:25–34. This is too long to quote in full, but Jesus gives His bird's-eye view of the Father's attitude toward His own children.
+ This was written for the new creation. The Jews could not understand it. Notice this: "*Be not anxious for your life, what ye shall eat, or what ye shall drink, nor yet for your body, what ye shall put on*" (Matthew 6:25).
+ He illustrates it by the Father's care for the birds, and says, "*Are not ye of much more value than they?*" (verse 26).
+ And then we show lack of wisdom in worrying over our finances, "*Consider the lilies of the field, how they grow; they toil not, neither do they spin*" (verse 28).
+ Then, in verses 30–32:

  > But if God doth so clothe the grass of the field, which to-day is, and to-morrow is cast into the oven, shall he not much more clothe you, O ye of little faith? Be not therefore anxious, saying, What shall we eat? or, What shall we drink? or, Wherewithal shall we be clothed? For after all these things do the Gentiles seek; for your heavenly Father knoweth that ye have need of all these things.

+ And then we have the climax in the thirty-third verse: "*But seek ye first his kingdom and his righteousness; and all these things shall be added unto you.*"
+ We are in His kingdom. Colossians 1:13: "*Who delivered us out of the power of darkness, and translated us into the kingdom of the Son of his love.*"
+ We have found His righteousness. Second Corinthians 5:21: "*Him who knew no sin he made to be sin on our behalf; that we might become the righteousness of God in him.*"
+ Then we are in the family. (Romans 8:14–16.)

- And in 1 John 3:1–2, we read, *"Behold, what manner of love the Father hath bestowed upon us, that we should be called children of God…Beloved, now are we children of God."*

- And now only are we sons, but we are heirs of God and joint heirs with Jesus Christ. God is our actual Father.

- John 16:27: *"For the Father himself loveth you, because ye have loved me."*

- If we are His children and if He is our Father, then He is responsible for us. If we take our place as sons, He is bound to take His place as a Father.

- John 14:23: *"If a man love me, he will keep my word, and my Father will love him, and we will come unto him, and make our abode with him."*

- *"If a man love me, he will keep my word."* That means that we are taking our place as sons. We will take the responsibility of sons. We will bear the burden of it, and we will enjoy the privileges of it. If we do that, then He will assume His place as a Father and will make His home with us, take care of us, and enable us to meet our obligations, enable us to walk in love and in wisdom, and to walk in the fullness of His fellowship.

- Philippians 4:13: *"I can do all things in him that strengtheneth me."*

- Here is the ability of God that becomes ours the moment that we come into the family.

- Write out Philippians 4:19:

_____

_____

_____

- That will be the end of worry, the end of fear. That will mean that God, our Father, has assumed the responsibility that came to Him when He gave us eternal life. Study this section very carefully.

- Proverbs 3:5–6: *"Trust in Jehovah with all thy heart, and lean not upon thine own understanding: in all thy ways acknowledge him, and he will direct thy paths."*

WE ARE HIS LOVE SLAVES

- This is the Master speaking to His love slaves. He is saying to us, in essence, "I want your heart trust, your fullest confidence. I make you wiser than your enemies. I can make you a master over circumstances."

- Philippians 4:11: *"I have learned in whatsoever state I am therein to be independent of circumstances"* (TWENTIETH).

- He wants us to know that we have His ability, that 2 Corinthians 3:4–5 is ours, written especially for us. *"And such confidence have we through Christ to Godward; not that we are sufficient of ourselves, to account anything as from ourselves; but our sufficiency is from God."*

- You have His ability in life's fight… it in the office, in the store, in the schoolroom, in the home. The mechanic has His wisdom at the bench. The judge and the lawyer both have access to His ability. There isn't a walk in life in which the believer finds himself, but what God's ability belongs to him, and that his Father is not watching over him, meeting his every need in every crisis.

- Psalm 27:1 belongs to this dispensation. *"Jehovah is my light and my salvation; whom shall I fear?"*

- Light means wisdom. Salvation is our redemption from Satan. I have no fear then, of anything that can happen. *"Jehovah is the strength of my life; of whom shall I be afraid?"* (Psalm 27:1)

No matter the condition—physical, spiritual, mental, or financial—your succor is at hand, your strength is God's ability at your disposal. You can sing Psalm 56:9, 11: *"This I know, that God is for me. …In God have I put my trust, I will not be afraid; what can man do unto me?"*

OUR FEARLESS SONG

+ Psalm 46:1 is yours: *"God is our refuge and strength, a very present help in trouble."*

+ He is able to meet every financial obligation when you trust Him utterly. But it will be necessary for you to go into business with Him, for you to be partners.

+ Malachi 3:10 should become a part of your daily consciousness:

> *Bring ye the whole tithe into the storehouse, that there may be food in my house, and prove Me now herewith, saith Jehovah of hosts, if I will not open you the windows of heaven, and pour you out a blessing, that there shall not be room enough to receive it.*

+ Now you people that have not been able to meet your obligations: you have had to make and to get loans, had sickness and expenses that should not have come to you. Notice the eleventh verse: *"I will rebuke the devourer for your sakes, and he shall not destroy the fruits of your ground: neither shall your vine cast its fruit before the time in the field, saith Jehovah of hosts."*

+ Satan has tried to keep you in bondage. One thing after another has happened that has kept your pocketbook drained. Now the Father has promised to watch over your finances so that you will have no unnecessary bills to meet. If you have a fearless confidence in Him, He will see that blessings shower in upon you. But if you are vacillating and trust Him today and doubt Him tomorrow, you will find yourself walking alone.

THE SENSE OF MASTERY

+ When you know that you are tied up with Him and that He is back of you, it gives you a sense of superiority. Isaiah 41:10 is peculiarly yours. *"Fear thou not, for I am with thee; be not dismayed, for I am thy God. I will strengthen thee; yea I will help thee; yea I will uphold thee with the right hand of my righteousness."*

+ Now notice this sentence: *"I am with thee."* He is in the home with you; He is in the shop with you; He is in the school with you. In essence, "Fear thou not for I am God Almighty, creator of the universe. I am your Father; I am watching over you. Be not dismayed, for I am thy God." I know of no other statement in Scripture that thrills me like that. "I am thy God—thy Father-God, the strength of your life, your wisdom, your ability. I am your 'bread provider.' I am your caretaker. I am all you need."

+ And then He whispers, "I will strengthen you, no matter what your work may be."

+ If it is physical strength, He is your sufficiency. If it is mental strength, He meets you. And if it is spiritual strength that will give you courage to face the impossibilities, He is there.

+ You notice, *"I am with thee,"* but that is in the old covenant. Now He says, *"Greater is he that is in you than he that is in the world"* (1 John 4:4).

REMEMBER THE GOD INSIDE

+ Israel could conquer all the armies that came against them, for God was with them. How much more can God do through us when we are conscious of His indwelling presence. When things press hard, we whisper softly, "He is inside of me, and the God inside of me is mightier than all the forces that can come against me." So, we rest quietly.

- And He says, *"I will uphold thee with the right hand of my righteousness"* (Isaiah 41:10).

- Well, Jesus is my righteousness so I am upheld by God's ability, and God's own righteousness invested in His Son, Jesus for me.

- There is one phase of this life that we haven't mentioned. It is so vague in the minds of most of us that we are the righteousness of God, and that 2 Corinthians 9:8 is ours: *"And God is able to make all grace abound unto you; that ye, having always all sufficiency in everything, may abound unto every good work."*

- You are not only going to meet your obligations, but you are going to be able to help in the cause of Christ. You will be able to distribute literature and books that will build up faith in others. You may be able to scatter abroad the message of eternal life. You will be able to give to the poor.

- And now notice the tenth verse. And you are going to increase the fruits of your righteousness. You are the righteousness of God. You can take Jesus's name. You know Mark 16:17–20. You know that the secret of Jesus's domination over demons, over the laws of nature over the works of the adversary, was because He was righteous. Now you have become righteous with His righteousness, just as you become strong with His strength, just as you can love because His love is shed abroad in your heart. Read Romans 5:5.

- You can love as He loved. You can rule the forces of darkness as He ruled them. You are not afraid of disease. You are not afraid of anything that may come. You are a master. You see, when we take these Scriptures seriously, knowing that God means exactly what He says to us, it lifts us out of the old ream of the weakness and failure. It is no longer "I can't," but, "I can do all things through Him who is my ability."

- He is anxious for us to increase the fruits of our righteousness in Christ so that we are enriched in everything. We are able to minister to the needs of those about us. Some of you have never been able to give much money. You may be able to, if you let Him loose in you. He can enable you to give. He can enable you to earn. He can cause people to give to you. It all depends upon your attitude toward what you are in Christ. Can you do all things through Him who strengthens you? Have you a right to use the name of Jesus?

- Don't you see, *"I am the vine and ye are the branches"* (John 15:5). Meditate upon this.

- Didn't He say, *"If ye abide in me, and my words abide in you, ask whatsoever ye will, and it shall be done unto you"* (John 15:7)?

- Can't the branch bear vine fruit? Is there any limitation?

- If you do not limit Him then you are limitless. If you let the limitless One dominate you and rule you, if you let His will be carried out in you, it would mean that you are taking responsibilities and privileges that you have never assumed before, if you will dare to say, "I can do all things. His ability is mine. His wisdom is mine. Therefore, I am what He says I am."

HOW MUCH DO YOU REMEMBER?

1.   What work does the living Word do in us?
2.   What does Romans 10:11 mean to us in our daily life?
3.   a. What is God's responsibility to us His children?

    b. What is our responsibility to Him as Father?
4.   What are the benefits of this righteousness?
5.   With what are His children equipped?
6.   What is the vocation of God's children?
7.   What promise is ours in keeping Malachi 3:10?
8.   What is the contrast between Isaiah 41:10 and 1 John 4:4?
9.   What work will you be able to do with the consciousness of being the righteousness of God?
10.   What will hinder the limitlessness of the living Word?

LESSON 5 NOTES

_____

_____

_____

_____

_____

_____

_____

_____

_____

_____

_____

_____

_____

_____

_____

_____

_____

_____

_____

_____

Lesson 6
THE REALITY OF REDEMPTION

Redemption has been a theological word in the minds of most believers.

We knew the Greek word. We knew its literal meaning, but we did not know the new meaning that the Father has put into it. So many of the Greek words used in the classical Greek have now a new and richer meaning in the Pauline Revelation, and so we are going to study redemption from perhaps a new angle. We will begin with Romans 3:21.

You remember that the key word for Romans is righteousness, or the ability to stand in the Father's presence without a sense of guilt or inferiority—stand there without condemnation or the sense of sin consciousness.

THE REASON

+ That could not be as long as we were under the dominion of an enemy. It could not be as long as that enemy's nature was in our spirits; so there must come a redemption from the nature of Satan and a redemption from the fear of Satan and of his works.

+ So the Spirit through the apostle, tells us a righteousness of God has been discovered, has come to light, and that righteousness comes to man through faith in Jesus Christ, and belongs to all those who acknowledge Christ as Savior and confess Him as their Lord. They are justified freely on the grounds of grace, through the redemption that God wrought in Christ. That redemption is based upon the fact that God laid our sins and diseases upon Jesus—that "Him who knew no sin, God made to become sin that we might because the righteousness of God in Him" (see 2 Corinthians 5:21).

HE PUT SIN AWAY

+ Not only did He become the sin-bearer, but God accepted His substitutionary sacrifice on our behalf. He was delivered up on account of our trespasses, for God made Him sin without sins. He was raised from the dead because He had put sin away; He had satisfied the claims of justice. After that, He was made alive in Spirit, that is, recreated. He was the firstborn out of death. After that, He was declared righteous and made a new creation by the life God imparted to Him. Then He met the adversary in his own kingdom and stripped him of his authority and took from him the dominion that he had over the world. When Jesus arose from the dead, He arose, not only because He had put sin away, but also because He had, as a substitute, conquered Satan. It was as though we, individually, had been the conquerors, just as though we had been there in that dark region and had conquered Satan, stripped him of his authority, and risen from the dead. Then Christ rose from the dead and redemption became a settled fact, a closed issue.

+ Now you can understand Ephesians 1:7–8:

_____

_____

_____

"IN WHOM WE HAVE"

+ Note carefully, *"In whom we have."* That means in Christ we have (present tense) our redemption out of the hand of the enemy, so that Satan no longer has dominion over us. We have our redemption from sin and its judgment. *"Sin shall not lord it over us because now we have entered the realm of grace through the new birth"* (Romans 6:14 TWENTIETH).

+ Write out Colossians 1:13–14: *"Who delivered us out of the power of darkness and translated us into the kingdom of the Son of his love; in whom we have our redemption; the forgiveness of our sins."*

+ Note carefully that we have been delivered out of the authority of Satan. He has no dominion over us. Don't let the opinions of theologians take away the reality of this fact. You are redeemed. Satan has no more right to reign over you than the Pharaoh of Egypt had to reign over delivered Israel in Palestine. We have been delivered out of Satan's authority, and we have been translated over into the kingdom of the Son of His love. Our all is now in Christ, the Son of His love, in whom we have our redemption. It is ours just as the money you have in your pocketbook that you earned honestly is yours. Now this redemption from Satan is a present-tense face, for you have the redemption now.

AN ETERNAL REDEMPTION

+ Hebrews 9:11–12:

    > But Christ having come a high priest of the good things to come, through the greater and more perfect tabernacle, not made with hands, that is to say, not of this creation, nor yet through the blood of goats and calves, but through his own blood, entered in once for all into the holy place, having obtained eternal redemption.

+ In the tenth chapter, it says that He not only obtained an eternal redemption for us, but that He sat down at the right hand of the Majesty on High. He carried His blood into the Holy of holies, and our redemption was sealed. The supreme court of the universe passed upon it and declared that whosoever accepted Jesus as Savior and confessed Him as Lord could come into God's family, and be free from condemnation.

+ Satan is eternally defeated. That redemption is an eternal redemption. God wrought it in His Son. That Son satisfied the claims of justice. That Son is seated at the head of the new creation at the right hand of the Father, and the new creation is free from the dominion of Satan. Christ is the head. You will enjoy your rights in this redemption as you know its reality.

+ Hebrews 9:15:

    > And for this cause he is the mediator of a new covenant, that a death having taken place for the redemption of the transgressions that were under the first covenant, they that have been called may receive the promise of the eternal inheritance.

+ It is very important that we know that Christ's death on that cross and His substitutionary sacrifice not only met our needs, but it reached back and cancelled all the promissory notes of that first covenant, so that every man that believed in the blood of bulls and goats and was covered by that blood was perfectly redeemed by the blood of Jesus carried into the Holy of holies. They were redeemed as servants; we are redeemed as sons.

+ Hebrews 9:26: *"But now once at the end of the ages hath he been manifested to put away sin by the sacrifice of himself."*

+ As long as one holds his redemption as a theory or as a doctrine, it will bring him no sense of reality, but as soon as he looks up and says, "Father, I thank Thee for my perfect redemption, that this body of mine is no longer under the dominance of Satan, that my mine and senses are no longer to be dominated by the adversary; I am free and by Thy grace I will not be entangled again in the yoke of bondage"—then, it is real.

THE NEW CREATION

+ As long as Christianity was simple forgiveness of sins to me with a theological justification, there was no sense of reality in it, but when I came to know that Jesus was recreated, and read, "*Thou art my Son, this day have I begotten thee*" (Acts 13:33), I know that He raised Him from the dead, now no more to return to corruption.

+ Colossians 1:18: "*And he is the head of the body, the church: who is the beginning, the firstborn from the dead; that in all things he might have the preeminence.*"

+ You see, Jesus was made sin with our sin. He became our substitute. We died with Him. We were buried with Him. We were judged with Him. He went to the place where we should have gone, and He suffered there until the claims of justice against us were met, until all the claims were satisfied. Then the grave could hold Him no longer.

+ First Peter 3:18 declares that He was made alive in spirit, that is, not of the Holy Spirit, but His own spirit; for He had died in spirit and His body had become mortal, so He must be made alive.

+ First Timothy 3:16 declares that He was justified in spirit. Now we understand the miracle of His substitution, for when He was recreated, we in the mind of justice were recreated.

+ Ephesians 2:10: "*For we are his workmanship, created in Christ Jesus for good works, which God afore prepared that we should walk in them.*"

+ That new creation took place just as our redemption took place, just as righteousness took place. Our new creation became a fact in the mind of justice the moment He was made alive in spirit.

+ Then, before He arose from the dead, He conquered Satan as our substitute. After Satan was conquered, his authority broken, Jesus arose from the dead and shouted to the disciples, "All Hail." Then He said to Mary, "*Touch me not, for I am not yet ascended unto the Father: but go unto my brethren, and say to them, I ascent unto my Father and your Father; and to my God and your God*" (John 20:17). In this we have the substitutionary work of God in Christ to make natural man a new creation.

+ Now we understand John 3:3. Jesus says to Nicodemus: "*Except a man be born anew from above, he cannot see the kingdom of God.*"

+ He answered Jesus, "*How can a man be born when he is old?*" (verse 4).

+ Jesus replied, "*Except a man be born of water and the Spirit he cannot enter the kingdom*" (verse 5).

+ Water, no doubt, means the Word. So, if a man is born of the Word and of the Spirit, he enters the kingdom of God.

+ You see, the difference between the natural birth and the new birth is that one of them is physical, and the other, spiritual. It is your human spirit that is recreated.

+ Now you can turn to 2 Corinthians 5:17: "*Wherefore if any man is in Christ, he is a new creature: the old things are passed away; behold, they are become new.*" Here is a description of the new creation that is unveiled to us in Romans 6:1–16, where we have the legal side of the new birth.

THE VITAL SIDE

+ This man that is in Christ is a new creation, a new species. He has received into his spirit the nature and life of God. When He did, the old nature that had dominated him passed away and a new nature took its place. "*But all things are of God, who reconciled us to himself through Christ, and gave unto us the ministry of reconciliation*" (2 Corinthians 5:18).

- But note carefully now that this man is in Christ. He has accepted Christ as his Savior and confessed Him as his Lord. (See Romans 10:9–10.) Second Peter 1:4 says that he made us *"partakers of the divine nature."*

- First John 5:13: *"These things have I written unto you, that ye may know that ye have eternal life, even unto you that believe on the name of the Son of God."*

- You can see that the new creation is brought into being by the life and nature of God, and this new creation is awaiting every unsaved man. The work is accepted, finished by Jesus when He sat down at the right hand of the Father. It was not finished on the cross. It was begun on the cross, but it was consummated when the blood was accepted and Christ was seated.

- It is necessary that we notice Ephesians 2:8–9: *"For by grace have ye been saved through faith; and that not of yourselves, it is the gift of God; not of works, that no man should glory."*

- The new creation does not come through our repentance or the surrendering of ourselves or the confessing of our sins, but it comes by grace pure and simple. All we do is to accept it. It is ours, a gift based upon legal grounds.

- What is grace? It is love unveiled in our redemption. It is the hungry heart of God assuming man's sins; yes, assuming the responsibility of man's creation, acting as though He were guilty of every sin that man committed.

- Now we understand Galatians 6:15: *"For neither is circumcision anything, nor uncircumcision, but a new creature."*

- No works that man could do would have any value. Why? Because every man was spiritually dead and the good things that he would do to redeem himself would be the works of a spiritually dead man. But God comes into the sense realm in the person of His Son, and that Son becomes sin on our behalf, assumes all that man had ever done and ever was and meets the claims of justice, satisfies the need of fallen man. Then He sits down at the right hand of the Father, and sends the Holy Spirit, who convicts men through the Word, and recreates them.

THE REVELATION OF GRACE

- He gave to Paul the revelation of His grace. This revelation is an unveiling of the finished work of Christ that is consummated in the new birth.

- You understand that all the plans of God were unveiled to us in the first covenant. He is pointing to the great event when God on the legal grounds can impart to man His own nature and make him a new creation. You can see how that forgiveness of sins would not touch the issue, that the confirming of a child by a priest could not reach the issue. There must be a new creation. That child must receive eternal life, the nature of God, for the natural man is without God. He is without hope, and he is in the world. He is Satan-ruled.

- It is very important that we understand the difference between forgiveness and the remission of sins. A man receives remission of sins when he is born again. He may receive forgiveness of sins after he is born again as often as he sins.

- You remember 1 John 1:9: *"If we confess our sins, he is faithful and righteous to forgive us our sins, and to cleanse us from all unrighteousness."*

HOW MUCH DO YOU REMEMBER?

1. What is the difference between theological redemption and Christ's actual redemptive work?

2. How does Christ's sitting at the right hand of the father affect us?

3. What does Jesus's victory over Satan mean to us?

4. Explain Hebrews 9:15.

5. Explain the expressions, "Jesus is the firstborn from among the dead."

6. Where does the Word tell us that sin had been put away?

LESSON 6 NOTES

_____

_____

_____

_____

_____

_____

_____

_____

_____

_____

_____

_____

_____

_____

_____

_____

_____

_____

_____

_____

_____

_____

_____

Lesson 7
OUR SOLID FRONT

Most of us have never realized the vital place that our testimony or confession holds in our daily life.

Colossians 2:5 (WEYMOUTH): *"For although, as you say, I am absent from you in body, yet in spirit I am present with you and am delighted to witness your good discipline and the solid front presented by your faith in Christ."*

Their solid front was a persistent, intelligent confession of what they were in Christ.

Philippians 1:27–28:

> *Only let the lives you live be worthy of the Good News of the Christ, in order that, whether I come and see you or, being absent, only hear of you, I may know that you are standing fast in one spirit and with one mind, fighting shoulder to shoulder for the faith of the Good News. Never for a moment quail before your antagonists.* (WEYMOUTH)

The twenty-eighth verse illustrates beautifully our solid front. *"Your fearlessness will be to them a sure token of impending destruction, but to you it will be a sure token of your salvation—a token coming from God"* (WEYMOUTH).

The Philippian believers had had a hard battle. The church was located in the prison keeper's home. It had come into being when Paul and Silas were imprisoned and God had set them free in such a miraculous way that the keeper had turned to God and a church had been formed in his own home. (See Acts 16:11–34.)

They had to put up a solid front or Satan would have absolutely overwhelmed them. The same thing is true today. Many are sick and weak and total failures because of their public confession. The Spirit speaks of that type of Christian.

BABES IN CHRIST

+ Hebrews 5:12–14 (WEYMOUTH):

> *For although, considering the long time you have been believers, you ought now to be teachers of others, you really need someone to teach you over again the very rudiments of the truths of God, and you have come to require milk instead of solid food. By people who live on milk I mean those who are imperfectly acquainted with the teaching concerning righteousness. Such persons are mere babes. But solid food is for adults—that is, for those who through constant practice have their spiritual faculties carefully trained to distinguish good from evil.*

+ This is a remarkable statement. When by reason of time we ought to be teachers, leaders, helpers of men, praying with the sick, we are still where others have to do the prayer for us. We are like the body of believers of whom James writes in James 5:14–16:

> *Is any among you sick? let him call for the elders of the church; and let them pray over him, anointing him with oil in the name of the Lord: and the prayer of faith shall save him that is sick, and the Lord shall raise him up; and if he have committed sins, it shall be forgiven him. Confess therefore your sins one to another, and pray one for another, that ye may be healed. The supplication of a righteous man availeth much in its working.*

+ These babes in Christ were sick. They needed to see the elder, feel the anointing oil upon their heads, hear the prayer, and feel the hands that were laid upon them. They lived in the realm of the senses. They had never developed to the point where they believed the Word that declared that *"with his stripes we [were] healed"* (Isaiah 53:5).

THEY HAD SENSE KNOWLEDGE FAITH

+ Isaiah 53:4–5 had never become a part of their lives. They mentally assented to it. They agreed that it was true; they acknowledged that it was true, but it wasn't theirs.

+ Let us read it:

> *Surely he hath borne our griefs, and carried our sorrows; yet we did esteem him stricken, smitten of God, and afflicted. But he was wounded for our transgressions, he was bruised for our iniquities; the chastisement of our peace was upon him; and with his stripes we are healed.*

+ You see, that is a settled thing. When Jesus arose from the dead and carried His blood into the heavenly Holy of holies, and that blood became the red seal upon the document of our redemption, He sat down, because His earthly work was finished. Our sin problem was settled; the righteousness problem was settled; the disease problem was settled; and Satan was defeated.

+ Hebrews 9:11–12 states that He had obtained an eternal redemption. That redemption reached down to this day and is ours. Satan knows that he is eternally defeated. Now every believer has a legal right to perfect healing and deliverance on the grounds of the finished work that Christ wrought.

+ It is not necessary to call for the elders or anyone else. All he needs to do is to turn to John 14:13–14: *"And whatsoever ye shall ask in my name, that will I do, that the Father may be glorified in the Son. If ye shall ask anything in my name, that will I do."*

+ The word "ask" is better translated "demand." All you need to do is to demand that Satan leave you, that he take with him the disease that he brought to you. Mark 16:17 tells us that *"In My name shall they cast out demons."* You are a master of demons because you and Jesus conquered Satan when you were raised together with Him and His resurrection.

+ Ephesians 2:4–6 makes the case clear:

> *But God, being rich in mercy, for his great love wherewith he loved us, even when we were dead through our trespasses, made us alive together with Christ (by grace have ye been saved), and raised us up with him, and made us to sit with him in the heavenly places, in Christ Jesus.*

YOU STAND BY YOUR CONFESSION

+ You can see now that you have a confession of a perfect deliverance, of a perfect healing from disease, of your dominion over the adversary; and in your confession now you can make a solid front before the world and the powers of darkness. They have no dominion over you.

+ You remember that Jesus said, *"The prince of the world cometh; and he hath nothing in me"* (John 14:30).

+ The same thing is true in your case. 2 Corinthians 5:17–19:

> *Wherefore if any man is in Christ, he is a new creature: the old things are passed away; behold, they are become new. But all things are of God, who reconciled us to himself through Christ, and gave unto us the ministry of reconciliation; to wit, that God was in Christ*

reconciling the world unto himself, not reckoning unto them their trespasses, and having committed unto us the word of reconciliation.

- If you are a new creation, Satan has nothing in you. That new creation is all of God. The old thing that Satan owned and controlled is all passed away, and the things that are in you now are all of God.

- When you know this as you know the multiplication table, you will have something that will absolutely put to flight the forces of Satan. There isn't any reason why we should live in constant fear of sin and doubt when we are the very sons and daughters of God.

- Write out Romans 8:15–16:

_____

_____

_____

- Then the old bondage of fear and want and disease is gone. You have another spirit now, a recreated spirit. God is no longer God to you: He is your Father, and as a Father, He is your lover and caretaker. You aren't afraid of anything now. You are absolutely fearless, and now you "put up a solid front" before all your enemies. You lift your banner; you shout His praises; you stand complete in Him over every circumstance and every attack of the enemy.

SOME FACTS OVERLOOKED

- When you came into the family of God, you made a confession of Romans 10:9: *"For ye received not the spirit of bondage again unto fear; but ye received the spirit of adoption, whereby we cry, Abba, Father. The Spirit himself beareth witness with our spirit, that we are children of God."*

- When you confess His Lordship, it is not only His dominion over you, but "lord" means "the bread-provider," the caretaker, the protector from all your enemies. He becomes at once the Lord of your life. His ability is back of you to protect. You actually become a partaker of the divine nature. (See 2 Peter 1:4.)

- And as you become a partaker of His nature, you become a partaker of His ability. God's ability becomes your ability. God's strength becomes your strength, and Jesus is the Surety of that new covenant for you. (See Hebrews 7:22.)

- When you acknowledge Him as your Lord, then God becomes automatically your very Father. All the resources of heaven are at your disposal.

- You ought to turn to 2 Corinthians 3:4–6:

  And such confidence have we through Christ to God-ward: not that we are sufficient of ourselves, to account anything as from ourselves; but our sufficiency is from God; who also made us sufficient as ministers of a new covenant.

- We have tried to conquer the adversary with our own strength. We have tried to overcome temptation with our own wills. That is unnecessary, for His will has become ours; His sufficiency is ours; His ability is ours. Now we become efficient as a member of the body of Christ with His efficiency.

- You have learned to yield to the God inside of you. As you walk on with Him, you become "God-inside minded" so that again and again during the day as you face life's problems, you remember that the Greater One is in you.

GOD-INSIDE MINDED

- Philippians 2:13 illustrates this for us: *"for it is God who worketh in you both to will and to work, for his good pleasure."*

- He is as work within you, solving your problems, building His strength into you, making His wisdom your wisdom, His ability your ability, His strength your strength.

- You can understand now that you are not common anymore. You belong to an unusual order of beings. You are a new creation created in Christ Jesus (see Ephesians 2:10), and you are created to an end to enter into a certain realm, to do His will, carry out His purposes here on the earth. You have a testimony now that is thrilling. You remember that your faith will keep pace with your testimony, that you will never have faith beyond what you confess; for there is a relation between your faith and your confession.

- If you are afraid to confess your oneness with Him, that His very life is your life, that His ability is your ability, that His strength is your strength, that His wisdom is your wisdom—if you are afraid to confess it, it is not yours. It is what you boldly say before the enemy that fills him with fear and you with courage and victory, that is yours in reality. If you are halting and have a negative confession, your faith will never rise above it.

- A negative confession shows a lack of appreciation on your part of Christ's victory over Satan. You are identified with Christ. When He conquered Satan, before He arose from the dead, you were with Him in that combat, and the victory that He achieved is laid to your account. All you have to do is to assume your place and say, "Satan, in His name leave me now;" or, "You leave that loved one."

- And when you quote Jesus's word, it is exactly as if He were speaking it Himself. You remember when Jesus said, in essence, "The words that I speak are not Mine, but the Father's" (see John 14:10). So, when Jesus commanded diseases to leave those bodies, it was the Father speaking. So, when you order disease to leave bodies in Jesus's name, it is as though the Father were speaking. But when you have a negative testimony and you talk about your lack and your weakness, the adversary takes advantage of your confession and brings you down to the level of it.

A VICTORIOUS CONFESSION

- In the school of Christ, you learn to say, "Thanks be unto God who always leadeth me in triumph in Christ!" In the school of Satan, you have learned a neutral or negative confession. And that neutral confession will bring you down to Satan's dominion and keep you there. Your life will be a failure. You will become a preacher of unbelief and of doubt and of fear.

- Learn to say with fearlessness, *"God is our refuge and strength, a very present help in trouble"* (Psalm 46:1).

- You have learned to shout with Isaiah 41:10: *"Fear thou not, for I am with thee; be not dismayed, for I am thy God; I will strengthen thee; yea, I will help thee; yea, I will uphold thee with the right hand of my righteousness."*

- That is victory. That is the conqueror. That is a positive testimony that shakes the very foundations of Hell. That brings glory to the Father; that brings joy to Jesus; that brings victory to our own spirit.

- As you maintain your "solid front," your testimony becomes richer and more helpful. The living Word becomes a part of your very being. Now you are acting and speaking the Word that lives in you, that is becoming a part of you. You are not bearing the fruits of righteousness.

- Second Corinthians 9:10: *"And he that supplieth seed to the sower and bread for food, shall supply and multiply your seed for sowing, and increase the fruits of your righteousness."*

HOW MUCH DO YOU REMEMBER?

1. What is meant by the term "solid front"?
2. How does Paul describe a babe in Christ?
3. Explain why we have a right to perfect healing and victory.
4. What part does our testimony or confession have in deliverance?
5. Explain Philippians 2:13.
6. What is the relation between your faith and your confession?
7. What is a negative confession?
8. What is a victorious confession?
9. What are the rewards of a victorious testimony?

LESSON 7 NOTES

_____

_____

_____

_____

_____

_____

_____

_____

_____

_____

_____

_____

_____

_____

_____

_____

_____

_____

_____

_____

_____

_____

Lesson 8
THE LAW OF PROSPERITY

God never planned that we should live in poverty, either physical, mental, or spiritual.

He made Israel the head of the nations financially.

When we go into partnership with Him, and we learn His way of doing business, we cannot be failures. Failures are not God-made. God never made a weakling or an inefficient man. He is purely a human product.

CO-LABORERS WITH GOD

+ Second Corinthians 6:1: *"And working together with him we entreat also that ye receive not the grace of God in vain."*

+ Few have ever taken advantage of this invitation and statement of fact. We are laborers with Him. We are partners with Him in carrying out His dream for the world.

+ First Corinthians 3:9: *"For we are God's fellow-workers: ye are God's husbandry, God's building."* The marginal rendering says, *"Ye are God's tilled land."*

+ Notice that this is a threefold statement:

+ First, you are God's fellow workers. He has called you to labor with Him; so whatever your work is, as long as you are in His will, He is a partner with you. You can't be a failure, for His wisdom is your wisdom; His ability in every department of life is your ability. All you need to do is to study the Word and get the knowledge that is imparted to you there. Then He will give you the ability to use that knowledge to make your life a success.

+ You see, He created all the vegetable world, so He knows everything that is in those vegetables. There isn't a single plant that He does not know about; and, we have reached a place in our chemistry where we need to know what is in those things. We know that woods that we have burned up have materials that can be made into planes and many other materials necessary to our advantage.

+ Well, God is our fellow worker so there isn't any limit to where we can go in chemistry. There isn't any limit in biology, because we have the wisdom and ability of God; and God created the chemicals and minerals, the oils, and the gases. He knows what is in them and He knows how to change them and to bring what we need out of them.

+ We may not know it, but His ability is our ability; and we know this: that no country where the Bible has not gone has ever had a patent law. They do not need one, for they have never created anything. But we new creation folks have the mind of Christ, and the ability of Christ. (See 2 Corinthians 2:16.)

+ We are getting to know these things. Can't you see now how we can become God's fellow workers?

+ We have been told that God would stand off at a distance and kind of order us around, but that isn't true. He has made himself one with us.

+ Take Jesus's illustration that we are all familiar with: *"I am the vine, ye are the branches"* (John 15:5). There is a oneness that cannot be challenged. The branch is just as much a part of the vine as the vine is a part of the branch, and the life flows into the branch and causes the branch to bear fruit. The branch will be like the vine now.

+ As God imparted to you His nature and His ability, that nature and ability will produce in you and through you the same kind of works that Jesus would do in our place.

- Jesus would know how to get the elements that we need out of the air, the vegetable world, or out of the water.
- We are laborers together with Him. We are fellow workers. He is interested in our progress and development. Then, if we will cultivate a close fellowship with Him, an intimacy, there is no limit to where we can go.
- First Corinthians 2:10–12:

  But unto us God revealed them through the Spirit: for the Spirit searcheth all things, yea, the deep things of God. For who among men knoweth the things of a man, save the spirit of the man, which is in him? even so the things of God none knoweth, save the Spirit of God. But we received, not the spirit of the world, but the spirit which is from God; that we might know the things that were freely given to us of God.

- Now those things are not spiritual things altogether. They are also things connected with chemistry, with biology, with metallurgy. For the Spirit created matter; the Spirit created chemicals and minerals.
- Now the Spirit has come into you and has brought to you the life and nature of the Father God.
- He wants to take over your senses, those five channels to your brain—seeing, hearing, tasting, smelling, feeling—and through these contacts with the earth, with physical things, He wants to unveil to you the treasures that He hid away in these natural things. You may seek His blessings, but as long as you refuse to cooperate with Him, He can't bless you.
- Notice that He said, "You are God's tilled land."
- The seed is not going to be sown, then, upon the rocky soil, nor the weed- and thorn-choked soil; but it is going to be sown in the heart that is responsive to the Spirit's uplifting pull.
- You are going to let Him draw you out; you are going to let Him unveil Himself to you; then you are going to bear fruitage that will glorify Him. You are to be the hundredfold soil.
- Think what it would mean to us if we would let God freely use us, and I believe that we are going to let Him do it.

RESURRECTION ABILITY

- You see, the natural man cannot understand the things of the Spirit of God, for they are foolishness to him. (See 1 Corinthians 2:14.)
- It requires a recreated spirit to grasp the things of God, whether those things be in the mental, physical, or spiritual realm.
- I think we ought to turn for a moment to Romans 5:17 and notice the Weymouth's Translation:

  For if, through the transgression of the one individual, Death [spiritual death] made use of the one individual to seize the sovereignty [here on earth], all the more shall those who receive God's overflowing grace and gift of righteousness [in the new birth] reign as kings in Life through the one individual, Jesus Christ.

- You understand now, that the gift of grace means the gift of eternal life that was given to us when we were made new creations, that is, when God's nature was imparted to us. You cannot separate God's nature from His ability, so when He imparted His nature to us, He expected that we would let that nature loose in us. It would then govern our entire intellectual processes, and our minds would be renewed in Him. Have you ever thought of that?

- Romans 8:29: *"For whom he foreknew, he also foreordained to be conformed to the image of his Son."*
- Write out Colossians 3:9–10:

_____

_____

_____

- Then Colossians 1:9–10 tells us, *"That ye may be filled with the knowledge of his will in all spiritual wisdom and understanding, to walk worthily of the Lord unto all pleasing, bearing fruit in every good work, and increasing in the knowledge of God."*

- Now we can understand that we have not only become partakers of the divine nature, but that divine nature can so absorb our intellectual processes that we have knowledge beyond anything that the natural senses can teach. We will have a knowledge greater than can be gained in any school or university. Natural processes cannot touch us, because God has become the source of a new type of knowledge.

- Let me illustrate: A friend of mine had been very anxious to find a certain alloy that would react upon metals and produce a certain result. The metallurgical world has been searching for that alloy for two generations. Some of the big companies had spent millions of dollars in research. This friend is a very devout man. One day he was up in the Rockies prospecting, as he always does when he has a few days off; and he cried: "Lord, won't You show me where that alloy is?" And a voice said, "It is in that rock."

- He took it for granted that it was the Lord and he said, "No, it isn't in that rock." The voice said again, "It is in that rock."

- He took it and put it in the smelter, but nothing came of it. However, as he kept trying, he discovered a secret. He put another metal with it, and lo and behold, he discovered a new alloy. He discovered that that rock was 80 percent a new alloy.

- How did he do it? His mind had become attuned to God's mind. God could talk to him. After years of experimentation, he produced the metal that the world had been looking for. No one could believe it until they saw the demonstration. He had arrived because he walked with God. That is the secret.

- Now, notice Romans 6:5 (weymouth) carefully: *"For since we have become one with Him by sharing in His death, we shall also be one with Him by sharing in His resurrection."*

- As you share in His resurrection, you share in the supernatural victory over death, over Satanic power, over everything that has held man in bondage throughout the ages. That resurrection meant a new kind of life—a resurrection life with a new kind of ability—resurrection ability. You are sharing this with Him as you let Him come into your life and share with you.

- John 14:23: *"If a man love me, he will keep my word: and my Father will love him, and we will come unto him, and make our abode with him."*

- That is God sharing with you. That is God coming into your life, into your home, and becoming one with you. Do you think that He likes to live in a home of poverty and want, in a house that is not properly heated, where children are not properly fed or clothed? Never.

- The law of prosperity is discovered in His making Himself one with us, and in our identification with Him in our earth walk. In that you will find the law that governs prosperity of the highest order. It is not the prosperity of the senses, which thinks that gold and political favor is prosperity. No, it is the ability to use the ability of God to help humanity.

+ God so loved the world that He gave His only begotten Son in order to help humanity back into prosperity and success.

+ Now John 3:16 has a new meaning for you. You can say, "I share in His resurrection. I share in His ability. I share in His grace. I share in His love."

WHAT IS PROSPERITY

+ Some say, "It is love. I am prosperous because I have a home of love. My children are love children. We live in a miniature heaven."

+ Yes, that is true; but hear what Jesus said in John 14:21: *"He that loveth me shall be loved of my Father, and I will love him, and will manifest myself unto him."*

+ That is prosperity; that is success, to have the Father love you, and Jesus love you, and Jesus unveil Himself to you. He does not unveil Himself as a man only, nor does He unveil Himself as God only, but in blessing and saving and giving to the world a new vision of life. He manifests Himself as a successful self, a victorious self, unto you.

+ Let us go back for a moment to the old covenant.

+ Malachi 3:10 tells us, *"Bring ye the whole tithe into the store-house, that there may be food in my house, and prove me now herewith, saith Jehovah of hosts, if I will not open you the windows of heaven, and pour you out a blessing, that there shall not be room enough to receive it."*

+ That is dollars and cents. That is grain. That is production in factories. That is a happy home. That is a victorious life.

+ What have you done? You have brought one tenth of your income, whether it is grain, coal, wood, materials, or manufactured goods. You brought one tenth to the storehouse, and upon the nine tenths God began to pour out His blessings.

+ He told you how to buy and how to sell. He told you how to save and how to accumulate. He made you efficient in your home, in mending and cooking. He made you wise in your business ability. His strength became your strength, His all-seeing eye was finding new prospects, new opportunities, new ways of doing things, shortcuts here and shortcuts there in production.

+ You are a partner, now, with the Creator's ability, and that ability is yours. (See 1 Corinthians 1:30.) All these things are yours. Now you rest in quiet confidence for you have within you the ability of the God who created the universe.

+ Now you can say with Paul, *"I can do all things in him that strengtheneth me"* (Philippians 4:13).

+ There is no power of Satan that can defeat you, for the Father has made you more than a conqueror through Jesus Christ.

HOW MUCH DO YOU REMEMBER?

1. On what grounds can we claim God's ability as ours in our daily work?
2. Explain Jesus's illustration of the vine and the branches in terms of His partnership with us.
3. What is the Holy Spirit's work in a successful Christian life?
4. Why is it necessary to have eternal life in order to be truly successful?
5. What does it mean to "share in His resurrection"?
6. What is the secret of the law of prosperity?
7. What is the Word's definition of prosperity? How does it differ from sense knowledge prosperity?
8. How can Malachi 3:10 apply to prosperity?

LESSON 8 NOTES

_____

_____

_____

_____

_____

_____

_____

_____

_____

_____

_____

_____

_____

_____

_____

_____

_____

_____

_____

_____

_____

_____

_____

_____

Lesson 9
THE SENSE-RULED MIND

The unrenewed mind is always waging war against unbelief, ever praying for faith but never arriving; always talking unbelief yet struggling to get faith; ever confessing failure, but at the same time confessing faith in the Word and denying it in actions; trying to believe, yet never acting on the Word.

James 1:5–8 describes this type of spiritual infant in Christ: *"But if any of you lacketh wisdom, let him ask of God, who giveth to all liberally and upbraideth not; and it shall be given him"* (verse 5).

Wisdom really belongs to you. The adult believer unconsciously turns to 1 Corinthians 1:30, where Jesus is made unto us wisdom; but the babe in Christ, the undeveloped believer, has not yet learned the secret of trusting the Word. He feels that he must do something in order to enjoy his privileges in Christ.

Verses 6–8 describes him: *"But let him ask in faith, nothing doubting: for he that doubteth is like the surge of the sea driven by the wind and tossed. For let not that man think that he shall receive anything of the Lord; a doubleminded man, unstable in all his ways."*

This sense-ruled mind is the companion of a recreated spirit, but the mind has never been renewed, so there is no real fellowship between the recreated spirit and the mind that is in contact with the world and largely ruled by it.

This believer does not know anything about Ephesians 1:3: *"Blessed be the God and Father of our Lord Jesus Christ, who hath blessed us with every spiritual blessing in the heavenly places in Christ."*

Here the believer is blessed with every spiritual blessing—wisdom, divine ability, strength, love, and every other thing that is necessary to make the believer's life beautiful, helpful, and victorious.

THE TWO CONFESSIONS OF THE DOUBLE-MINDED

+ First Kings 18:21 gives us a graphic description of that kind of a believer. Write out this verse:

_____

_____

_____

+ *"And Elijah came near unto all the people, and said, How long go ye limping between the two sides? if Jehovah be God, follow him; but if Baal, then follow him. And the people answered him not a word."*

+ Elijah was confronted with the problem of dealing with double-minded men. In the modern church, we have the same problem.

+ John 20:24–29 gives us a picture of the sense-ruled Thomas. You remember that after the resurrection, Jesus had appeared to a number of disciples. Thomas had not been with them and he cried, *"Except I shall see in his hands the print of the nails, and put my finger into the print of the nails, and put my hand into his side, I will not believe."*

+ He was a sense knowledge believer. He had to see in order to believe. His senses had to be satisfied. He could not take the Word of God independent of his senses.

+ We are confronted continually with that type of believer.

+ Now God in His great grace came down into the realm of the senses in the person of Christ. Then Christ arose from the dead and appeared among the disciples—let them see Him, hear Him, and feel Him.

+ First John 1:1–3:

> *That which was from the beginning, that which we have heard, that which we have seen with our eyes, that which we beheld, and our hands handled, concerning the Word of life (and the life was manifested, and we have seen, and bear witness, and declare unto you the life, the eternal life, which was with the Father, and was manifested unto us); that which we have seen and heard declare we unto you also, that ye also may have fellowship with us: yea, and our fellowship is with the Father, and with his Son Jesus Christ.*

+ You notice that *"that which we have seen and heard declare,"* is sense knowledge evidence. That was all right in the early church. During the first fifteen years, the early church lived very largely in the realm of sense knowledge faith. We have many today that cannot believe beyond what their senses register.
+ God let them see signs and wonders on the day of Pentecost because they were babes, just newborn. They knew nothing of the finished work of Christ. None of them believed or knew about His substitutionary work. That was to come later through the Pauline Revelation.

THE LAW OF THE SENSES

+ Galatians 5:16 gives us a very graphic picture of the senses and of the spirit: *"But I say, Walk by the Spirit, and ye shall not fulfil the lust of the [senses]."*
+ This Scripture will be of infinite value to you, for the senses war against the recreated spirit, and the recreated spirit is warring against the senses.
+ *"For these are contrary the one to the other; that ye may not do the things that ye would"* (Galatians 5:17).
+ The word, *"flesh,"* should have been translated, *"senses."* Then we could have understood it. You see, the five senses—seeing, hearing, smelling, feeling, and tasting—are all physical doors that lead to the brain. I know a thing is sweet because I tasted it. I know a thing is fragrant because I smelled it. I know it is hard because I struck it. What we call the sins of the flesh are sins of the senses. They are sins connected with the physical body, and this body of ours is the laboratory where we have learned all we know of secular knowledge.
+ The eighteenth verse goes further: *"But if ye are led by the Spirit, ye are not under the law."*
+ The Mosaic covenant had to do only with the senses. The new law that Jesus gave in John 13:34–35 has to do altogether with our recreated spirits.
+ So Paul continues in Galatians 5:19: *"Now the works of the flesh are manifest."* And he gives a long list of them. We are all familiar with it.
+ The battle that we fight in our daily walk is with our senses. I want the thing that I see. I may want to drink it. I may want to eat it. I may want to feel it. My spirit must govern my senses. My mind must be so renewed by knowing the Word and acting on the Word that I can easily conquer my senses.
+ Romans 12:1–2:

> *I beseech you therefore, brethren, by the mercies of God, to present your bodies a living sacrifice, holy, acceptable to God, which is your spiritual service. And be not fashioned according to this world: but be ye transformed by the renewing of your mind, that ye may prove what is the good and acceptable and perfect will of God.*

+ Here He is asking that our senses be turned over to Him.
+ You see, our bodies are really our universities, and our technical schools. How do I know anything about metallurgy except through the senses? How do I know anything about mechanics except through the senses?

- If a man is totally blind, he cannot be a mechanic. If you go a step beyond that and rob him of his hearing, now he is locked up to his senses of taste, smell, and feeling because sight and hearing are gone. Suppose you go a step beyond that, and he is paralyzed so that he has no feeling in his body. Now he is helpless. You see how utterly we are dependent on our senses and how all the knowledge we have comes through the senses.

THE NEW KIND OF KNOWLEDGE

- We have a new kind of knowledge—revelation knowledge. It is spiritual knowledge. It is knowledge that has come to use through the recreated spirit by acting on the Word and living in it.
- You understand that the mind cannot be renewed by the study of the Word. There must be a continual practice of the Word. The Word must live in me so that it becomes part of me. Just as my blood is a part of me, just as my muscles are a part of me, the Word must become a part of my very being.
- Romans 8:1–2 gives us a contrast: *"There is therefore now no condemnation to them that are in Christ Jesus"* (verse 1).
- Why? *"For the law of the Spirit of life in Christ Jesus made me free from the law of sin and of death"* (verse 2).
- The Ten Commandments were the law of sin and of death. The law had to do with spiritually dead men. The recreated man, this new man in Christ, has a new law, which is the law of the spirit of life.
- That is love. He is governed by love. The other man is governed by fear. If you will read carefully the Old Testament, you will find that God says, again and again, in essence, "There is no fear of Jehovah before you." He does not say "love."
- Malachi 3:16: *"Then they that feared Jehovah spake one with another."*
- And in Malachi 4:2: *"But unto you that fear my name."*
- And in verse 6, He says, *"And if I am a master, where is my fear? saith Jehovah of hosts unto you, O priests, that despise my name."*
- The law of Moses begat fear in spiritually dead men. The law of the new covenant begets love, faith, and confidence in the new creation. So, the law of the spirit of life is the law of love.
- Romans 8:6–9:

  > *For the mind of the flesh is death; but the mind of the Spirit is life and peace: because the mind of the flesh is enmity against God* [that is the reason that it is death]; *for it is not subject to the law of God* [as is the new law of love], *neither indeed can it be: and they that are in the flesh cannot please God* [that is, they that are ruled and governed by the senses cannot please God]. *But ye are not in the flesh but in the Spirit, if so be that the Spirit of God dwelleth in you.*

- Then He says the most remarkable thing, *"But if any man hath not the Spirit of Christ, he is none of his"* (verse 9).
- In other words, if he is not ruled by the spirit that dominated Jesus—not the Holy Spirit—he does not have a part with Him. That spirit was love. That spirit drove Jesus to the cross, and no man that does not walk in love and live the love life and who is not governed by love has any knowledge of the things of the new creation.
- You want evidence for it? First John 4:7–8: *"Beloved, let us love one another: for love is of God; and every one that loveth is begotten of God, and knoweth God. He that loveth not knoweth not God; for God is love."*
- The new creation is a love creation, and the man that is not born again can't understand this love life.

- First Corinthians 2:14: "*Now the natural man understandeth not the things of the Spirit of God for they are foolishness to him.*"
- And in verse 12: "*But we received, not the spirit of the world, but the spirit which is from God; that we might know the things that were freely given to us of God.*"
- And you cannot know the things that are freely given to us of the Father until you are recreated and the law of the new creation becomes a part of your very being. That law of love becomes instinctive in you so that you do it just as a hungry man eats, as a thirsty man drinks. So, you live the love life.

THE DARKNESS OF THE SENSE-RULED MIND

- First John 2:9–11:

   He that saith he is in the light and hateth his brother, is in the darkness even until now. He that loveth his brother abideth in the light, and there is no occasion of stumbling in him. But he that hateth his brother is in the darkness, and walketh in the darkness, and knoweth not whither he goeth, because the darkness hath blinded his eyes.

- Here is the condition of the believer whose mind has never been renewed. He is walking according to the senses.
- John 8:12 is utterly unknown to him: "*I am the light of the world: he that followeth me shall not walk in the darkness, but shall have the light of life.*"
- The light of life is love. God is light. In Him is no darkness at all because God is love. We love now; we have received the love nature, and love is to dominate us. When it does, the mind becomes renewed, comes into harmony with the recreated spirit.
- Sense knowledge governs the recreated man whose mind is renewed. He walks in love.

THE NEW CREATION

- The new creation man is described in Ephesians 3:20: "*Now unto him that is able to do exceeding abundantly above all that we ask or think, according to the power* [or ability] *that worketh in us.*"
- It is the ability of God that is at work in the new creation, building into him the love nature of the Father, the wisdom of Jesus, the grace and beauty of the Man of Galilee.
- In our daily walk, the Holy Spirit is building into us a fearless confidence in the Word. We require no physical evidence to prove that we are healed. When He says, "*Surely he hath borne our griefs, and carried our sorrows*" (Isaiah 53:4), that settles it for us, for we are governed by the Word—not by the five senses.
- When He tells us in 1 Peter 5:7: "*Casting all your anxiety upon him, because he careth for you,*" with loving joy we throw off our burdens upon the Lord as one lays down a heavy load from his shoulder. We say, "Thank you father, for bearing this load. Thank you for carrying it for me." Anxiety has stopped and we rest with quiet confidence in that living Word.
- You see, this renewed mind understands John 15:7–8: "*If ye abide in me, and my words abide in you, ask whatsoever ye will, and it shall be done unto you. Herein is my Father glorified, that ye bear much fruit; and so shall ye be my disciples.*"
- A disciple means a student—one that sits at the feet of a master. So, He says, "If my words are a part of your daily life so that you are acting them and living them, then you will be able to ask what you will."
- You see, the renewed mind realizes that John 15:5 is absolutely true, in essence, "I am the Vine and you are the fruit-bearing part of Me. I am seated up here at the Father's right hand, meeting your every need, and you are down there on the earth bearing love fruit in your ministry of helping men and women."

HOW MUCH DO YOU REMEMBER?

1. Why is there no fellowship between the unrenewed mind and the recreated spirit?
2. What are the two confessions of the double-minded man?
3. Why is the old covenant law called the law of the senses?
4. What should be the relation between the senses and the renewed mind of an adult Christian?
5. Explain Romans 12:1.
6. What is the difference between "sense knowledge" and "revelation knowledge"?
7. What was the nature of the spirit that dominated Christ?
8. What is the work of the Spirit in the walk of the new creation?
9. What are some of the advantages of prayer for the new creation?
10. Explain John 15:5 in the light of the ministry of the new creation.

LESSON 9 NOTES

Lesson 10
JESUS'S THREEFOLD VICTORY OVER SATAN

Satan was the reason for redemption. There could be no redemption without defeating Satan. Satan's eternal defeat was a part of the redemptive plan.

Hebrews 9:11–12:

> But Christ having come a high priest of the good things to come, through the greater and more perfect tabernacle, not made with hands, that is to say, not of this creation, nor yet through the blood of goats and calves, but through his own blood, entered in once for all into the holy place, having obtained eternal redemption.

His redemptive work can be thought of only in terms of that Scripture. Satan is eternally defeated.

But I want you to study with me now His threefold ministry—His victory over Satan in His earth walk, His victory over Satan in His substitutionary sacrifice, and His victory of Satan in the new creation.

JESUS'S VICTORY IN HIS EARTH WALK

- John 1:14: "And the Word became flesh, and dwelt among us (and we beheld his glory, glory as of the only begotten from the Father), full of grace and truth."
- This was God's invasion of the sense realm. Here natural man lived. It could not work without an incarnation. An angel's visit would not help. God had to come Himself.
- His first combat with Satan with which we are familiar is recorded in Matthew 4:1–11 and in Luke 4:1–13. In both of these records we have Satan attempting to overcome the incarnate One as he had overcome Adan in the garden. He tempted Jesus through the senses the same as he tempted Adam, but Jesus met him with the Word, and conquered him when He came down out of the mount.
- Matthew 4:23–24:

> Jesus went about in all Galilee, teaching in their synagogues, and preaching the gospel of the kingdom, and healing all manner of disease and all manner of sickness among the people. And the report of him went forth into all Syria: and they brought unto him all that were sick, holden with divers diseases and torments, possessed with demons, and epileptic, and palsied; and he healed them.

- From that day until Jesus gave Himself up to the high priest as our substitute, He met Satan under every possible form of disease that he could bring to man, and in every place, He conquered him. He conquered him as a new creation does today.
- Matthew 14:13–21 is the story of feeding the multitude in the wilderness. Satan had brought want and hunger to humanity. Jesus answers that hunger in His love.
- In the same chapter, from the third to thirty-third verses, there is a story of Jesus walking upon the sea. He was Master of every law of nature. He conquered the storm. He bade Peter come and walk with Him and become a master with Him of the laws of nature. Peter failed because he had not yet been born again.
- John 11 gives us a picture of Jesus raising Lazarus from the dead. This is not a resurrection of Lazarus. No one had been resurrected. Many had been raised from the dead.

- You notice that the author clearly states that he had been in the grave four days already, and Martha said, "*The body decayeth*" (John 11:39).
- Jesus proved that He was the master of the adversary who had the authority of death.
- Hebrews 2:14: "*That through death he might bring to nought him that had the power of death, that is, the devil.*"
- Perhaps the most striking sentence is in Luke 12:5: "*But I will warn you whom ye shall fear: Fear him who after he hath killed hath power to cast into hell; yea, I say unto you, fear him.*" Jesus is talking about the adversary whom He had conquered so many times.
- In Luke 13:11–16, we have the story of the woman with the infirmity. Jesus said to the woman, "*bowed together, and could in no wise lift herself up…Woman, thou art loosed from thine infirmity. And he laid his hands upon her: and immediately she was made straight, and glorified God*" (verses 12–13).
- And in the sixteenth verse Jesus said, "*Ought not this woman, being a daughter of Abraham, whom Satan had bound, lo, these eighteen years, to have been loosed from this bond on the day of the sabbath?*"
- In every contact with the adversary, Jesus conquered him.

HIS SUBSTITUTIONARY SACRIFICE

- Man is a spirit being. The real things about man are not his body. When Jesus said, "*If therefore the Son shall make you free, ye shall be free indeed*" (John 8:36), He meant the liberation of the spirit of the man.
- He did not have reference to physical slavery but to spiritual. Man's deliverance is threefold. He delivers man spiritually from the hand of the enemy. He delivers him physically from disease, hunger, and want. He delivers him mentally from being ruled by the senses and brings his spirit, which has been a slave through all the ages, to dominate his thinking and his physical actions.
- But let us look at the substitutionary sacrifice.
- First Corinthians 15:3–4: "*For I delivered unto you first of all that which also I received: that Christ died for our sins according to the scriptures; and that he was buried; and that he hath been raised on the third day according to the scriptures.*"
- God's revelation to Paul of the substitutionary sacrifice of His Son is the most amazing document in any language.
- Second Corinthians 5:21: "*Him who knew no sin he made to be sin on our behalf; that we might become the righteousness of God in him.*"
- Isaiah 53:4–6:

  > *Surely he hath borne our griefs, and carried our sorrows; yet we did esteem him stricken, smitten of God, and afflicted. But he was wounded for our transgressions, he was bruised for our iniquities; the chastisement of our peace was upon him; and with his stripes we are healed. All we like sheep have gone astray; we have turned every one to his own way; and Jehovah hath laid on him the iniquity of us all.*

- This is His substitutionary work in history and it governs the three parts—His spirit, soul, and body. But the strange thing is that He began with His body and then He leads us through the rest of the chapter showing man's threefold deliverance from the authority of the adversary.
- Romans 3:21 is the Spirit's revelation of man's deliverance from the hand of the enemy through the substitutionary sacrifice of Christ. It is climaxed with Romans 4:25–5:1: "*Who was delivered up for our trespasses, and was raised for our justification. Being therefore justified by faith, we have peace with God through our Lord Jesus Christ.*"

- Study carefully Romans 3:21–26. Read how a righteousness from God has been brought to light.
- Conybeare's translation of Romans 3:21 is striking:

  > But now, not by the law, but by another way God's righteousness is brought to light, whereto, the Law and the prophets bear witness; God's righteousness which comes by faith in Jesus Christ, for all, and upon all, who have faith.

- You see, righteousness is the key to the substitutionary work of Christ. The object of Christ's finished work was that He might make it possible for natural man to become a new creation and by that new creation become the righteousness of God in Christ.
- Righteousness means the ability to stand in God's presence as though sin had never been—stand there without any sense of inferiority or condemnation. That means now—not after death.
- Colossians 2:15 with Revelation 1:18 gives us a picture of the combat that Jesus had with the adversary after He had satisfied the claims of justice and had been made alive in spirit.
- First Peter 3:18: *"Christ also suffered for sins once, the righteous for the unrighteous, that he might bring us to God."*
- You see, Jesus had been made sin. Two things had to take place in Him after the claims of justice had been satisfied.
- He must first be justified in spirit. First Timothy 3:16: *"Who was manifested in the flesh, justified in the spirit."*
- Then He must be made alive, as we have just read in Peter. Then after He was justified and made alive, the Father spoke to Him. Acts 13:33–34:

  > *That God hath fulfilled the same unto our children, in that he raised up Jesus; as also it is written in the second psalm, Thou art my Son, this day have I begotten thee. And as concerning that he raised him up from the dead, now no more to return to corruption, he hath spoken on this wise, I will give you the holy and sure blessings of David.*

- That was done in Hades where Christ was suffering as our substitute.
- The next step in the drama is when He meets Satan in the combat and conquers him.
- Colossians 2:14–15 (WEYMOUTH) gives us a graphic picture of this:

  > *The bond, with its requirements, which was in force against us and was hostile to us, He cancelled, and cleared it out of the way, nailing it to His Cross. And the hostile princes and rulers He shook off from Himself, and boldly displayed them as His conquests, when by the Cross He triumphed over them.*

- You can see that in the great combat where Jesus meets the entire Satanic force and overwhelms them, strips them of the authority, He takes from Satan the authority that he has had ever since the fall of man.
- We get another graphic picture of that in Revelation 1:17–18: *"I am the first and the last, and the Living one; and I was dead, and behold, I am alive for evermore, and I have the keys of death and of Hades."*
- This could only come after He had conquered the adversary and taken the keys of death and of Hell—of Hades—from the enemy.
- Hebrews 9:26: *"But now once at the end of the ages hath he been manifested to put away sin by the sacrifice of himself."*

- Hebrews 10:12: *"But he, when he had offered one sacrifice for sins forever, sat down on the right hand of God."*
- He had carried His blood into the heavenly Holy of holies, the supreme court of the universe had accepted it, and then He who had been made sin, who had been made righteous, sits in God's presence without the smell of that awful sin of the world that had been laid upon Him.

HIS VICTORY OVER SATAN IN THE NEW CREATION

- Ephesians 2:10: *"For we are his workmanship, created in Christ Jesus."*
- When Jesus was recreated down in that dark region as the head of the church, we, in the mind of justice, were recreated, too, when Jesus conquered the adversary, when He put Satan to naught, it is as though we alone had done it. When He arose from the dead, it was our resurrection. And as He appeared among men, it was a type of our resurrection life that we live today.
- Write out 2 Corinthians 5:17:

_____

_____

_____

- The new creation is absolutely a master over the adversary. The prince of this world came to Jesus but could find nothing in Him. And the prince of the world, Satan, can come to the new creation and can find nothing in him.
- If he could find anything in him, he would have dominion over him; but there isn't for he has the nature and life of God.
- First John 4:4: *"Ye are of God, my little children, and have overcome them: because greater is he that is in you than he that is in the world."*
- The One who raised Jesus from the dead is in you—the new creation. You have the life and nature of God, and the One that is in you is greater than any force or power outside of you.
- First John 5:4: *"For whatsoever is begotten of God overcometh the world: and this is the victory that hath overcome the world, even our faith."*
- Your faith that brought you into the family of God has made you Satan's master, for *"who is he that overcometh the world, but he that believeth that Jesus is the Son of God?"* (1 John 5:5).
- Do you believe that? You see, Satan was conquered by you and Jesus before Jesus arose from the dead because you are identified with Him and now are a master.
- *"I can do all things in him who strengtheneth me"* (Philippians 4:13). The ability of God is in your hands.
- Psalm 27:1: *"Jehovah is the strength of my life."*
- Philippians 4:19: *"And my God shall supply every need of yours according to his riches in glory in Christ Jesus."*
- The new creation is a master. Why? Because Jesus said, in essence, "In My name you shall cast out demons." (See Mark 16:17.)
- He has given to the believer the use of His name and all authority has been given to Jesus. Now that "all authority" belongs to the church. Now we are masters.
- Second Peter 2:24 seals the issue. The believer's healing is guaranteed because it is a part of the redemptive work of Christ.
- James gives us a picture of the babe in Christ who needs the elder to pray for him and he does. But the full-grown believer knows he is perfectly healed by the finished work of Christ.
- Philippians 4:19 shows us how God supplies our financial needs.
- And Matthew 6:31–34 gives us Jesus's revelation of the Father's attitude toward His children.

HOW MUCH DO YOU REMEMBER?

1. In what three ways did Jesus defeat Satan?
2. What did Jesus use to combat Satan in His temptation?
3. What are three instances of Jesus defeating Satan during his earth ministry?
4. What is man's threefold deliverance through Christ's substitutionary sacrifice?
5. How was this threefold deliverance consummated?
6. Explain Hebrews 10:12.
7. How is the new creation identified with Christ's victory over Satan?
8. Why cannot Satan lay anything to the charge of the new creation?
9. Explain what Jesus meant when He said, "In My name."
10. Explain the place of healing in our victory over Satan.

LESSON 10 NOTES

_____

_____

_____

_____

_____

_____

_____

_____

_____

_____

_____

_____

_____

_____

_____

_____

_____

_____

_____

_____

Lesson 11
THE PRAYER OF FAITH

We are combating demons and disease with the Word. The Word is the sword of the recreated spirit. That Word can slay disease, and that Word can heal the sick.

The man who walks by faith in the Word requires no evidence of the senses. He has proof that the thing he is praying for has come.

You understand that there are two kinds of faith: sense knowledge faith that demands physical evidence to satisfy the senses before he can see that he is healed or that he has the thing for which he prayed; and the other kind of faith that depends upon the Word alone. He finds a passage that covers his need and he makes that his own.

Prayer based upon the Word rises above the senses and contacts the Author of the Word.

Second Corinthians 10:3–7 is a vital Scripture: "For, though living in the flesh [or senses], my warfare is not waged according to the flesh [or senses]. For the weapons which I wield are not fleshly weakness, but mighty in the strength of God to overthrow the strongholds of the adversaries" (CONYBEARE).

THE WORD VERSES SENSE KNOWLEDGE

+ The mightiest enemy of the prayer life is sense knowledge. And the weapon that we use against sense is the Word of God. It is the Word of the recreated spirit.

+ Ephesians 6:17 tells us how we overthrow reasoning of the disputer and we will pull down all the lofty bulwarks. *"And take the helmet of salvation, and the sword of the Spirit, which is the word of God."* We show the world that we are absolutely masters in Christ.

+ We have never as a church realized the authority and might of the Word.

+ This Pauline Revelation takes the place of the absent Christ and we act upon the Word as Jesus acted upon the Word of His Father. Jesus used the Father's words to defeat the adversary, to heal the sick, to raise the dead, and to feed the multitudes.

+ We use the Word of God to defeat the enemy. When we approach the throne, we come with our mouths filled with His Word. Then, when we go before the world, we make our public confession. We cast down reason based on the senses.

+ These senses have evidence of fever, pain, and cancer. These things exalt themselves against the Word of God. As though the cancer spoke, it says: "You cannot unseat me. I have authority over this body. I am holding this one captive. I have filled his heart with fear, and his mouth with a confession of my strength and my ability to slay him." (Read Ephesians 6:10–18 carefully.)

+ Now you bring the living Word of God to combat the reasonings of the senses. You are not swayed by the things you see—an empty purse, a weak body, or a lack of work. You must never think of your combat as against the thing that you can see or hear or feel. Your combat is with the prince of the power of the air that rules people's feelings and fills them with fear.

+ You are a master. When want faces you, you read Psalm 23:1–3. Write out this verse:

_____

_____

_____

+ You see, I am by the waters of plenty. There is no need that He cannot supply. You say it over and over again, "The Lord is my shepherd—my bread-provider, my rent-payer."

+ The world's lord may lead one into want, into pain and heartache; but the Lord leads into green pastures.

+ Isaiah 41:10: *"Fear thou not, for I am with thee; be not dismayed, for I am thy God; I will strengthen thee; yea, I will help thee; yea, I will uphold thee with the right hand of my righteousness."*

+ Go over that carefully. *"Fear thou not for I am with thee."* He is with you—the Creator of the universe, the Master who conquered the storm. Who is in you? The great, mighty Spirit who raised Jesus from the dead.

+ Don't you know John 15:5: *"I am the vine and ye are the branches?"*

+ Don't you realize that you are the fruit-bearing part of the Christ today? Hear Him whisper, *"I am thy God."*

+ That settles it. He opened the Red Sea. (See Exodus 12.) He held the Jordan back by the word of His power.

+ He sent His beloved Son here in the form of a babe to grow up so that He would be tempted in every point like as we are that He might learn the awful lessons that the bride, or the church, has to learn. And He said, *"Lo, I am with you always"* (Matthew 28:20) and, *"All authority hath been given unto Me"* (Matthew 28:18).

+ In essence, "I am backing you to the limit."

THE AUTHORITY OF THE NAME

+ John 14:13–14: *"And whatsoever ye shall ask in my name, that will I do, that the Father may be glorified in the Son. If ye shall ask anything in my name, that will I do."*

+ You remember, this is not prayer; but here Jesus is giving you a legal right to use His name to cast out demons, to heal the sick, to meet the forces of darkness in every field and to meet them as a conqueror. That is beautiful.

+ John 16:23–24:

> *And in that day ye shall ask me no question. Verily, verily, I say unto you, If ye shall ask anything of the Father, he will give it you in my name. Hitherto have ye asked nothing in my name: ask, and ye shall receive, that your joy may be made full.*

+ This is the ground for prayer. There is no power this side of Hell that can withstand it. You have a legal approach to God. You have a legal ground for prayer. Prayer is not based upon sufferance or pity, but upon the Word of God.

+ He has said that *"Whatsoever ye shall ask in my name, that will I do"* (John 14:13).

+ This is the legal power of attorney. Several times Jesus said, *"In my name."* He has given us the right to use that name against the forces of darkness and that name is identical with Himself. That name has the same power that was in Christ in His earth walk.

+ In Mark 16:17–18:

> *And these signs shall accompany them that believe: in my name shall they cast out demons; they shall speak with new tongues; they shall take up serpents, and if they drink any deadly thing, it shall in no wise hurt them; they shall lay hands on the sick, and they shall recover.*

+ So, after the Lord Jesus had spoken these words to them: *"They went forth and preached everywhere, the Lord working with them, and confirming the Word by the signs that followed"* (verse 20).

- Now you can see that no demons or disease can stand against the Word.
- You give out the Word in your lips. Remember, it is the Word in your lips that heals and saves. It is the Word in your lips when you speak to the Father that gives you the answer to your petition. It is the name in your lips that casts out demons, that breaks the power of Satan, that sets the captive free, that gives you a standing in the Father's presence. Never forget that.

FREEDOM IN CHRIST

- In Hebrews 4:14–16 and 10:19, He asks us to come boldly unto the throne of grace. He asks you to visit Him, to fellowship with Him.
- There is no ground for sin or sin-consciousness because you have become the very righteousness of God in Christ. Let that be a basic thing in your mind. Say it over and over again: "I am the righteousness of God in Christ. I have a legal right to stand in the Father's presence with the same liberty and freedom that Jesus had. I am now maintaining my confession before the world that I am what He says I am in the Word." (See 2 Corinthians 5:21.)
- *"Beloved, now are we the sons of God"* (1 John 3:1).
- I am a son of God. *"There is therefore now no condemnation to them that are in Christ Jesus"* (Romans 8:1). I am free. I can stand in the Father's presence just as Jesus did. I don't have to die to get my liberty. I have it now. Cancers can't resist the Word in the lips of faith.
- Your lips are the lips of faith.
- Tuberculosis can't resist the Word. It must yield. It is of the devil, and you are a master of demons and their works.
- Psalm 107:20: *"He sent his word and healed them."*
- That Word was Jesus. Then that Word was given to us by revelation and we have it in the New Testament. That Word is in your heart and lips.
- Romans 10:8–11; you want to remember this: *"The word is nigh thee, in thy mouth, and in thy heart: that is, the word of faith, which we preach"* (verse 8).
- And then He tells a man that if he confesses the Lordship of Jesus and believes in his heart that God raised Him from the dead, he is saved.
- And in the eleventh verse, *"For the scripture saith, Whosoever believeth on him shall not be put to shame."*
- You have it. You are a master. You are absolutely an overcomer.
- That makes men masters where they served as slaves. We are taking Jesus's place and acting for Him.
- Your renewed mind must agree with your spirit and the Word. Remember Romans 12:1–2. Your mind will be ruled by sense knowledge. Your spirit will repudiate it. The Word repudiates it.
- Come, take your place and stand your ground, that you are what Jesus says you are.

THE LAW OF FAITH

- Mark 11:23–24:

  Verily I say unto you, Whosoever shall say unto this mountain, Be thou taken up and cast into the sea; and shall not doubt in his heart, but shall believe that what he saith cometh to pass; he shall have it. Therefore I say unto you, All things whatsoever ye pray and ask for, believe that ye receive them, and ye shall have them.

- That is the law of faith. He was giving it to the Jews that could not understand it any more than the modern Christian can. But you can.

- Your faith requires no evidence but the Word, requires no proof from the senses. Faith is blind to all but the Word. It rises above the realm of the senses. It has its own way, its own weapons, its own ground for assurance. It is the Word.

- Second Corinthians 5:7: *"For we walk by faith and not by sight* [or senses]."

- The believer is a believer. He is not a doubter.

- It is the most natural thing in the world for him to act on the Word and to take his place as a son or daughter when he knows his place. He does not walk according to the senses, for the testimony of the senses cannot be trusted, but the Word can be.

- The believer has a legal right to the use of the Word. He has a legal right to the use of the name. He has a legal right as a child in the Father's family to take his place and to take his rights.

- The only thing that he asks is, "Does the Word say that?" Yes. "Well, that ends it."

- "Can the Word be trusted?" Yes, as fully as God himself can be trusted.

- The man of faith is like the Master. He is continually confessing before the world what he is in Christ and the integrity of the living Word.

- He fearlessly faces the impossible as a conqueror. He knows that his resources are all in God.

- Second Corinthians 2:14 is the Father's message to his heart: "But thanks be to God who leads me on from place to place in the train of his triumph" (CONYBEARE).

- We are His victories over the enemies of Christ, and by us He sends forth the knowledge of Himself, a steam of fragrance throughout the world, for Christ is the fragrance that we offer up to God in our prayer life, in our faith walk.

- James 5:15–16 says, *"The prayer of faith shall save him that is sick and the Lord shall raise him up"* (verse 15). And, *"The supplication of a righteous man availeth much in its working"* (verse 16).

- We have been made righteous, so we are the righteous ones that walk by faith.

- Hebrews 10:38: *"My righteous one shall live by faith: and if he shrink back, my soul hath no pleasure in him."*

- That is, if he draws back from the faith life to the sense life, from the Word to feelings, he brings no joy to the Father.

- You are righteous and you are walking according to the Word. You are walking in the realm of the Word. The Word has become one with you and you have become one with the Word.

- John 15:7–8: *"If ye abide in me, and my words abide in you, ask whatsoever ye will, and it shall be done unto you* [or brought into being]. *Herein is my Father glorified, that ye bear much fruit; and so shall ye be my disciples."*

- What kind of fruit? Why, the fruit that Jesus bore in His earth walk.

- You are going to take Jesus's place in His absence. You are going to act as He acted, speak as He spoke, do as He did.

- The world is going to be conscious that He is in you. You are another Jesus man or woman.

- You are not struggling to be righteous; you are not struggling to have faith. You have faith; you have the Word, and faith comes by the Word.

- The unsaved man may have to struggle to get faith, but you do not. All you have to do is to act upon what He has said. Your faith can only grow as you act upon the Word.

- Every time you act on the Word, something enters into your spirit that increases your assurance. Every time that you fail to act on the Word, you lose.

- You stand in the presence of someone that is sick and you know that they want you to pray for them. You fearlessly do it no matter who is with you or what your surroundings may be. You act on the Word. God honors you and backs up the Word.

- You do not need faith for the things that are possible to the senses. Faith is needed only for the impossible, and you dare to act on the Word as though the impossible had become a possibility...a reality.

- Jeremiah 1:12: *"I watch over my word to perform it."*

- And Luke 1:37: *"For no word from God shall be void of power."*

- Act on these fearlessly, and God will unveil Himself to your spirit.

HOW MUCH DO YOU REMEMBER?

1. Explain why there are no unanswered prayers.

2. Show how the Pauline Revelation takes the place of the absent Christ.

3. Tell why sense knowledge is the greatest enemy of faith.

4. Why is it that we are not to combat sickness, fear, want, or weakness?

5. Explain why prayer is not based on sufferance or pity.

6. Show how the recreated spirit and the Word repudiate sense knowledge.

7. What did Jesus mean when He said, *"If ye abide in me and my words abide in you"*?

8. What is your attitude toward impossibilities?

9. Show what Jeremiah 1:12 means to the new creation.

10. Tell in your own words what this lesson means in your prayer life.

LESSON 11 NOTES

_____

_____

_____

_____

_____

_____

_____

_____

_____

_____

_____

_____

_____

_____

Lesson 12
THE LAW OF LIFE VERSUS THE LAW OF DEATH

The law of Moses is called the law of death.

The reason it is called the law of death is because it was God's law that ruled spiritually dead men.

Romans 8:2: *"For the law of the Spirit of life in Christ Jesus made me free from the law of sin and of death."*

Paul could say, "I had been under the law of sin and death ever since I was circumcised as a child."

On his way to Damascus, he met Jesus and was circumcised in his heart, or born again. In other words, he received there eternal life, became a child of God, and came into the new covenant that Jesus established when He had fulfilled the old covenant.

The new covenant has a new law, a new priesthood, new sacrifices, and a new walk.

It is vitally important that we understand that the Ten Commandments were not written for Christians, the new creation; neither is the law of the new covenant written for men outside of Christ.

Let us notice that Scripture again; for the law of the recreated spirit of life in Christ Jesus is love.

Love is the nature of the Father, so when Paul received eternal life, the new love law entered into his spirit and became a part of his very nature.

Now we will read it: For the love law of the recreated spirit is the life that Jesus brought to us from the Father, and this new life made Paul free from the law of sin and of death because the Ten Commandments could not rule or govern the new creation.

As long as he was a Jew outside of Christ he was under that law, but now he is born again. God has become his Father, and he has come into a new covenant under another regime.

THE LAW OF THE NEW COVENANT

+ John 13:34–35: *"A new commandment I give unto you, that ye love one another; even as I have loved you, that ye also love one another. By this shall all men know that ye are my disciples, if ye have love one to another."*
+ The word "love" here is *agape*, the new word that Jesus evidently coined.
+ The new covenant came into being in the resurrection of the Lord Jesus. He had fulfilled the old covenant with its laws, ceremonies, and priesthoods, and had laid it aside. That is, when He said on the cross, *"It is finished"* (John 19:30).
+ Now God raises Him from the dead, the Head of a new covenant. He Himself is the High Priest, and we are the holy priesthood and the royal priesthood.
+ The rules for our daily walk are found in Jesus's teachings and in Paul's revelation.
+ John 15:9–10: *"Even as the Father hath loved me, I also have loved you: abide ye in my love. If ye keep my commandments, ye shall abide in my love; even as I have kept my Father's commandments, and abide in his love."*
+ This new love law is interpreted in a special way in 1 Corinthians 13. It is a revelation of the grace of God. It is a revelation to the sons of God.
+ You are to walk, not as the son of Abraham walked in the realm of the senses, but as a new creation man you are to walk in the spirit.

- Galatians 5:16: *"But I say, Walk by the Spirit* [the resurrected human spirit], *and ye shall not fulfil the lust of the flesh* [senses].*"*
- This recreated spirit is to dominate the senses and to govern the individual.
- Romans 5:5: *"Because the love of God hath been shed abroad in our hearts through the Holy Spirit."*
- We have become partakers of the divine nature. (See 2 Peter 1:4.) That divine nature is love.
- First John 4:8: *"He that loveth not knoweth not God; for God is love."*
- And we have received this love nature into our spirits. This love nature now is to govern us as the Ten Commandments governed the Jew.
- The old covenant was a covenant of death; the new covenant is a covenant of life.
- The old covenant commanded man to love God, but he could not. The only thing that a Jew could give to God was fear and reverence.
- The new creation gives Him real love.
- You hear us singing, "I love Him; I love Him." Yes, we do—we love Him. We can't help but love. Our spirits are filled with Himself, with His own love nature.

BELIEVING IN LOVE

- First John 4:16: *"And we know and have believed the love which God hath in us. God is love; and he that abideth in love abideth in God, and God abideth in him."*
- Now you can understand how this walk of ours is going to be governed by a new Lord. Satan has governed men because men choose to walk in hatred and selfishness. Now a new authority has taken us over in the new birth, and our daily life is to be lived in love.
- Ephesians 5:1–2: *"Be ye therefore imitators of God, as beloved children; and walk in love."*
- If I am an imitator of God, I will so love that I will give. As He walked in love, I will walk as Jesus walked.
- In John 14:9, Jesus said, *"He that hath seen me hath seen the Father."*
- As we see Jesus walk in His earth walk, we see love walking. Love healed the sick. Love fed the hungry. It was love at work; it was God in Christ unveiling Himself. Love is the dominant law of God.
- Write out Romans 13:10:

_____

_____

- Jesus is the love that fulfilled the old commandment and set it aside. Love established now another commandment of love. God does not command the man in Christ to love Him. If he walks in fellowship, he cannot help but love Him. Man has become a lover.
- Can't you see how this is a solution of the human problem? If love governed, there would be no more wars; there would be no more lawsuits; jails and prisons would cease to be. What an object for us to aim at, to bring this old world to a knowledge of Jesus Christ!
- First Corinthians 12:24–26:

  Whereas our comely parts have no need: but God tempered the body together, giving more abundant honor to that part which lacked; that there should be no schism in the body; but that the members should have the same care one for another. And whether one member suffereth, all the members suffer with it; or one member is honored, all the members rejoice with it.

What a law of love!

- First Corinthians 10:24: *"Let no man seek his own, but each his neighbor's good."*
- And in verses 32–33: *"Give no occasion of stumbling, either to Jews, or to Greeks, or to the church of God: even as I also please all men in all things, not seeking mine own profit, but the profit of the many."*

IMITATORS OF GOD

- In Ephesians 5:1–2, he told us that we are to imitate God. Now Paul says to "imitate me." Paul could not say that unless he was an imitator of God.
- What does it mean to imitate God? It means to walk in love.
- First Corinthians 13 tells us that *"Love seeketh not its own"* (verse 5); *"Beareth all things"* (verse 7). The marginal rendering is *"covers closely all things"* so that no one can see or hear the unsightly scandal. And above all things, *"love never faileth"* (verse 8).
- Sense knowledge has failed, but here is something that cannot fail. Children brought up in the atmosphere of this new kind of love never become criminals. You cannot find a criminal in any of our penal institutions today whose father and mother walked in this new kind of love before that child was born and in its early years; for this Jesus kind of love does not produce criminals. Hatred and selfishness produce criminals. Love produces beautiful people.
- Ephesians 1:4–5: *"Even as he chose us in him before the foundation of the world, that we should be holy and without blemish before him in love: having foreordained us unto adoption as sons through Jesus Christ unto himself."*
- You see, the believer is a love creation. Away back before the foundation of the earth of heaven were laid, love said, "I will have a family." And then love said, "Whosoever will may come into that family. That is going to be a new kind of folk."
- God was unhappy over His first creation, so He brings in a new creation created in His own Son.
- The failure of Christianity is not the failure of the nature of God in man, but it is because man has substituted church organization for the new creation.
- Sense knowledge has gained the supremacy in the church, and Jesus is no longer Lord or Head of the church. Worldly-minded men rule most of the churches.
- Second Corinthians 2:17: *"For we are not as the many, corrupting the word of God* [or, as it reads in the margin, making merchandise of the Word of God]."
- Conybeare says, "For I seek no profit (like most) by setting the word of God to sale [or by selling for retail], but I speak from a single heart, from the command of God, as in God's presence, and in fellowship with Christ."
- It must be fully understood that the Ten Commandments were never given to the new creation, and that the new commandment was never given to natural men. This, if it were known, would save much confusion among those who are teaching the law today.

LAW OF LIGHT AND DARKNESS

- First John 2:9–10: *"He that saith he is in the light and hateth his brother, is in the darkness even until now. He that loveth his brother abideth in the light, and there is no occasion of stumbling in him."*
- There is no place for hatred in the new creation. We are born in love; we are to walk in love; we are to speak the new love language; we are to bear the burdens of the weak.
- The eleventh verse is striking: *"But he that hateth his brother is in the darkness, and walketh in the darkness, and knoweth not whither he goeth, because the darkness hath blinded his eyes."*

- The moment we step out of love, we step into darkness. All those "out of fellowship" are out of love. All the unseemly and wicked things that people do, who once walked in fellowship, are done through selfishness. Sense knowledge rules them. Satan governs through selfishness.

- First John 3:14: *"We know that we have passed out of death into life, because we love the brethren. He that loveth not abideth in death."* That is, he lives in the realm of spiritual death and he is ruled by the prince of the powers of the air. (See Ephesians 2:1–3.)

- Verse 15: *"Whosoever hateth his brother is a murderer: and ye know that no murderer hath eternal life abiding in him."* You cannot commit a murder. Murder would be stopped if men would receive eternal life.

- Here is God's solution for the human problem.

- Then, 1 John 3:16: *"Hereby know we love* [or in this manner we know what love is], *because he laid down his life for us: and we ought to lay down our lives for the brethren."*

LIVING THE NEW LAW

- He laid down His life for us. We are to live for the brethren. He poured His life out. We are to pour ours out in love.

- First John 3:17–23. In this portion we see why prayer is not answered, why the sick often are not healed. We have not walked in love. We have not borne the burdens of the weak. We haven't helped them in their financial distress. We have looked at them and said, "God bless you. Go, and the Lord will meet your needs," when we were to take Jesus's place and meet the needs.

- In verses 22–23, it says, *"If our heart condemn us not, we have boldness toward God; and whatsoever we ask we receive of him, because we keep his commandments and do the things that are pleasing in his sight."*

- The commandments here are not the Ten Commandments, but new commandments of loving one another and bearing one another's burdens.

- Galatians 6:2 gives us a suggestion in the marginal rendering: *"Bring ye one another's burdens and so fulfill the law of Christ."* The literal translation gives it: "Bear ye one another's overload."

- Some are overloaded. Some cannot carry the load that they face. God help us to be ready to take the overload.

- Do you want to be a soul winner? Do you want to be a teacher of the Word? Let love rule your life. You can never amount to anything unless you do, for you can never be a blessing to the world until love dominates you.

- First John 4:7–9:

    > Beloved, let us love one another: for love is of God; and every one that loveth is begotten of God, and knoweth God. He that loveth not knoweth not God; for God is love. Herein was the love of God manifested in us, that God hath sent his only begotten Son into the world that we might live through him.

HOW MUCH DO YOU REMEMBER?

1. Give Scripture and show how the law of life set man free from the law of death.
2. How does the law of the new covenant rule man's life?
3. Tell why God does not command the man in Christ to love Him.
4. Explain why children who are brought up in the new covenant never become criminals.
5. Tell how Christianity has failed.
6. Explain 2 Corinthians 2:17 and tell what Paul means by corrupting the Word of God.
7. How have we become burden-bearers?
8. What is God's solution for the human problem?
9. What gives us boldness toward God?
10. How does one become a teacher of the Word and a soul-winner?

LESSON 12 NOTES

_____

_____

_____

_____

_____

_____

_____

_____

_____

_____

_____

_____

_____

_____

_____

_____

_____

_____

_____

_____

_____

_____

Lesson 13
UNUSED ABILITIES

The finished work of Christ has been little understood by the church. It is like the undeveloped resources of China and India.

We have not realized what it means to be a partaker of the divine nature.

SOURCE OF OUR ABILITY

+ Second Peter 1:3–4:

    Seeing that his divine power hath granted unto us all things that pertain unto life and godliness, through the knowledge of him that called us by his own glory and virtue; whereby he hath granted unto us his precious and exceeding great promises; that through these ye may become partakers of the divine nature.

+ Notice carefully now, that He has granted unto us all things that pertain unto life and godliness and that we have become partakers of His very nature. That nature is called eternal life: and Jesus said, *"I came that they may have life, and may have it abundantly"* (John 10:10).

+ That life is the substance and being of God. Who knows what that might mean if it could be harnessed, utilized by every man who has received it?

+ The creative ability as seen in creation, is imparted to us in the new creation. Heathen nations do not have it.

+ That is the reason there have been no creative inventions in any of the heathen countries until Christ has been revealed to the people, until they have received the nature of God. The German, Scandinavian, and Anglo-Saxon peoples were not creative until this nature of God was given to them.

THE CREATIVE ABILITY IN THE RECREATED HUMAN SPIRIT

+ The reasoning faculties have no creative ability.
+ First Corinthians 3:9 says, *"For we are God's fellow-workers: ye are God's husbandry, God's building."*
+ John 15:5: *"I am the vine, ye are the branches."*
+ The branch is the fruit-bearing part of the vine. Now we are His tilled land where He produces, develops things. This tilled soil is the creative energy manifesting itself in inventions, art, and what we call the sciences. We are God's fellow-workers. We are working together with Him. (See 2 Corinthians 6:1.)
+ You and God are working together. You are in a machine shop. You are developing, discovering, and creating new machinery. You and God are working, laboring together as partners.
+ You see, there is no limit where we may go with this. *"Wherefore if any man is in Christ, he is a new creature: the old things are passed away; behold, they are become new"* (2 Corinthians 5:17).
+ The old things of ignorance have passed away, and the new things of wisdom and God's ability have been imparted to us.
+ Our partnership with Him enables us to utilize His abilities.
+ First Corinthians 1:30: *"But of him are ye in Christ Jesus, who was made unto us wisdom from God."*

- He is made unto us ability to use knowledge gained through our contact with physical and mental things. Through the five senses, humanity has acquired an immense amount of knowledge, but that knowledge is of no value without wisdom to direct its use. So, Christ in us becomes wisdom to use this knowledge.

- We should not omit Philippians 2:13: *"Or it is God who worketh in you both to will and to work, for his good pleasure."*

- What is God doing in us? He is thinking in us, illuminating our spirits, illuminating our minds—renewing them so that they become responsive to His indwelling presence.

- We all know that inspirations like poetry are not the product of cold reason. Poetry comes leaping, thrillingly touching our whole being. Where does it come from? Out of our spirits.

- Where does that invention, that startling discovery in metallurgy or chemistry come from? We have been looking at it through cold reason, but it lay there cold and inert. The spirit now begins to reveal to us its secrets—not the Holy Spirit, but our recreated spirits are the mothers of every invention. And you have that ability in you.

- Every person who has received the nature and life of God has divine prerogatives that thrill us.

EXACT KNOWLEDGE

- Colossians 1:9–14 is a gold mine. *"For this cause we also, since the day we heard it, do not cease to pray and make request for you, that ye may be filled with the [exact] knowledge of his will in all spiritual wisdom and understanding"* (verse 9).

- It will enable you *"To walk worthily of the Lord unto all pleasing, bearing fruit in every good work, and increasing in the [exact or perfect] knowledge of God"* (verse 10).

- And you are going to be *"strengthened with all power, according to the might of his glory, unto all patience and longsuffering with joy"* (verse 11).

- And we have the background for a super-mind—a superman. You have perfect knowledge.

- The Greek word *epignosis* means more than knowledge. It is a perfect, exact, and complete knowledge and spiritual wisdom that God gives us, so that we can understand how to use the elements around us to advantage.

- Here is a new realm for serious men and women. We are really become supermen.

- Notice the twelfth verse: *"Giving thanks unto the Father, who made us meet to be partakers of the inheritance of the saints in light."*

- This word *"light"* here means a new type of mental efficiency—wisdom that can grasp the things that ordinary minds have never seen.

- You remember in 1 John 1:5: *"God is light, and in him is no darkness at all."*

- And Jesus said in John 8:12: *"I am the light of the world: he that followeth me shall not walk in the darkness, but shall have the light of life"*—or *zoe*, God's nature.

- That darkness is a spiritual thing that develops in a mental darkness—ignorance.

- Since Jesus is the Light, and we have Him in us, we have this Light of life. In other words, we have God's ability to face human needs and circumstances that surround us. It is just as though Jesus were here in person, actually superintending and guiding us.

DIVINE ABILITY UTILIZED

- Few of us have realized that we have in us divine ability. You ask, "How can this be utilized?" It is suggested in Colossians 1:12.

- He has given us the ability to enjoy our share of our inheritance of the saints that walk in this realm of light.

- I am acting now upon His Word. I am taking, by grace, Him to lead me into all the fullness of my inheritance.

- In the next verse, He says, "*Who delivered us out of the power of darkness* [that is, Satan's dominion], *and translated us into the kingdom of the Son of his love* [the kingdom of light, this realm of revelation knowledge]" (verse 13).

- And God is at work within us, thinking through our minds, operating through our recreated spirits. He has actually taken over us. Let Him rule!

- First Peter 2:9: "*But ye are an elect race, a royal priesthood, a holy nation, a people for God's own possession, that ye may show forth the excellencies of him who called you out of darkness into his marvelous light.*"

- Here is a gold mine. We are an elect people. We are a royal priesthood. We are a set-apart people, and we are for God's own possession. Why? That we may unveil the hidden treasures of grace by God at work within us. He is illuminating us, leading us into all the truth and reality. Why? In Colossians 2:3 it says, "*In whom are all the treasures of wisdom and knowledge hidden.*"

- And He has given us light and ability to know what these treasures are. Notice that there are treasures of "*wisdom and knowledge.*" Knowledge of what He has done; knowledge of what He is to do in us; knowledge of what we are; knowledge of what we may do with His ability. And then there is wisdom to utilize all this varied knowledge.

- It is a sin for us to be commonplace. It is wrong for us to be weak. It is a lack of wisdom for us to depend longer upon simple sense knowledge when we have the ability of God to put us over.

- Colossians 1:27: "*To whom God was pleased to make known what is the riches of the glory of this mystery among the Gentiles, which is Christ in you, the hope of glory.*"

- Note the language: the riches of the glory of the sacred secret that had been hidden through the ages, but now is unveiled to us in Christ. Christ unveils to us the ability of God we have in us.

BRINGING TO REMEMBRANCE

- How few of us have taken advantage of John 14:26: "*But the Comforter, even the Holy Spirit, whom the Father will send in my name, he shall teach you all things, and bring to your remembrance all that I said unto you.*"

- What is He going to teach us? All things. That would include mechanics and mathematics. That would include mineralogy, the treasures hidden in the earth. We become masters of the mysteries that surround us. What plastics we would discover! The plant life would unveil to us the hidden treasure there.

- I don't suppose there is a single weed but has within it something that is of benefit, something that we could use in life's work. Every tree, every shrub, every rock, and the ground we walk upon, is teeming with unknown wealth. And He is going to be our teacher.

- All the time I have been working on this, I have been conscious of this Scripture, Matthew 28:20: "*Lo, I am with you always, even unto the end of the world.*"

- He is here with us today, the Teacher of teachers, the One who knows every law of nature, every chemical. We don't have to theorize with Him. There is no longer any hypothesis. We are walking on sure ground of absolute knowledge.

- Much of what we call science is absolute conjecture, but when He leads us, we walk out of the realm of uncertainty to absolute certainty.

+ Jesus said, *"Howbeit when he, the Spirit of truth, is come, he shall guide you into all the truth"* (John 16:13).

+ This is not only the reality of Christ, but the reality of all that surrounds us—this great world in which we walk and live and move and have our being.

+ Ephesians 3:20: *"Now unto him that is able to do exceeding abundantly above all that we ask or think, according to the power that worketh in us."*

+ There is ability that has never been utilized. There is mental strength and spiritual strength in us. Once more, *"For it is God who worketh in you"* (Philippians 2:13).

+ We have thought only of Him working to build into us the love nature and the graces of the Lord Jesus. That will make us beautiful in our spiritual life; but there is all that, plus the illumination of our mind and spirit, to know the mysteries of creation that were created for our special uses.

THE INWARD MAN

+ In Ephesians 3:6, it says, *"That he would grant you, according to the riches of his glory, that ye may be strengthened with power through his Spirit in the inward man."*

+ This inward man is our spirit, and it is going to be strengthened with God's ability, and the Spirit is going to take charge of the up-building, the strengthening of our spirits through the Word.

+ He has recreated us; now He is going to build that Word into us.

+ You remember that *"in the beginning was the Word, and the Word was with God, and the Word was God"* (John 1:1).

+ So, He is going to build this Word, this Logos, into your spirit, and it will so dominate your inward spirit that you become like the Master.

+ You remember in John 1:3–4 that it says, *"All things were made through him; and without him was not anything made that hath been made. In him was life; and the life was the light of men."*

+ Then the life that is within Jesus is God's life, and that life is our light, our ability, our wisdom. It is God Himself becoming our tutor, leading us on from strength to strength; from success to success; from weakness into strength, and from failure into victory. It is God taking us over, building Himself into us until we can say with Paul: *"It is no longer I that live, but Christ liveth in me: and that life which I now live in the flesh I live in faith, the faith which is in the Son of God, who loved me, and gave himself up for me"* (Galatians 2:20).

+ You remember in our teaching on identification that we saw how God came down here in the person of His Son and identified Himself with man. *"The Word became flesh and dwelt among us"* (John 1:14). Now He is dwelling in our midst. He is dwelling in us. He became incarnate in the flesh. Now He is incarnate in our spirits.

+ Would it not be worthwhile to learn to utilize this spirit that is in us? Would not it mean to the church and to ourselves and to our loved ones if these things that we have been studying would become part of our lives, and we would use them as we use simple mathematics?

HOW MUCH DO YOU REMEMBER?

1. Give Scripture and explain the source of ability.
2. Tell why the heathen nations do not have these abilities.
3. Show how God's ability operates in the new creation.
4. Tell what is meant by "You are God's tilled land."
5. Explain Colossians 1:9–14, and give meaning of the Greek word, *epignosis*.
6. What is the background for a super-mind?
7. How can the new creation utilize this divine ability?
8. What did Jesus mean when He said He would teach us all things?
9. How is the inward man strengthened with God's ability?
10. What can His dwelling in our midst mean to the church?

LESSON 13 NOTES

_____

_____

_____

_____

_____

_____

_____

_____

_____

_____

_____

_____

_____

_____

_____

_____

_____

_____

_____

_____

_____

_____

Lesson 14
WHY WE DON'T PRAY FOR FAITH

A prayer for faith would be a prayer of unbelief, and a prayer of unbelief has no ground for an answer.

The people who pray for faith always live in the realm of unbelief.

If I asked you to give me faith in yourself and I had known you for years, you would think it an insult. So, the believer's pray for faith is an insult to Christ and the Father.

But you say, "The disciples said, '*Lord, increase our faith*' (Luke 17:5); and the man who brought his son to the Master said, '*Lord, help thou mine unbelief*' (Mark 9:24)."

I don't think that our unbelief needs any special help. The devil is our only helper in that regard.

A BELIEVING ONE

+ Jesus said, "*All things are possible to him that believeth*" (Mark 9:23). The Greek word for "*believeth*" means a "believing one." Then all things are possible to the believer.

+ The Jews were not believers. There were no real believers, as we understand the term, until the day of Pentecost. The disciples were called believers.

+ Jesus urged the Jews to believe Him because they were God's covenant people. They had lived in doubt for generations.

+ You understand John 6:47, in which Jesus says, "*Verily, verily, I say unto you, He that believeth hath eternal life.*"

+ The believer has; the doubter has not. The believer is a possessor, an owner. We are believers.

+ Matthew 17:19–20:

    Then came the disciples to Jesus apart, and said, Why could not we cast it out? And he saith unto them, Because of your little faith: for verily I say unto you, If ye have faith as a grain of mustard seed, ye shall say unto this mountain, Remove hence to yonder place; and it shall remove; and nothing shall be impossible unto you.

+ Mark 11:23–24 gives the same message. Jesus says,

    Verily I say unto you, Whosoever shall say unto this mountain, Be thou taken up and cast into the sea; and shall not doubt in his heart, but shall believe that what he saith cometh to pass; he shall have it. Therefore I say unto you, All things whatsoever ye pray and ask for, believe that ye receive them, and ye shall have them.

+ This Scripture is not to a believer, a child of God. It was a message to God's covenant people. But, you say, "Why isn't it a message to us?"

ALREADY BLESSED

+ Because of Ephesians 1:3: "*Blessed be the God and Father of our Lord Jesus Christ, who hath blessed us with every spiritual blessing in the heavenly places in Christ.*"

+ Notice that He has blessed us with every spiritual blessing—that we are blessed. He doesn't say that we are blessed if we believe. We are blessed because we are believers.

+ Second Corinthians 9:8–11:

> *And God is able to make all grace abound unto you; that ye, having always all sufficiency in everything, may abound unto every good work, as it is written, He hath scattered abroad, he hath given to the poor; his righteousness abideth forever. And he that supplieth seed to the sower and bread for food, shall supply and multiply your seed for sowing, and increase the fruits of your righteousness: ye being enriched in everything.*

FRUITS OF RIGHTEOUSNESS

+ Jesus bore fruits of righteousness.
+ If you knew you were what the Word says you are, what fruits you would bear for Him!
+ Here the Spirit is unveiling "the riches of the sons of God." This is Conybeare's translation.
+ The believer is enriched with every blessing. The difficulty is that we haven't known it. The major part of our praying is for things that we already possess.
+ It may startle you if I tell you that you need not pray for your healing, but sick folks spend most of their time praying for their healing. Why should we not pray for it? Because Isaiah 53:4–5 tells us that we already have the healing.

> *Surely he hath borne our griefs, and carried our sorrows; yet we did esteem him stricken, smitten of God, and afflicted. But he was wounded for our transgressions, he was bruised for our iniquities; the chastisement of our peace was upon him; and with his stripes we are healed.*

+ And in the tenth verse we read, *"Yet it pleased Jehovah to bruise him; he hath put him to grief."*
+ If He bore our diseases and put them away, God declares that *"with his stripes we are healed."* Then, what should we do? We should not pray for our healing because He would answer us, "I have already healed you. I have laid your sickness on My Son. Don't you appreciate what I have done for you?"
+ You can understand that He actually laid that disease on His own Son, and that that Son put that disease away. Now He bids us to look up and thank Him for it.
+ It is not a problem of faith at all. The only problem that confronts you is that of the integrity of that Word.

THE REVELATION OF THE WORD

+ Jeremiah 1:12: *"I watch over my word to perform it."*
+ Isaiah 55:10–11:

> *For as the rain cometh down and the snow from heaven, and returneth not thither, but watereth the earth, and maketh it bring forth and bud, and giveth seed to the sower and bread to the eater; so shall my word be that goeth forth out of my mouth: it shall not return unto me void, but it shall accomplish that which I please, and it shall prosper in the thing whereto I sent it.*

+ There is also Luke 1:37. The angel is speaking to Mary about the incarnation, about the child Jesus, and he says, *"For no word from God shall be void of power."* And what does Mary say? *"Behold, the handmaid of the Lord; be it unto me according to thy word"* (verse 38). And the angel departed from her.
+ You see, under the old covenant, God could not talk to the Jews as He talks to us through our spirits, so an angel was sent. But to us today, we have His living Word.

- John 6:63: *"The words that I have spoken unto you are spirit, and are life."*
- You understand that we are recreated through this Word, that the Word is the food on which our recreated spirits feed. So, you see, a believer is a possessor, and this new covenant man, this recreated man (see 2 Corinthians 5:17), has been invited to come into the very presence of the Father.

OUR STANDING

- Hebrews 4:16: *"Let us therefore draw near with boldness unto the throne of grace, that we may receive mercy, and may find grace to help us in time of need."*
- You see, you have a perfect right to stand in the Father's presence. You are invited into the throne room. There you can stand face to face with your Father, make your requests known, and receive an answer for your prayer.
- You understand that the believer has been given a legal right to the use of Jesus's name. He has the power of attorney. The difficulty is that we haven't recognized our rights. The average believer has no higher conceptions of the finished work of Christ that he has of the blood of bulls and goats under that first covenant.
- Romans 3:21: *"But now apart from the law a righteousness of God hath been manifested, being witnessed by the law and the prophets."*
- What does he mean? He means that by this righteousness you have the right to stand in the Father's presence without a sense of guilt or inferiority or a sense of sin consciousness. The believing one is a new creation. He is no longer under the dominion of Satan or condemnation. He has received God's very nature and life. (See 1 John 5:12–13.)
- That nature makes him a branch of the vine. He and Jesus are one. They are so much one that when Jesus met Saul on the way to Damascus in Acts 9:1–9, it says, *"And as he journeyed, it came to pass that he drew nigh unto Damascus: and suddenly there shone round about him a light out of heaven: and he fell upon the earth, and heard a voice saying unto him, Saul, Saul, why persecutest thou me?"* (verses 3–4).
- Saul was persecuting the Christians, but the Christian and Jesus are one.
- *"I am the vine; ye are the branches"* (John 15:5).
- When they persecute the branch, they persecute the vine; so, the believer and Jesus are one.
- That means that you can go into the Father's presence with the same freedom that Jesus did when He walked the earth. You do not need faith. All you need to know is your rights in Christ.
- How do you get it? Study the Word.
- Write out 1 John 5:1:

_____

_____

_____

- Read Romans 8:14–17. *"The Spirit himself beareth witness with our spirit, that we are children of God: and if children, then heirs; heirs of God, and joint-heirs with Christ"* (verses 16–17).
- You see, the Spirit bears witness with our spirits through the Word. This Word you are now reading is the Spirit's message to your spirit, and He is telling you that you are a son; and if a son, then you have a son's place and a son's rights as well as a son's responsibility.
- Galatians 3:26: *"For ye are all sons of God, through faith, in Christ Jesus."*
- As a sinner, you would have to have faith in Christ; but now, having come into the family, all things are yours.

ALL THINGS ARE YOURS

+ First Corinthians 3:21–22: "*Wherefore let no one glory in men. For all things are yours; whether Paul, or Apollos, or Cephas, or the world, or life, or death, or things present, or things to come; all are yours.*"

+ He has unveiled to you your rights and privileges in Christ.

+ Psalm 23:1: "*Jehovah is my shepherd; I shall not want.*"

+ That word Jehovah is a word of three tenses—past, present, and future.

+ It is Jesus, as Son, in Hebrews 13:8. It is the Jesus of today, the Jesus of yesterday, and the Jesus of tomorrow; and that Jesus is my shepherd, my caretaker, my protector, my burden bearer, and my lover.

+ Galatians 2:20: "*I have been crucified with Christ; and it is no longer I that live, but Christ liveth in me: and that life which I now live in the flesh I live in faith, the faith which is in the Son of God, who loved me, and gave himself up for me.*"

+ He loved me and gave Himself up for me, so now it is no longer I that live, but this new life of Christ is making me a branch of the vine.

+ Praying for faith is an absurdity when you have all things, when you are a very son of God. What would you have thought of Jesus's asking the Father to increase His faith? No, beloved, now are we the very sons of God.

ESTABLISHED IN THE FAITH

+ Colossians 2:6–7: "*As therefore ye received Christ Jesus the Lord, so walk in him, rooted and builded up in him, and established in your faith.*"

+ You see, Christianity is called "*your faith.*" Now you are to be built up in your faith. How? By being built up in Christ through the Word.

+ Notice the third verse of Colossians 2: "*In whom are all the treasures of wisdom and knowledge hidden.*"

+ So, you are to study the Word, pore over the Word, feed on the Word, act on the Word until the Word is built into you and becomes a part of your prayer life. Then it is no longer an exercise of praying for faith but a fellowship with the Father.

+ Colossians 1:9–12. You ought to read it carefully. Take this translation: "*That you may be filled with a clear [or perfect] knowledge of His will accompanied by thorough wisdom and discernment in spiritual things*" (verse 9 WEYMOUTH).

+ What is the object? "*To walk worthily of the Lord unto all pleasing, bearing fruit in every good work*" (verse 10). That is because you are a branch of the vine, and it is the branch who bears the fruit.

ENJOYING OUR SHARE OF THE INHERITANCE

+ "*And increasing in the knowledge of God; strengthened with all power, according to the might of his glory, unto all patience and longsuffering with joy*" (Colossians 1:10–11).

+ Now read this: "*Giving thanks unto the Father, who made us meet to be partakers of the inheritance of the saints in light*" (verse 12).

+ Notice the next two verses: "*Who delivered us out of the power of darkness, and translated us into the kingdom of the Son of his love; in whom we have our redemption, the forgiveness of our sins*" (verses 13–14).

+ From today, you are taking your place in Christ. You recognize that you have been delivered out of Satan's dominance. You recognize that you have been translated into the kingdom of the Son of His love. You are in the Father's family. You have a perfect right to the throne room now, and you have seen that every sin that you have ever committed has been wiped out as though it had never been. You stand complete in Him.

HOW MUCH DO YOU REMEMBER?

1. Why do we not have to pray for faith?
2. Explain why Mark 11:23–24 is not written to the believer.
3. Explain 2 Corinthians 9:8.
4. By knowing what the Word says we are, what are the fruits we can bear?
5. Tell what the relation of Jeremiah 1:12 is to Isaiah 55:10–11, and what is meant to us?
6. What standing in your prayer life does Hebrews 4:16 give you?
7. What is the Spirit telling us through the Word?
8. Tell how Jesus is the same today as He was when He walked the earth.
9. Tell how we can enjoy our share of the inheritance.
10. Tell how Jesus becomes manifested in you.

LESSON 14 NOTES

_____

_____

_____

_____

_____

_____

_____

_____

_____

_____

_____

_____

_____

_____

_____

_____

_____

_____

_____

_____

_____

_____

Lesson 15
THE REVELATION ACCORDING TO PAUL

What have the Gospels according to Matthew, Mark, Luke, and John. In Romans 2:16, the Spirit, through Paul, says this: *"In the day when God shall judge the secrets of men, according to my gospel, by Jesus Christ."*

From anyone but Paul this would be almost blasphemy. But the spirit-ruled heart has a consciousness that Paul is telling the truth.

Romans 1:1: *"Paul, a servant of Jesus Christ, called to be an apostle, separated unto the gospel of God."*

"Paul" means "the little one." The Greek word *dulos* means "a love slave"—the little love slave of Jesus the Messiah; and he is called by Jesus, Himself, to be an apostle and has been separated by Jesus Christ unto the good news of God.

If you will notice carefully, he was called; but there were fourteen years of separating before the separation was complete. Then he was commissioned and sent out as an evangelist of Christ.

SEPARATION

+ Many of us are called, but we are never separated. That separation is a threefold thing. First, the new creation separates us from the old life. Second, as the Word is built into us, we are separated unto Christ.

    1. First, there is a separation from the world;

    2. Now there is a separation unto the Master. Jesus becomes the Lord of our lives. His Word dominates us.

    3. Third, in our walk, there comes our own choice in which we separate ourselves from that which is not sinful in itself but is unnecessary, and this separation continues year after year, until the world has lost its dominion over us.

+ We are giving up good things for the best. We are learning to walk in the fullness of His fellowship.

+ Paul was called to be an apostle.

+ The four Gospels give us a picture of the incarnation of the Son of God. Each one of the four gives us a different vision of the incarnate One. Matthew gives us a picture of the kingdom; Mark, of service; Luke, of fellowship; and John, of Sonship. In John we catch a vivid picture of the Father. Jesus said, *"He that hath seen me hath seen the Father"* (John 14:9).

THE FATHER'S WORDS

+ Again, He declares, *"I and the Father are one"* (John 10:30). In the gospel of John, many times He says, in essence, "The Words that I speak of not mine, but the Father's." (See John 7:16, 12:49, 14:10.)

+ John 12:45: *"And he that beholdeth me beholdeth him that sent me."* Jesus is introducing the Father.

+ Perhaps you get a clearer picture in John 1:18: *"No man hath seen God at any time; the only begotten Son, who is in the bosom of the Father, he hath declared him."*

+ Rotherham puts it, "The only begotten Son who is now in the bosom of the Father has introduced Him."

+ Jesus comes with a revelation of the Father, but the Jews cannot understand it. When He calls God His Father, they try to stone Him.

- John 5:18: *"For this cause therefore the Jews sought the more to kill him, because he not only brake the sabbath, but also called God his own Father."* This is the only charge they brought against Him.

- John 19:7: *"We have a law, and by that law He ought to die."*

- The Jew could not accept the revelation of God as a Father because they were natural men.

- John 1:14: *"And the Word became flesh, and dwelt among us (and we beheld his glory, glory as of the only begotten from the Father), full of grace and truth."*

- In the four Gospels, there is no substitutionary sacrifice taught. Had it been taught, no one would have understood it. Nowhere do any of the Gospels speak of Jesus's being made sin on our behalf.

- The great unfoldings of the church are sometimes spoken in parable form, but no one could have understood them if the Master had attempted to teach them. When Jesus was arrested, the disciples hoped in some way He would perform a miracle and save Himself from their hatred. They have only sense knowledge faith in Jesus.

- John 6:30: *"They said therefore unto him, What then doest thou for a sign, that we may see, and believe thee? what workest thou?"*

- And as they stood about the cross, the disciples could not see Jesus as a substitute. None of them believed that He was dying for their sins. To them, He was dying as a martyr; and during the three dark days that His body was lying in the tomb, no one believed that He was to rise from the dead. No one understood; and when He arose from the dead, no one believed it.

- Luke 24:11–12. When Joanna and Mary, the mother of James, and the other women told them that Jesus arose from the dead, their words appeared to them as idle talk. They disbelieved them.

- After the resurrection and His talk with them, they did not yet grasp the significance of His substitutionary sacrifice. Why? Because they were spiritually dead. Eternal life had not yet come to them.

- Write out John 10:10:

_____

_____

ABUNDANT LIFE

- That new life would make them new creations. You understand now that the disciples had only sense knowledge faith in Jesus. They believed that He was the Messiah, the Son of God; but they did not believe that He was to die for their sins and be raised for their justification. That was to come when they had been liberated from their darkness, disbelief, and doubt.

THE MIRACLE OF PENTECOST

- Pentecost must always stand as the most outstanding miracle of grace ever manifested. No one could stand in the upper room and tell that group of 120 that Christ had died for their sins according to the Scriptures, and that He had risen again for their justification. No one could stand then and tell them that Satan had been defeated and conquered, that Jesus had carried His blood into the heavenly Holy of holies, and that the Father had accepted it. No one had explained to them about the new creation.

- They sat there in the upper room waiting as the Master told them. During that time, they had tried to find someone to take the place of Judas. They had cast lots as natural men do, and had selected a man to take Judas' place. God never accepted their choosing. Paul was to take Judas's place, but they did not know that. They were in that upper room as natural men.

- They were hoping that Jesus would restore the kingdom of Israel and break the rule of Rome over them. The spiritual kingdom was utterly out of the range of their thought.
- The Spirit came to that upper room where they had gathered waiting. Suddenly the room was filled with a sound from heaven as the rushing of a mighty wind, and it filled the whole house wherein they were sitting. They were immersed in the Holy Spirit. Jesus told them that they were to be immersed.
- Then, a second thing happened. Tongues of fire appeared on the head of each one, indicating that the gospel was going to be preached with tongues anointed by the Spirit, which would be irresistible.
- Men could not resist them. This is what caused the persecutions to come. When man cannot answer, he uses brute force.

SPIRIT-FILLED MAN

- But the spirit recreated them. The Spirit comes and chooses the men for the propagation of the gospel. Then He filled them with the Holy Spirit. You notice that He recreated them before He filled them.
- Then they spoke in tongues as the Spirit gave them utterance. No one understood the phenomena of that day, but the Spirit had filled them. Now they go with tongues of fire to tell the world what has happened. Fifteen years or more go by, and yet there is no revelation of what happened from the time that Christ was made sin on the cross until He sat down on the right of the Father on high.
- They preached what God gave them. There was nothing taught about substitution. So far as we know as recorded in the book of Acts, there was nothing taught about the body of Christ until God gave it to the man, Paul, by revelation.
- One of the most beautiful things about the early church was the way that John and Peter and the other apostles received Paul's revelation.
- You remember in 2 Peter 3:15–16, Peter says,

  And account that the longsuffering of our Lord is salvation; even as our beloved brother Paul also, according to the wisdom given to him, wrote unto you; as also in all his epistles, speaking in them of these things; wherein are some things hard to be understood, which the ignorant and unsteadfast wrest, as they do also the other scriptures, unto their own destruction.

- In Galatians 1:18–19, Paul says, "*Then after three years I went up to Jerusalem to visit Cephas, and tarried with him fifteen days. But other of the apostles saw I none, save James the Lord's brother.*"
- Those must have been wonderful days, when Peter told Paul all about his fellowship and walk with the Master, and Paul told peter about the revelations that he had received of Jesus and of His finished work.
- Now let Paul speak to us in Galatians 1:6–12:

  I marvel that ye are so quickly removing from him that called you in the grace of Christ unto a different gospel; which is not another gospel: only there are some that trouble you, and would pervert the gospel of Christ. But though we, or an angel from heaven, should preach unto you any gospel other than that which we preached unto you, let him be anathema. As we have said before, so say I now again, If any man preacheth unto you any gospel other than that which ye received, let him be anathema. For am I now seeking the favor of men, or of God? or am I striving to please men? if I were still pleasing men, I should not be a servant of Christ. For I make known to you, brethren, as touching the gospel which was preached by me, that it is not after man. For neither did I receive it from man, nor was I taught it, but it came to me through revelation of Jesus Christ.

+ Notice that he says, *"Though we, or an angel from heaven, should preach unto you any gospel other than that which we have preached unto you, let him be anathema."*

REVELATION OF JESUS CHRIST

+ And in the twelfth verse: *"Neither did I receive it from man, not was I taught it, but it came to me through revelation of Jesus Christ."*
+ Paul knew that the message he had was not of man.
+ In Ephesians 3:1, we read, *"For this cause I Paul, the prisoner of Christ Jesus in behalf of you Gentiles."*
+ Notice that he is a prisoner of Jesus, yet he is locked in a Roman jail. Is there any incongruity in this? No. Paul is being shut away, a guest of the Roman authorities, that he might have an opportunity to write these marvelous epistles, gives to us this revelation.
+ Ephesians 3:2–5:

> *If so be that ye have heard of the dispensation of that grace of God which was given me to you-ward; how that by revelation was made known unto me the mystery, as I wrote before in few words, whereby, when ye read, ye can perceive my understanding in the mystery of Christ; which in other generations was not made known unto the sons of men, as it hath now been revealed unto his holy apostles and prophets in the Spirit.*

+ Paul dared to confess that he was what God had made him to be.
+ Romans 16:25–27:

> *Now to him that is able to establish you according to my gospel and the preaching of Jesus Christ, according to the revelation of the mystery which hath been kept in silence through times eternal, but now is manifested, and by the scriptures of the prophets, according to the commandment of the eternal God, is made known unto all the nations unto obedience of faith: to the only wise God, through Jesus Christ, to whom be the glory forever.*

+ Paul believed in the gospel that he preached. Let me give you Scriptures from Conybeare's translation of 1 Thessalonians 1:3: "Remembering in the presence of our God and Father, the working of your faith, and the labors of your love, and the steadfastness of your hope in our Lord Jesus Christ."

IN THE FATHER'S PRESENCE

+ Note, "remembering the presence of our God and Father." Paul recognized that he was in the Father's very presence.
+ First Thessalonians 2:3–4: *"For our exhortation is not of error, nor of uncleanness, nor in guile: but even as we have been approved of God to be intrusted with the gospel, so we speak; not as pleasing men, but God."*
+ He dared to say that God had proved his fitness for this revelation, that God Himself had prepared him, Paul, to be this instrument of God's grace to unveil what He did in Christ from the time that He was made sin on the cross until He sat down on God's right hand.
+ In 1 Thessalonians 2:13, we see another startling statement: *"And for this cause we also thank God without ceasing, that, when ye received from us the [spoken] word of the message, even the word of God, ye accepted it not as the word of men, but, as it is in truth, the word of God, which also worketh in you that believe."*
+ Paul knew that the Word that he spoke to them in his public ministry was the very Word of God. He called it the "spoken Word of God," and the people of Thessalonica received it. It worked in them

effectually and produced in them a faith and a life that glorified the Father. Why is it that the Word spoken today does not have the same effect upon the hearts of men that the Word did when Paul preached it?

+ First Thessalonians 3:9: *"For what thanksgiving can we render again unto God for you, for all the joy wherewith we joy for your sakes before our God."*

+ You can understand now Hebrews 4:16, in which he invites us to come boldly into the throne room. Paul lived in the throne room. *"Let us therefore draw near with boldness unto the throne of grace."*

+ He lived in the presence of God and of Christ upon that throne of grace.

"THE THRONE OF GRACE"

+ First Thessalonians 3:12: *"And the Lord make you to increase and abound in love one toward another, and toward all men, even as we also do toward you."*

+ Paul dared to say he loved as Jesus loved.

+ And in the thirteenth verse we read, *"To the end he may establish your hearts unblamable in holiness before our God and Father, at the coming of our Lord Jesus with all his saints."*

+ If we could remember that we are living in the actual presence of God, our Father, and of Jesus all the time, we would see things differently.

+ Jesus says, in John 15:5, *"I am the vine and ye are the branches."* Well, the branch is a part of the vine and is in the presence of the vine all the time.

+ First Thessalonians 4:8: *"Therefore he that rejecteth, rejecteth not man, but God, who giveth his Holy Spirit unto you."*

+ Paul believed that his words were God's words.

HOW MUCH DO YOU REMEMBER?

1. Why did Paul have to wait fourteen years after he was called before he was commissioned as an evangelist of Christ?

2. Give the different visions of the Gospels of the incarnate One.

3. Why did the Jews try to kill Jesus when He called God His Father?

4. Why did the disciples ask for a sign that they might see and believe?

5. Explain why Pentecost is the most outstanding miracle of grace ever manifested.

6. How did Paul know that the message he had was not of man?

7. Explain the mystery that was made known to Paul in this revelation.

8. Explain 1 Thessalonians 1:3.

9. Show how the Word works effectually in those who believe.

10. What is shown in 1 Thessalonians 4:8?

LESSON 15 NOTES

_____

_____

_____

_____

Lesson 16
GOD'S REVELATION OF JESUS ACCORDING TO PAUL

No one knew the Father until Jesus introduced Him; no one knew Jesus until the Father had introduced Him.

This introduction is given to us in Paul's revelation. The Father is unveiling to the church what they really are in Christ. He is unveiling what He did for us in His Son.

I once wondered why Paul never quoted from the Master; then I noticed that Jesus said in John 12:50, *"The things therefore which I speak, even as the Father hath said unto me, so I speak."*

The same thing was true of Paul. He had no choice of the thing he wrote. His message was fresh from the Father's heart.

Read Galatians 1:6–12 carefully. Paul here declares he was not taught of man; so, his message did not come from Peter nor from John, but came fresh from the Father.

Paul did not know about the substitutionary sacrifice until it was revealed to him.

TWO PHASES OF SUBSTITUTIONARY SACRIFICE
+ There are two phases of the revelation: one is the legal side of the plan of redemption, and the other is the vital.
+ The legal is what God did in Christ for us, what legally belongs to us as new creations. The vital is what the Spirit through the Word is doing in us in the new creation. It is His indwelling, His building the Father's nature into us through the Word.

GOD WORKING WITHIN US
+ Philippians 2:13: *"For it is God who worketh in you both to will and to work, for his good pleasure."*
+ God is working within us. He is building Himself into us. He is building His love nature, His righteousness, His faithfulness, His longsuffering, His gentleness. As we contact the world, these qualities are necessary, and He builds them into us.
+ First Corinthians 1:30: *"But of him are ye in Christ Jesus, who was made unto us wisdom from God, and righteousness and sanctification, and redemption."*

JESUS MADE OUR WISDOM
+ He made Jesus to be wisdom unto us so in this revelation we have discovered that Jesus is our wisdom. We don't have to have prayer for wisdom as James tells us; but as we meditate in the Word, this revelation is the wisdom of God. It is an unveiling of the Father's ability. He lives in that revelation, and as you feed on it and meditate on it, you become wiser than your enemies.

JESUS MADE OUR RIGHTEOUSNESS
+ He not only is made unto us wisdom, but He is made unto us righteousness. This is the most difficult thing that I ever had to accept—that God had made Jesus to be my righteousness. Righteousness here means the ability to live in the Father's presence as I live in the presence of people here in the office, without any sense of inferiority or condemnation or guilt. I could not understand how the Father could do that.

+ But He makes it clear in His redemption spoken of in Colossians 1:13. Write out this verse:

_____

_____

_____

+ Darkness is Satan's family relationship. His kingdom is darkness. Darkness is hatred, jealousy, bitterness—everything that Satan can impart to man.
+ We have been delivered out of that and have been delivered out of the authority of it, so that it no longer dominates us or rules us.
+ This is the new creation that has come into the family of love of which Jesus is the Lord and Head, the Firstborn out of death, in whom we have our redemption.

FIRSTBORN FROM THE DEAD

+ The church has had a limited redemption. It has been more occupied in the meaning of the Greek word than it has in the reality of our deliverance from the dominion of the devil.
+ You notice that we have been delivered out of the authority of Satan and we have been redeemed. Two things have taken place: the penalty has been paid that we owed to justice. Jesus met it when He was made sin on our behalf, and He went to the place of justice where He suffered for the Spirit. (See 1 Peter 3:18 and 1 Timothy 3:16.)
+ As soon as He was justified and made alive, He met the adversary, conquered him, and stripped him of his authority. You see, there is a perfect legal redemption.
+ Jesus actually conquered our enemy and delivered us out of his dominion. When He did that, He made possible our new creation, and when we were made new creations we received the nature of God in our spirits.
+ Second Corinthians 5:18–21. Read this carefully down to the twenty-first verse and see how God made Jesus to be sin on our behalf to the end that we become the righteousness of God in Him.
+ Now you can understand how Jesus has been made our righteousness. There are three phases in that revelation.
+ Romans 4:25 says that He was delivered up on account of our trespasses and was raised when we were declared righteous or justified.
+ He wasn't raised until justification became the property of the unsaved world. Just as God so loved the world that He gave His only begotten Son—made the world a present of Jesus—now God not only makes the world a present of Jesus, but He makes the world a present of righteousness. But Jesus is of no value to the sinner until he confesses Him as Lord.
+ Romans 10:9–10:

> Because if thou shalt confess with thy mouth Jesus as Lord, and shalt believe in thy heart that God raised him from the dead, thou shalt be saved: for with the heart man believeth unto righteousness; and with the mouth confession is made unto salvation.

+ The moment that he does it, redemption becomes reality, and righteousness becomes a reality. All that Jesus is is stored up and waiting for the unsaved man to take. The moment that the unsaved man says, "I take Jesus as my Savior and as my Lord," he is made a new creation. Not only is righteousness reckoned unto him, but he has the righteousness of God.
+ The new nature that is imparted unto him is God's nature, and that nature is righteousness.

- Now you can understand Romans 3:26. God in speaking of Himself, says, *"That he might himself be just, and the justifier of him that hath faith in Jesus."*
- You see, God actually becomes the righteousness of the man who believes in Jesus.
- One can hardly grasp the significance of this—that God has become our righteousness.
- Now you can understand Romans 8:33: *"Who shall lay anything to the charge of God's elect? It is God that justifieth."* When anyone lays anything to your charge, God becomes your vindicator.

JESUS, OUR ADVOCATE

- Did you ever notice that if a man sins, he has an *"Advocate with the Father, Jesus Christ, the righteous"* (1 John 2:1)?
- Any man who commits sin loses his sense of righteousness and is ashamed to go into the presence of the Father. Then he asks forgiveness, and the Father listens to his advocate, Jesus. You see, Jesus is our Advocate and can plead for us who have lost our sense of righteousness, and our righteousness is restored.
- *"If we confess our sins, he is faithful and righteous to forgive us our sins, and to cleanse us from all unrighteousness"* (1 John 1:9).
- He forgives our sin; He is faithful and righteous to forgive us our sin and to cleanse us from all unrighteousness and restores to us fellowship with Himself.
- You see, the whole things moves around this fact of righteousness. God becomes my righteousness, now He makes Jesus to be my righteousness.
- Romans 4:25: *"Who was delivered up for our trespasses, and was raised for our justification."*
- He was raised up when our substitute had obtained righteousness for us. Righteousness is reckoned, then, to the unsaved man. That gives him a legal right to approach God as a sinner, and to accept Christ as his Savior. The moment that he does it, God becomes his righteousness, Jesus becomes his righteousness, and by the new birth he becomes the righteousness of God in Christ.

BECOMING A REALITY

- Meditate on this until it becomes a reality to you. You can't get it the first time you hear it or the first time you read it. I went over these Scriptures again and again. My heart craved it, but my reason rejected it. But after a while I knew that God had not only made Jesus wisdom unto me, but Jesus was my righteousness.
- The third thing it says is that Jesus is made unto us "sanctification." We have made sanctification a hobby, a doctrine, a part of our creeds, and we have said that sanctification was something that we obtained because we prayed and surrendered and consecrated ourselves until God was able to sanctify us.
- That is sense knowledge interpretation. You can't do anything; neither did God ask you to do anything to make you worthy.
- Romans 4:4–5 declares this: *"Now to him that worketh, the reward is not reckoned as of grace, but as of debt. But to him that worketh not, but believeth on him that justifieth the ungodly, his faith is reckoned for righteousness."*
- You see, God gave His Son to the ungodly. Romans 5:6 clears the case: *"For while we were yet weak, in due season Christ died for the ungodly."*
- And in the tenth verse we read, *"For if, while we were enemies, we were reconciled to God through the death of his Son, much more, being reconciled, shall we be saved by his life."*

+ What does it mean? It means that same thing as Ephesians 2:8: *"For by grace have ye been saved through faith; and that not of yourselves, it is the gift of God."*

ETERNAL LIFE, A GIFT

+ In other words, sanctification is a gift. You can't do anything to merit it. It is yours when you are recreated. It belongs to you as much as eternal life belongs to you. God gave eternal life. God gave redemption. God gave wisdom. God gave the sanctification, and God gave Himself in the person of His Son to us so that "He that has the Son has the life." (See 1 John 5:12.)

+ If you have eternal life, you have the nature of God. If you have the nature of God, you have righteousness. If you have righteousness, you have sanctification.

+ What does sanctification mean? It means being set apart—separation. Who set you apart? God set you apart.

+ Then what do you do to accept it? As soon as you are born again and the spirit comes to make His home in you and begins to build Jesus's nature and life into your spirit, you begin to separate yourself from the unnecessary things that have held you in bondage and kept you so occupied that you didn't' have time for the best things.

+ A woman said to me, "I haven't time to study the Word. I have so many things to do in my home." A year or two afterward she was taken very, very ill. Doctors said that an operation was the only hope, but that she had just very little chance—one in one thousand. I said, "You have plenty of time now for studying the Bible." And she remembered.

FIRST THINGS FIRST

+ "I should have put first things first," she said.

+ The most important thing to any man—I don't care what his business is—is to know his Father and to know his rights and privileges in Christ. That is the most important thing in life.

+ This Pauline Revelation is the most marvelous thing given to man, but it is of no value to you until it becomes a part of your life.

+ He was not only made unto us wisdom from God, and righteousness from God, and sanctification from God; but He is made redemption from God.

+ What does redemption mean? It means, first, the satisfying of the claims of justice against you so that you are redeemed from the sentence that falls upon unregenerate man. God did that in Christ.

+ Now the unsaved man filled with satanic nature cannot believe in the sense that you as a believer believe, so the message is presented to him, and he acts upon it. He may not understand all of it, but the moment that he acts upon the Word, he receives eternal life. Then his spirit becomes illuminated and his mind renewed, and he can understand what has taken place in his life.

+ You see, believing means acting on the Word. A sinner cannot have faith in the sense that you have faith as a believer, but God reckons it to him as faith when he acts upon the Word that God has given him.

+ Our preaching to the unsaved to believe and believe is unwise. What we are to do is to give him something to believe or act upon. Make it clear to him how Christ died for our sins according to the Scripture, how He arose from the dead according to the Scripture, how God gave Jesus to him as a gift, and how he should take Him as his Savior and Lord.

+ Don't mention "believe" or "believing" to him. If you do, you confuse him. You understand what God means by believing, but he doesn't.

HOW MUCH DO YOU REMEMBER?

1. Explain the two phases of our redemption.
2. Tell how He has been made wisdom unto us.
3. Explain Colossians 1:13–14.
4. Explain how Jesus is the firstborn from the dead.
5. Show how God is the righteousness of him that believeth on Jesus.
6. Explain why reason will reject our being the righteousness of God.
7. Show how "works" limit God.
8. What is meant by "first things first"?
9. Explain how the unregenerate man has been redeemed.
10. What does God mean by "believing"?

LESSON 16 NOTES

_____

_____

_____

_____

_____

_____

_____

_____

_____

_____

_____

_____

_____

_____

_____

_____

_____

_____

_____

_____

_____

_____

Lesson 17
HOLDING FAST TO OUR CONFESSION

It is of vital importance that after we have prayed, we never go back on our prayers. Many repudiate the Word by the confession of a doubt or admission of a doubt into their consciousness.

Isaiah 55:11: *"So shall my word be that goeth forth out of my mouth: it shall not return unto me void, but it shall accomplish that which I please, and it shall prosper in the thing whereto I sent it."*

STAND BY YOUR PRAYER

+ The heart must be rooted and grounded in the Word so that what He says is final with us.
+ You prayed and you know it was His will.
+ First John 5:14–15: *"And this is the boldness which we have toward him, that, if we ask anything according to his will, he heareth us: and if we know that he heareth us whatsoever we ask, we know that we have the petitions which we have asked of him."*
+ That word *"boldness"* means *"successful."* It means a fearless confidence. We prayed according to His will. Then we are assured that He heard us; and if He hears, that is as good as an answer.
+ But how can you know that He heard you? Because it was His will and you are here to do His will. You and He are cooperating. You pray according to instructions given by Him. You approach Him through the name.
+ John 16:23: *"And in that day ye shall ask me no question. Verily, verily, I say unto you, If ye shall ask anything of the Father, he will give it you in my name."*
+ Jesus has given to us a legal right to use His name, and His name is the same as Himself.
+ When you come to the Father in Jesus's name, it is as though Jesus Himself were standing there.
+ John 6:38: *"For I am come down from heaven, not to do mine own will, but the will of him that sent me."*
+ You are acting in Jesus's stead. You have no selfish desires that prompted your prayer. Your prayer is for someone who desperately needs His help, and you come as the mediator between him and the Father. You are taking Jesus's place, acting in His stead. You know that Jesus would do exactly as you are doing.
+ The Father hears you. His Word guarantees that, for you have prayed according to His will.
+ Now you stand by that prayer. You do not let the enemy steal it away from you.
+ In Genesis 15:9–11 there is a wonderful illustration. Abraham and Jehovah were entering into a covenant. Jehovah had said,

> *Take me a heifer three years old, and a she-goat three years old, and a ram three years old, and a turtle-dove, and a young pigeon. And he took him all these, and divided them in the midst, and laid each half over against the other: but the birds divided he not. And the birds of prey came down upon the carcasses, and Abram drove them away.*

+ The offering lay upon the altar. It was God's offering. Birds of prey would steal it before it was consumed, so Abraham watched over it.
+ This living Word that has been given to us is from God. It is God's part of the prayer-life. It is like the animals laid upon the altar.

- You have prayed in Jesus's name, and the answer has not yet come; it had not come to Abraham yet. Now the birds of prey, demons, would steal that Word from your heart, that God-given message; but you watch over it. You won't let the adversary touch it.

- Then you turn to Philippians 4:6: *"In nothing be anxious; but in everything by prayer and supplication with thanksgiving let your requests be made known unto God."*

- You have done this. The requests have been made known. Now with thankful quietness, you wait.

- Someone says, "But your prayer is not yet answered." The fever is still there, or the bill is still unpaid.

- You drive the birds away. You refuse to let them alight upon the Word and destroy it. The Word is God's part of the offering, and you know that "no Word from God is void of ability to make good." (See Isaiah 11:55.)

- Your heart knows that the case is settled. You asked for rain, so you put on your raincoat and your rubber boots. You are ready when the rain comes. You asked for money, so you made provision to pay the bill. You asked for healing, so you didn't get out of bed and walk.

- Didn't He say if you ask anything according to His will, He hears you? Yes!

- Didn't that give you the boldness to go and act as though the prayer were already answered? Yes.

- When you know that He hears, that you have His attention, you know that you have the petition. What would you naturally do? You would praise Him, wouldn't you?

- You are certain that it is settled. Satan cannot hinder the answer.

- First Peter 5:7 is yours: *"Casting all your anxiety upon him, because he careth for you."*

- Notice that "Word," because that is the secret. He loves you and He gave you His word, and you are resting on that Word.

- There is a slang word that has become a part of our language. You have the answer "in the bag." It is just as though you had the money in your hands. You are as certain of it as though the Master had come into the room and had said, "Here is the thing for which you have been praying."

- This morning, I needed four dollars. I had said that I expected that He would stir the hearts of men and women who had been blessed by His ministry through me, and that they would send the money. A man living outside of town heard His call and brought the four dollars. That is the secret. I knew that He would do it. I thanked Him for it, and I got it.

- Write out Mark 11:24:

_____

_____

_____

BELIEVING IS POSSESSING

- You see, believing is possessing. When I believe His Word, I possess the thing that His Word has guaranteed. I made my request and boldly made provision to use that request at once.

- Jesus showed us this in John 14:13: *"And whatsoever ye shall ask in my name, that will I do, that the Father may be glorified in the Son."*

- When you pray in that name, Jesus takes it over. Then it is in His care. It is no longer your burden as long as you do not repudiate it by a wrong confession. He is your standby. Your prayer is based upon His Word. It is His business to make it good.

- But supposing the answer is delayed? You remember Abraham. Romans 4:16–22. Read the whole of this carefully. In the eighteenth verse it says, *"Who in hope believed against hope, to the end that he might become a father of many nations, according to that which had been spoken."*

- Hope is always future. Faith is always now. He had hoped for a son. Now faith takes the place of hope. Hope is pushed aside. He remembered the God that *"calleth the things that are not as though they were"* (Romans 4:17).

- It is God who looked into the empty space and said, "There is a sun shining there"; and the sun becomes. "A constellation of stars is there," and it becomes.

- You remember Matthew 18:19. Jesus said, *"If two of you shall agree on earth as touching anything that they shall ask, it shall be done for them of my Father who is in heaven."*

- Your word, then, in Jesus's name, makes things come into being, or come to pass.

- Abraham, then, *"without being weakened in faith, considered his own body now as good as dead (being about a hundred years old) and the deadness of Sarah's womb"* (Romans 4:19).

- Sense knowledge could see that, but an angel had spoken from God. So *"Looking unto the promise that God had made, he wavered not through unbelief, but waxed strong through faith, giving glory to God"* (verse 20).

- And his faith told him that God would give him anything that He promised. So, his son was born to him. Abraham considered the promise and acted upon it.

- Jeremiah 33:3: *"Call unto me, and I will answer thee, and will show thee great things, and difficult [or fenced in], which thou knowest not."*

- You take Him at His Word, and your heart overflows with you that He has given you His Word. The thing for which you have prayed simply **is**. You have called into being a thing that was not because His Word had given you the assurance of it.

- Jeremiah 1:12: *"I watch over my word to perform it."*

- You have held up His Word to Him. You say, "Father, here is what You said through Jesus. Here is what you said through Paul. Here is what you said through your prophets and disciples. Here is what you said through your beloved disciple, John. I have acted upon it and I do thank you for making it good."

- You have taken Jesus's place. You are acting as Jesus would have acted. You are doing the Father's own will just as Jesus did it in His earth walk. You and Jesus are one. You act for Him. Your will and His will are harnessed. They make a unit. How beautiful it is.

- You can say, "Father, just as Jesus came down from heaven to do your will, so I have been born from heaven to do your will."

A MASTER OF CIRCUMSTANCES

- Arthur Way translated Philippians 4:11–13 this way:

  I have learned, in whatsoever condition I am, to be independent of circumstances. I am schooled to bear the depths of poverty, I am schooled to bear abundance. In life as a whole, and in all its circumstances, I have mastered the secret of living—how to be the same amidst repletion and starvation, amidst abundance and privation. I am equal to every lot, through the help of Him who gives me inward strength.

- Did you notice he said, "I have mastered the secret of living;" "I am to be independent of circumstances"?

- When one is master of circumstances, he has taken on his rights and privileges in Christ. The Word has become a reality. He says fearlessly, "I can do anything that my Father wishes me to do, because greater is He that is in me than he that is in the world." (See 1 John 4:4.)

- Just as Jesus said, "I came down from God" (see John 6:38), you say, "I am from God, and I am an overcomer; because great is He that is in me than he that is in the world."

- So, you see the secret of living is living in His Word. That is His will.

- Philippians 4:19: *"And my God shall supply every need of yours according to his riches in glory in Christ Jesus."*

- God is your supply. Its limit is His will. His will only limits your ability. "My Father does supply," you whisper over and over again.

- Matthew 6:26–33: *"Your heavenly Father feedeth them"* (verse 26). He is using the birds as an illustration. Then He says, *"shall he not much more clothe you?"* (verse 30).

- The thirty-second verse says, *"For your heavenly Father knoweth that ye have need of all these things."*

- Your heavenly Father knows your needs, knows your surroundings, the opposition, knows the whole thing.

- You rest in Him. You are His child; you are in His family; you are a branch of the Vine. He is the Husbandman. He cares for the vineyard. He knows about it. You are His fruit-producer. You are His connection with the unsaved world. You are His connection with the church and the people in your community. You have His life, His nature. You have His light and wisdom. You have His love. You have Him. He lives in You. By giving Him His place, you let Him have freedom in you.

- First John 3:2: *"Beloved, now are we children of God."*

- Take your place as a child; act your part. Assume your rights and responsibilities. You are His righteousness. Yes, you are His righteous one. (See Hebrews 10:38.)

- You are to act by faith, live by faith, show the faith walk. Why? You glorify Him. You make men know that He can be trusted, and you are bearing now the fruits of righteousness.

- Righteousness means your ability to stand in the Father's presence with no sense of guilt or inferiority.

- He made you righteous, and you do not discredit what He has made you to be. You are what He says you are.

- First John 5:4: *"For whatsoever is begotten of God overcometh the world: and this is the victory that hath overcome the world, even our faith."*

- Our faith took us into the family of overcomers. Our faith made us sons and daughters of God. Our faith has made us the very righteousness of God, has made us new creations of God.

- *"And who is he that overcometh the world, but he that believeth that Jesus is the Son of God?"* (1 John 5:5.)

- You stand before the world as God's overcoming son.

- Second Corinthians 10:4–5 (WAY):

  Very human as I am, I do not fight with merely human weapons. No, the weapons with which I war are not the weapons of mere flesh and blood [senses], but, in the strength of God, they are mighty enough to raze all strongholds of the foes. I can batter down bulwarks of human reason, I can scale every crag-fortress that towers up bidding defiance to the true knowledge of God.

- This translation startles you. We have never appreciated what we are in Christ. We have never appreciated His invitation in Hebrews 4:16 to come boldly to the throne of grace. That throne of grace is a throne of love gifts. It is a throne where love meets love. Love plans there to bless the world.

- He has made you righteous with His righteousness. He has made you strong with His own strength. Now you can face the foes of your Christ as a victor.
- The shield of faith, your quiet confidence in the Word of God, catches every fiery dart of the enemy. The sword of the Spirit is not used against men, flesh and blood, but is used against your enemies.
- What is this sword of the Spirit? It is the Word of God.
- Ephesians 6:10–18 is like an arsenal. There you equip yourself to meet your adversaries. You never use the sword to hurt folks, to cut them; but you use it as your face your enemy, praying *"with all prayer and supplication…in the Spirit"* (Ephesians 6:18), with a quiet confidence that your prayer will be answered just as Jesus's prayers were.
- You can look up and say as did Jesus at the grave of Lazarus, *"Father, I thank thee that thou heardest me. And I knew that thou hearest me always"* (John 11:41–42).
- Here is Way's translation of 2 Corinthians 2:14:

> *Not that my going was my own choosing: no, thank God, it is He who everywhere leads me, leads in Messiah's triumphant-procession. By me He wafts abroad through every land the knowledge of Jesus, the incense of His triumphal march. Yes, I am Messiah's incense, upwafted to God in the sight of all, alike of those who are going to deliverance, and of those who are going to destruction.*

HOW MUCH DO YOU REMEMBER?

1. Quote four definite prayer promises given to us in the Word.
2. How can we know God hears our prayers?
3. What must we do when prayers are not answered immediately?
4. What is the definition of hope?
5. What is God's definition for faith as given to us in His Word?
6. What example in prayer do we get from Abraham?
7. When do we give thanks for our answers to prayer?
8. What lesson does Matthew 6:26–33 hold for us?
9. How does a sense of righteousness help us toward a successful prayer life?
10. Can you give one or more distinct examples of any answers to your prayers or those of your friends?

LESSON 17 NOTES

_____

_____

_____

_____

_____

_____

_____

Lesson 18
THE SUPERMAN

The whole world has been expecting a superman.

The first superman came as a root out of dry ground. No one recognized Him. No one knew that God was manifested in the flesh. They didn't know that the Logos of God, who had been with God, and who was God, was with them. They didn't know that the quiet child who was growing up was the One of whom it was said that all things were made through Him and without Him was not anything made that has been made; and that in Him was life (*zoe*) and that that life was the light of men.

The world has not known that there is a superman in their midst today.

They don't know that every new creation is a superman in the embryo, that all that embryo needs is to know what it is, what it can do, what the Father expects it to do, and what the Father has empowered it to be and to do it in the world.

Hebrews 2:14 tells us what the first superman did to Satan: *"Since then the children are sharers in flesh and blood, he also himself in like manner partook of the same; that through death he might bring to nought him that had the power of death, that is, the devil."*

Hebrews 9:12: *"Nor yet through the blood of goats and calves, but through his own blood, entered in once for all into the holy place, having obtained eternal redemption* [or an eternal defeat of Satan].*"*

They haven't noticed Revelation 1:17–18: *"Fear not; I am the first and the last, and the Living one; and I was dead, and behold, I am alive for evermore, and I have the keys of death and of Hades."*

That is the message from Satan's conqueror.

THE FIRST SUPERMAN

+ Let us look for a moment at Jesus, the Superman.
+ The Superman is a faith man.
+ Jesus was peculiarly the faith Man. In Him, faith came to the world. Everything was waiting for faith.
+ Matthew 19:26. Jesus says here, *"But with God all things are possible."*
+ John 17:2: *"Even as thou gavest him authority over all flesh."* Master of all flesh, as well as of demons.
+ Luke 4:1–13. Here, we see Jesus meeting the adversary, Satan, and conquering him in every temptation.
+ In Matthew 4:23–25, we see Jesus casting out demons, healing all manner of disease, all manner of sickness, and setting men free who were holden with divers diseases and torments, palsy and epilepsy. He healed them all. Jesus was a Superman.
+ Matthew 8:23–27, we read, *"And the men marvelled, saying, What manner of man is this, that even the winds and the sea obey him?"* (verse 27).
+ He was crossing the Sea of Galilee in a boat, and the adversary brought a storm upon Him. The disciples cried, *"Lord, save! We perish"* (verse 25). He replied, *"Why are ye fearful, oh ye of little faith?"* (verse 26).
+ Then He arose and rebuked the winds and the sea, and there was a great calm.

- John 11:43–44 shows Him standing at the tomb of Lazarus. He had told them to take away the stone; and Martha, the sister, had said, *"Lord, by this time the body decayeth; for he hath been dead four days"* (verse 39).
- Jesus said unto her, *"Said I not unto thee, that, if thou believedst, thou shouldest see the glory of God?"* (verse 40).
- Then they took away the stone, and Jesus lifted up His eyes to heaven and said, *"Father, I thank thee that thou heardest me"* (verse 41).
- Here was a man who dared to thank God that He was heard whenever He spoke. And then He cried, *"Lazarus, come forth"* (verse 33).
- *"He that was dead came forth, bound hand and foot with grave-clothes; and his face was bound about with a napkin. Jesus saith unto them, Loose him, and let him go"* (verse 44).
- Here is the Master of death. The body was decaying; the flesh loosened from the bones. He came forth from the tomb with the flesh of a child. They were standing in the presence of a Superman.
- Not only was He a superman in His earth walk, but He is the head of the "super-race." This has never been believed by the church. She has had the theories of it. She has had more philosophy than reality. Her philosophers have been her enemies. They have given an interpretation of the Word that has robbed it of its reality.
- Colossians 1:15–18:

  Who is the image of the invisible God, the firstborn of all creation; for in him were all things created, in the heavens and upon the earth, things visible and things invisible, whether thrones or dominions or principalities or powers; all things have been created through him, and unto him; and he is before all things, and in him all things consist. And he is the head of the body, the church: who is the beginning, the firstborn from the dead; that in all things he might have the preeminence.

WHAT JESUS SAID ABOUT THIS NEW RACE

- Mark 9:23: *"And Jesus said unto him, If thou canst! All things are possible to him that believeth."*
- The word *"believeth"* means "a believing one." The Jews were not believers of the Word. They had sense knowledge faith. They believed that which they could see and hear and taste and feel. The superman believes in a Word of God independent of the senses.
- Matthew 17:20: *"And nothing shall be impossible unto you."* Jesus is not tantalizing us. He is not giving us a hyperbole. He is telling us the truth. He is laying down the law for the new man.
- You remember 2 Corinthians 5:17–18. Write out this verse:

_____

_____

_____

- Wherefore, if any man is in Christ, there is a new species—something new that has come into being.
- The old creation was a failure, a subject of Satan. This new creation, this new man, is a master of Satan and demons. The old creation lives in the realm of fear and doubt. The new creation lives in the realm of the new kind of life (*zoe*).
- Jesus spoke to Martha, *"If thou believedst, thou shouldest see the glory of God?"* (John 11:40.)

- But Martha didn't believe. All she ever saw was her brother, who had been dead four days, come out of the tomb. If the eyes of her understanding or heart had been illuminated, she would have seen the glory of God.

- Mark 11:23 shows the limitlessness of the faith life as illustrated by Jesus: *"Verily I say unto you, Whosoever shall say unto this mountain, Be thou taken up and cast into the sea; and shall not doubt in his heart, but shall believe that what he saith cometh to pass; he shall have it."*

- That leads you into the realm of creative faith.

- Hebrews 11:3 illustrates it: *"By faith we understand that the worlds have been framed by the word of God, so that what is seen hath not been made out of things which appear."*

THE NEW SUPERMAN

- Christianity is not a religion. It is not a system of ethics. It is not a set of rules to guide man's conduct, but it is union with Deity.

- One day I caught a glimpse of what the new creation meant. I asked my heart, "Why should we not be supermen?"

- John 5:24: *"Verily, verily, I say unto you, He that heareth my word, and believeth him that sent me, hath eternal life."*

- What is this eternal life? It is the nature of God. Well, if I have the nature of God, why can't I do God's works? That led me to study the new creation fact.

- We have just quoted that great Scripture, *"Wherefore if any man is in Christ, he is a new creature [a new kind of man]"* (2 Corinthians 5:17). A new man has come on the scene. He is a partaker of God's nature.

- Colossians 1:13–14: *"Who delivered us out of the power of darkness, and translated us into the kingdom of the Son of his love; in whom we have our redemption, the forgiveness of our sins."*

- This new creation has been delivered out of the authority of Satan by the new birth, has been translated into the kingdom of the Son of God's love. He has a perfect redemption from the hand of the enemy. Satan's dominion over him has been broken.

- You remember that Satan is eternally defeated. He is eternally conquered, and that the new creation has dominion over him.

- Mark 16:17–18: *"In my name shall they cast out demons… they shall lay hands on the sick, and they shall recover."*

- He is a master of Satan, a master of demons. This new creation is not a subject of demoniacal dominion. He has passed out of the realm of Satan into the realm of God. He is superior to Satan and demons.

- Philippians 4:11 (WAY) says that he becomes "independent of circumstances." He lives above want; he lives where affluence cannot sway him. In all things and in everything he is a master. He is a partaker of the divine nature. (See 2 Peter 1:4.)

- First John 5:13: *"These things have I written unto you, that ye may know that ye have eternal life, even unto you that believe on the name of the Son of God."*

- By your acting on that Word, you pass out of the realm of Satan, out of weakness, into the realm of God. God's life becomes your life.

- Here are a few snapshots of this new creation, this new man: He shall lay hands on the sick and they shall recover. He shall cast out demons. (See Mark 16:17–18.)

+ Romans 5:17: *"For if, by the trespass of the one, death reigned through the one; much more shall they that receive the abundance of grace and of the gift of righteousness reign in life through the one, even Jesus Christ."*

+ We reign as kings right here in the earth surrounded as we are with the work of the adversary, within the influence of the adversary. We are victors.

+ Can you understand what it would mean for a group of men and women to be "independent of circumstances," to know their Father God so intimately that they never thought of the need of faith, or the need of ability, or the need of power? Can you conceive of men to whom the Word is a living reality? Then you conceive of men who are masters, who are dominant.

+ Jesus told the disciples to tarry in Jerusalem until they received power from on high. (See Acts 1:8; Luke 24:49.) The word *"power"* is *dunimas*, which means "ability." This is thrilling. In essence, "I want you to tarry in Jerusalem until you receive God's ability."

+ God's ability comes to man through the new birth. You receive God's nature, God's very life. It sets you free from the dominion of Satan.

+ Jesus Christ becomes your wisdom. Wisdom is God's ability to utilize circumstances, to utilize knowledge, to take advantage of opportunities, to see the mind of God where others can only see impossibility.

+ Second Corinthians 3:4–6:

    And such confidence have we through Christ to God-ward: not that we are sufficient of ourselves, to account anything as from ourselves; but our sufficiency is from God; who also made us sufficient as ministers of a new covenant; not of the letter, but of the spirit.

+ God becomes your sufficiency. He renews your mind after receive eternal life so that you can grasp the significance of His revelation in the Word.

+ You can see yourself as a new creation, a new species with the ability of God, with the great and mighty Spirit that raised Jesus from the dead actually living in you. (See Romans 8:11.)

+ You can see yourself utilizing the authority that is invested in the name of Jesus.

+ Jesus said, in Matthew 28:18, *"All authority hath been given unto me in heaven and on earth."*

+ Then He gives to us the power of attorney to use His name.

+ John 14:13–14 and 16:23–24 show us the power of attorney to use the name that has back of it all authority in heaven and on earth.

+ That name heals diseases, breaks the dominion of Satan, conquers the very forces of the devil, makes the believer more than a conqueror in every field, takes him out of the realm of doubt and fear and gives him the courage of the faith of God. It takes him out of the realm of inefficiency and gives him the efficiency of God. It takes him away from the inefficiency of the word of man and gives him the efficiency of the Word of God.

+ You begin to see now that this new creation is no common being.

+ However, if he has no instruction to show him what he is in Christ, and what his rights and privileges are, he lives as a common man.

+ First Corinthians 3:1–3 gives us a pathetic picture:

    And I, brethren, could not speak unto you as unto spiritual, but as unto carnal, as unto babes in Christ. I fed you with milk, not with meat; for ye were not yet able to bear it: nay, not even now are ye able; for ye are yet carnal: for whereas there is among you jealousy and strife, are ye not carnal, and do ye not walk after the manner of men?

- Do you know who the Holy Spirit is? He raised Jesus from the dead. He is omnipotence. You have omnipotence abiding in you.
- What He did in the dead body of Jesus, He can do in your life. He can take your lips with God's Words filling them, and lead men to Christ, heal the sick, cast out demons, break the dominion of sin and fear over the minds of men and women.
- His Words in your lips make you a master of demons. That is a Superman!
- Hear Him whisper, "If God is for you, who can be against you? (See Romans 8:31.) I can do all things in Him who strengtheneth me. (See Philippians 4:13.) Lo, I am with you always. (See Matthew 28:20.) Nothing shall be impossible to you. (See Matthew 17:20.) God is the strength of your life. Who can condemn you? You are reigning with Him as the master of laws of nature."

HOW MUCH DO YOU REMEMBER?

1. Who was the first Superman, master of all flesh and demons?
2. What is referred to in our lesson as a "superman in embryo"?
3. Give four Scriptures showing Jesus's authority over demons, disease, and sickness.
4. Give a Scripture proving His mastery over the elements of nature.
5. Why did Martha feel sure that Jesus could not raise Lazarus from the dead?
6. What was Jesus's answer to Martha's unbelief?
7. Quote two Scriptures that show that the church may be supermen and masters today, if they but will.
8. What is your version of the possibilities wrapped up in the term "independent of circumstances"?
9. What other meaning may be given to the word "power" found in Acts 1:8 and Luke 24:49?
10. What is your confession today after reading about what God has made you through His Son?

LESSON 18 NOTES

_____

_____

_____

_____

_____

_____

_____

_____

_____

_____

_____

_____

Lesson 19
THE CONFESSION OF JESUS

As we study the life of the Man in the four Gospels, we are continually reminded of God.

He walked and talked and acted as though He and God were one.

He acted righteousness. He practiced it.

He was utterly unconscious of the need of anything. Whenever He needed faith, no matter what the circumstances were, whenever He needed love, whenever He needed wisdom, there was no sense of lack or limitation. In His walk, He had no sense of fear or sin, no sense of need of any kind.

He loved like God. He acted like God. He was unconsciously the Master of every circumstance.

He ruled the forces of nature like God. All these laws heard His voice. All of nature recognized Him as Master.

How it thrills us when we think of the winds and the waves obeying Him. (See Matthew 8:27.) He walked the waves. He turned water into wine. That was my Lord.

FIVE CONFESSIONS

+ Here are some confessions that I wish you would look up:
  1. *"I came out from the Father, and am come into the world: again, I leave the world, and go unto the Father"* (John 16:28).
     + You remember that the vital side of the plan of redemption is based upon confession.
     + In order to receive eternal life, you confess Jesus Christ as Savior and Lord, and your faith in His resurrection from the dead.
  2. *"Ye are from beneath; I am from above"* (John 8:23).
     + There is a fearlessness about these confessions that thrills us.
  3. *"A greater than Solomon is here"* (Matthew 12:42).
     + You sense no conceit or bigotry as you read these words.
     + If any other man had made these statements, his name would have been forgotten; but they fit into the life of the Man.
  4. *"I am the light of the world: he that followeth me shall not walk in the darkness, but shall have the light of life."* (John 8:12).
     + What a confession! He declares that He is the light and wisdom of the world; and the man who walks in His wisdom, His light, will not have been a failure. But perhaps the next one intrigues us more:
  5. *"I am the way, and the truth, and the life: no one cometh unto the Father, but by me"* (John 14:6).

FOUR MIGHTY FACTS

  1. First, He is the way to the Father. No other way, no other method, no other person, can lead a man to the Father but the Man of Galilee.
  2. Second, *"I am the truth"* or the reality.

- The wisest of humanity have sought for reality, but they have never found it until they find it in the Man. Jesus is the end of all search; He is reality.

3. Third, *"I am the life."*

- The Greek word, *zoe*, grips us. You remember, *"I came that they may have life, and may have it abundantly"* (John 10:10). This *zoe* is to be given to us in abundance. I now understand that when He said, *"Of his fulness we all received, and grace for grace"* (John 1:16), He means of the fullness of His life, of His nature, of His wisdom. That life was brought by Jesus, and He gives it to man.

- You understand that eternal life is the one thing that man must have. Forgiveness of his sins would not help him any. He would go on committing the same old sins. What he needs is eternal life, the nature of God, to displace his old fallen nature and make him a new creation in Christ Jesus.

- When Jesus said, *"No one cometh unto the Father, but by me"* (John 14:6), He is closing every door. The people who accept philosophy and metaphysics instead of eternal life are utterly lost. They can never stand in God's presence.

- Eternal life gives to man righteousness. Righteousness means the ability to stand in the Father's presence without the sense of guilt or inferiority. Eternal life makes us His very sons and daughters.

4. Fourth, when Jesus said, *"No one cometh unto the Father, but by me,"* we see it.

- The same truth is brought out by Peter, *"And in none other is there salvation: for neither is there any other name under heaven, that is given among men, wherein we must be saved"* (Acts 4:12).

- *"I am the good shepherd"* (John 10:11).

- What a confession! It makes you think of the twenty-third Psalm, *"Jehovah is my shepherd, I shall not want"* (Psalm 23:1). Then, He is my Caretaker, my Protector, my Bread-Provider. The shepherd is responsible for their food and water, and so my Shepherd, Jesus, says, *"I am the bread of life: he that cometh to me shall not hunger, and he that believeth on me shall never thirst"* (John 6:35).

HIS WORDS MEET EVERY NEED

- How that fits into the thought of the shepherd. He leads me down where the waters are gentle and quiet. He takes me back then where the alfalfa is rich. In every place in life He cares for me.

- You can almost hear Paul say, *"And my God shall supply every need of yours according to his riches in glory in Christ Jesus"* (Philippians 4:19).

- Or Ephesians 1:3: *"Who hath blessed us with every spiritual blessing in the heavenly places in Christ."*

- He is my Protector and Caretaker. He is my Shield. No enemy can touch me.

- Then you hear Him say, *"It is the spirit that giveth life; the flesh profiteth nothing: the words that I have spoken unto you are spirit, and are life"* (John 6:63).

- No other man ever talked that way, ever dared say that his words were spirit and life; that is, that they fed this human spirit, that they gave life to our bodies.

- You remember Psalm 107:20 says, *"He sendeth his word, and healeth them."*

- Then there in Romans 8:11: *"But if the Spirit of him that raised up Jesus from the dead dwelleth in you, he that raised up Christ Jesus from the dead shall give life also to your mortal bodies through his Spirit that dwelleth in you."*

- Here His words are food and strength and health. His words meet every need.

- You can understand Matthew 4:4: *"Man shall not live by bread alone, but by every word that proceedeth out of the mouth of God."* Now your heart can take this in as you feed on it, as you search it, and it becomes health and strength and healing to you.

- But this Scripture could mean so much to us: *"For I am come down from heaven, not to do mine own will, but the will of him that sent me"* (John 6:38).

WALK IN LOVE, FOR HIS WILL IS LOVE

- We have thought that the Father's will would be hard, and we shrank from doing it. But instead, it is a will of love. As you walk in the Father's will, you always walk in the light. You will never injure anyone. Your words will be saturated with love. You will walk in the light, for His will is the light. You will walk in love, for His will is love.

- Now you can understand, *"He that followeth me shall not walk in the darkness"* (John 8:12). In other words, He is saying to our hearts, "He that follows Me shall walk in the will of the Father; he will never step out of that will."

- *"I am the living bread which came down out of heaven: if any man eat of this bread, he shall live forever: yea and the bread which I will give is my flesh, for the life of the world"* (John 6:51).

- No unspiritually-minded person can understand this Scripture; but it is true. Spiritual hunger is just as real as physical or mental hunger, and your spirit can feed on Jesus. Your heart feeds on love, and you grow so lonely for it, until when love comes you feel so content and restful.

- But love springs from the recreated human spirit, and it is this recreated human spirit that receives the life of God. It is that part of us that feeds upon the love. Just as the lover feeds upon the object of his affection, you feed on Christ. He becomes the living bread for your spirit, the living water to quench your thirst.

- Of His fullness we have all received. That means of His love life, of His grace life, of His forbearance and gentleness, we have received. (See Colossians 2:9–10.)

- But there is something more. We have received His strength. Love is our strength to stand up under the heavy burdens and strains of life.

- Israel ate the bread that came down from heaven—*manna.* You need to eat the bread that will give you a mighty love, a mighty grace, and fortitude to stand in the midst of awful suffering and agony. Men will persecute us for righteousness' sake. Men never do that, but demons do. They shrink from the consciousness of your righteousness in Christ. They know that you are their master, and they fear you.

- Now you feed on the bread of the Mighty—this Word. You digest it until your whole being is saturated with His life, until it makes you victorious, fills you with victory, gives the sense of oneness with Him. You get so that after a while you recognize that it is in you. You remember that Jesus said, *"for he abideth with you, and shall be in you"* (John 14:17); and you become conscious of His indwelling presence. You meditate upon it.

- I love to think of your becoming God-inside-minded, knowing that *"greater is he that is in you than he that is in the world"* (1 John 4:4). Read that first sentence: *"Ye are of God."*

- Whisper it over in your heart, "I am of God; I am a master. I am a conqueror. I have been feeding on the bread of heaven. I have the vitamins of God. How they have strengthened my faith and built me up in Christ."

- *"He that hath my commandments, and keepeth them, he it is that loveth me: and he that loveth me shall be loved of my Father, and I will love him, and will manifest myself unto him"* (John 14:21).

- Jesus never said a greater thing as far as your daily walk is concerned. If you love Him, the Father will love you.
- In the next verse we read that Jesus and the Father will make their home in you. The Father and Jesus will live with you. That will ensure your rent and your taxes, your food and raiment; for they will never make their home with you without bearing the heavy end of the burden. That means that no disease can come into your home and find a lodging there.
- You have the very life and nature of God in you, and He is with you.
- *"And I will love him and will manifest myself unto him"* (John 14:21).
- How will Jesus manifest Himself to you? In His Word, in what we call providence. You will find blessing strewn all along the road, blessing that you never dreamed existed.
- He will manifest Himself as the Shepherd of your life, as your Bread-Provider, as your Keeper, as the One who loves you and gave Himself for you.
- He will come and make His home with you. You see, His love nature will dominate you. His love character will become part of you. He will build Himself into you. After a while, men will see Jesus in you, and they will call you the Jesus-man, the Jesus-woman.
- *"And we will come unto him, and make our abode with him"* (John 14:23).
- A man said the other day, "That is the work of the Master. I found a beautiful thing had taken place. Only Jesus could have brought that to pass."
- Let Him have His way with you. Let Him govern you. Don't be afraid of Him. No one loves you as He loves you. He is the strength of your life.
- *"I and the Father are one"* (John 10:30). *"He that hath seen me hath seen the Father; how sayest thou, Show us the Father?"* (John 14:9).
- Jesus dared to say that He and the Father were one!
- "Why, if the Father is like Jesus, I am perfect content," you say. What a joy it will be to live with Him eternally.

YOU AND JESUS, UTTERLY ONE

- But I want you to see another phase of this. Write out what Jesus said in John 17:21:

_____

_____

_____

- Now we are coming to the heart of it. You and Jesus are utterly one…identified.
- *"I am the vine and ye are the branches"* (John 15:5).
- How that truth grows into us. You are the fruit-bearing part of Jesus. If you are a branch, then you and Jesus are one.
- You remember 1 Corinthians 12:12: *"For as the body is one, and hath many members, and all the members of the body, being many, are one body; so also is Christ."*
- Here the body is called Christ. He is the head of the body. You are a member of His body. (See 1 Corinthians 6:15.) My hand is a part of me, and you are a part of Christ. You are a Christ-one. You and Christ are identified. You are the branch part of Him that bears the fruit of love. You are the part that says all the sweet, beautiful things, that does the kind deeds. You are the part of Him that sacrifices to give part of your money. You are the part of Him that bears the love fruit. You and He are one. (See John 15:5–8.)

- *"Herein is my Father glorified, that ye bear much fruit; and so shall ye be my disciples"* (John 15:8).

- A disciple is not only a convert, a new creation child of God, but he is a student. Then He said, *"Go ye therefore, and make disciples of all the nations, baptizing them into the name of the Father and of the Son and of the Holy Spirit: teaching them to observe all things whatsoever I commanded you: and lo, I am with you"* (Matthew 28:19–20).

- Now you are going to be a disciple of this Man who said all these wonderful things about Himself.

- The branch is going to be a light that will show men the way unto Christ. The branch is going to be a disciple that will bear fruit just like the Master, and will learn to know the Word so he can bless men with it.

- I want every one of you who is studying this course to get to know Him so well, and to know His Word so well, that you can bear the Jesus kind of fruit.

- Nearly all these references are from the gospel of John. I wish you would look them up. I want the Word to live in you. I want the Spirit to build it into you. He can do it only as you practice it. You can talk it, and learn it, and give it by heart, but until you practice it, until you live it, it will not mean much to you.

- Don't learn it to prove a doctrine, but learn it to live. Your doctrines are largely governed by the senses. You want to be governed by the Spirit through the Word.

HOW MUCH DO YOU REMEMBER?

1. In what things did the Master take His place?

2. a. If confession is the basis for the vital side of redemption, what do we confess?

   b. Give two Scriptures showing Jesus's confession.

3. a. Give a Scripture that assures us He will supply our needs.

   b. Give one that shows He has blessed us.

4. Tell the meaning of Romans 8:11.

5. What is the Father's will?

6. What three blessings has He given us from His fullness?

7. a. What three sentences can we repeat to help affirm our faith?

   b. What gives us strength?

8. If you allow the Father and Jesus to live with you, what will They manifest to you?

9. What does John 15:5 show us?

10. As a member of Christ's body, how are we to act?

LESSON 19 NOTES

_____

_____

_____

_____

_____

Lesson 20
SATAN, THE DEFEATED

Jesus vanquished Satan, not for Himself, but for man. His victory over Satan was purely a substitutionary act. So, Christ's victory is our victory, for all that He did in substitution, He did for us.

The Supreme Court of the universe looks upon the substitutionary work of Jesus as though it were actually ours. God did not need it, Jesus did not need it, the angels did not need it, but humanity needed the victory that He wrought. God sees Jesus as our perfect Redeemer and us as perfectly redeemed ones. He sees us entering into the fruits of the victory of Jesus, absolute conquerors over all the forces of darkness.

VICTORY OF THE MASTER

+ Hebrews 2:14: *"Since then the children are sharers in flesh and blood, he also himself in like manner partook of the same; that through death he might bring to nought him that had the power of death, that is, the devil."*

+ Way translates it:

> He did this, that he might be able to die, and by His death might annihilate the power of him who sways the scepter of death's terrors—that is, the devil—and so might transfer into a new existence those who through the haunting dread of death were all their lifetime bowed beneath a yoke of veritable slavery.

+ Colossians 2:14–15:

> *Having blotted out the bond written in ordinances that was against us, which was contrary to us: and he hath taken it out of the way, nailing it to the cross; having despoiled the principalities and the powers, he made a show of them openly, triumphing over them in it.*

+ These two Scriptures describe the victory of the Master before His resurrection.

+ Galatians 2:20 describes our place, *"I have been crucified with Christ."* It is not the same as the old version reads, for in the mind of justice, ever one of us was nailed to that cross in Christ. Then when He died, we died with Him. His death was a substitutionary death. It was our death.

+ Sin slew Him—our sin slew Him. I suppose, if the truth were known, we slew Him.

JESUS JUSTIFIED

+ Then Jesus, taking us and our sins with Him, went to the place where we should have gone alone, and there suffered until every claim of justice was fully met.

+ You remember 1 Timothy 3:16, which tells us that He was *"justified in the spirit."* He had been condemned in spirit. He had suffered in our stead in spirit. It means that He was actually begotten of God just as Acts 13:33 declares, *"Thou art my Son; this day have I begotten Thee."*

+ Peter tells us in 1 Peter 3:18 that He was made alive in spirit; that is, He received the life of God.

+ He had died spiritually. He had partaken of Satan's nature that we had. He became utterly one with us in His death, and now He is justified. He has met the claims of justice. He has met every claim that justice held against us.

+ But that is not all. *"For we are his workmanship, created in Christ Jesus"* (Ephesians 2:10).

- When Jesus was recreated, called the Son of God, then, in the mind of justice, our new creation became a reality.
- Notice what happened. He was justified in spirit. He was made alive in spirit; and in that justification, we see Romans 4:25: *"Who was delivered up for our trespasses, and was raised for our justification."*
- Then he was recreated, became the firstborn out of death—the Head of the new creation—and we are His workmanship, created that morning down in that dread place—made new creations in Jesus Christ.

SATAN DEFEATED

- Then our Master, Head, and Lord did the amazing thing found first in Hebrews and then in Colossians. He met the adversary who had reigned over the human race for more than four thousand years. He stripped him of his authority there in hell: He entered the home of that strong man and conquered him, defeated him, broke his dominion over the human race. What an hour it must have been! What a thing it must have been when Jesus actually paralyzed the death-dealing power of Satan!
- Revelation 1:18 became a fact: *"I was dead, and behold, I am alive for evermore, and I have the keys of death and of Hades."*
- Do you remember that Jesus said in Luke 12:5: *"Fear him, who after he hath killed hath power to cast into hell"?*
- When the believer knows that Satan has been conquered and that he is a conquered force today, he will begin to rise up and take his place in Christ.
- Write out Hebrews 9:12:

_____

_____

_____

- There could be no eternal redemption without an eternally defeated Satan to the new creation. You see, Jesus conquered the devil, actually defeated him on his own ground, and took from him the authority that Adam had given to him in the garden.
- That passage in Revelation 1:18 is a graphic picture of Jesus paralyzing the death-dealing power of Satan.
- Rotherham's translation of Hebrews 2:14: *"He paralyzed the death-dealing authority of the devil."*
- That left Satan, as far as the believer is concerned, a paralytic; and that is absolutely true with you walk in love as He tells us.
- First John 2:6, 10: *"He that saith he abideth in him ought himself also to walk even as he walked. …He that loveth his brother abideth in the light, and there is no occasion of stumbling in him."*
- So long as I walk in love, Satan is a defeated being as far as I am concerned. When I step out of love, I step over into no man's land, where Satan has access to me. When I walk in the light as he is in the light (see 1 John 1:7), Satan as no dominion over me.
- You understand that in Him is no darkness, and that if I walk in darkness I am playing into the devil's hands. (See 1 John 1:5–6.)
- Satan can't put diseases upon you any more than he could put them upon Jesus. As long as you take advantage of your place in Christ at the first intimation of Satan's touch, you have the authority to command his power to be broken over you. Satan is a defeated foe.

- Colossians 1:13: *"Who delivered us out of the power of darkness, and translated us into the kingdom of the Son of his love."*

- Satan has no authority over the new creation in the kingdom of the Son of God's love. Jesus is Lord and Head of that new creation. Jesus is the Vine and we are the branches. Do you think that Jesus would have the devil ruling one of the branches and curtailing the fruit-bearing ability of that branch? I can't accept that, for Satan has no legal right to rule over a branch of that vine.

- *"In whom we have our redemption"* (Colossians 1:14). From what were you redeemed? Why, from Satan of course! Was that just a temporary affair? No, it is an eternal redemption. It will last until the coming of the Master.

- We read in Ephesians 1:7, *"In whom we have our redemption through his blood, the forgiveness of our trespasses."*

- And what kind of redemption is it? It is *"according to the riches of his grace, which he made to abound toward us in all wisdom and prudence"* (Ephesians 1:7–8).

- It is a God-sized redemption. It is a God-arranged redemption, and it is a redemption of God's own possession. You are His possession. You are His sons and His daughters.

- Satan has no right to reign over you any more than he has a right to reign over Jesus.

- I wonder if you read carefully Hebrews 1:1–3:

> God…hath at the end of these days spoken unto us in his Son, whom he appointed heir of all things, through whom also he made the worlds; who being the effulgence of his glory, and the very image of his substance, and upholding all things by the word of his power, when he had made purification of sins, sat down on the right hand of the Majesty on high.

- He sat down because His work was finished. He conquered the adversary. He had a prize ring, and the great fight of the ages took place. He absolutely put Satan 'hors de combat.'

SATAN HAS NO RIGHTS TO US

- But perhaps the greatest thing ever spoken in connection with this was said in John 14:30: *"For the prince of the world cometh: and he hath nothing in me."* We would translate it today, "The prince of this world cometh to me, but he has nothing on me."

- What does that mean? It means that Satan found nothing in Jesus that he owned or had any right to. Jesus was absolutely righteous. There was nothing in Jesus that Satan could place his hand upon and say, "That is mine."

- Now what about the new creation? In 2 Corinthians 5:17–18 we read, *"Wherefore if any man is in Christ, he is a new creature: the old things are passed away; behold, they are become new. But all things are of God, who reconciled us to himself."*

- Who is the Spirit speaking of here? Of the man who has had satanic nature in him once, the man for whom Jesus died and suffered and conquered the devil.

- His former state is described in John 8:44:

> Ye are of your father the devil, and the lusts of your father it is your will to do. He was a murderer from the beginning, and standeth not in the truth, because there is no truth in him. When he speaketh a lie, he speaketh of his own: for he is a liar, and the father thereof.

- Jesus died and conquered Satan and wrought redemption for that demon-indwelt man, that man with the devil's nature in him.

- First John 3:10: *"In this the children of God are manifest, and the children of the devil: whosoever doeth not righteousness is not of God, neither he that loveth not his brother."*

- And, in 1 John 5:19, we read, *"We know that we are of God, and the whole world lieth in the evil one [or in the relationship of the evil one]."*

- Now come back with me to the Scripture in Corinthians. I want you to accept all that God has wrought in Christ. It is a perfect redemption that is waiting for humanity.

- Not only is it a perfect redemption, but a redemption of a perfect new creation; and with that new creation is a perfect righteousness. With that perfect righteousness is perfect fellowship, and with that perfect fellowship is absolute dominion over the adversary in the name of Jesus Christ.

- *"Wherefore if any man is in Christ."* Every man is in Christ who has acknowledged Him as Savior and Lord. That expression, "in Christ," is a legal phrase. It means that I have received the nature and life of God into my spirit and that I am now a branch of the vine. It means that the old things of my past life have stopped being and that all things have become new; and all these things are of God who has reconciled me to Himself. There could be no reconciliation without a new creation.

- God laid my diseases, my sins, and myself on Jesus. He bore them away. Now I accept that, and when I do, I receive a new nature that drives the old nature out.

- The world was justified, or granted, or reckoned justification, in the substitutionary work of Christ. That reckoned righteousness becomes real righteousness the moment we receive eternal life and become God's sons and daughters.

- Now notice that He has not reckoned unto the world their trespasses. Why? Because *"To wit, that God was in Christ reconciling the world unto himself, not reckoning unto them their trespasses, and having committed unto us the word of reconciliation. We are ambassadors therefore on behalf of Christ"* (2 Corinthians 5:19–20).

- We are going to the world and saying, "God laid your diseases and sins and yourself upon Jesus; and *'Him who knew no sin he made to be sin'* (verse 21) to the end that by your confessing Him as your Savior you might become the righteousness of God in Him, you have accepted, you have become the righteousness of God. You are alive in Christ."

- Way says, "Jesus knew not sin; yet God has made Him to be the world's sin for our sakes, that we, whose sin He had thus assumed, might become, by our union with Him, the very righteousness of God [in Christ]."

- Now then, Satan can come to you as he came to Jesus; and you can say, "Satan has come to me, but he has nothing in me. He has nothing on me."

- You are a new creation. If all you ever had was forgiveness of sins, Satan could claim you for his own. He could say, "You are mine." But now he has been defeated. He looks upon you as a new creation, a branch of the vine, Jesus, who conquered him.

- The only thing he can do now is to hinder that branch from bearing fruit.

- Matthew 5:10: *"Blessed are they that have been persecuted for righteousness' sake: for theirs is the kingdom of heaven."*

- Men won't persecute you for your righteousness; that will be Satan. He will bring scandal upon your life. He will make you look unrighteous. When he cannot make you to be unrighteous, he will scandalize you.

- But you remember Isaiah 54:17: *"No weapon that is formed against thee shall prosper; and every tongue that shall rise against thee in judgment thou shalt condemn."*

- You will find that the people through whom Satan persecutes you for righteousness' sake will suffer. You will outlive them. It will be a bitter thing to you to see them go down one after another, but they cannot touch you. They may rob you of your reputation, but they cannot touch your spirit. You stand invincible. You are the righteousness of God in Christ.

+ Satan will tempt you; but remember Ephesians 6:10: *"Finally, be strong in the Lord, and in the strength of his might* [or be made powerful in the Lord]."

+ Who can make you powerful? Why, the Lord, Himself. You are a partaker of His divine nature. He is your sufficiency; He is your ability; He is the strength of your life. Now you are made in the strength of His might, and you have on the armor of God. You are able to stand against all the cunning artifices of the devil.

+ You don't need sense knowledge wisdom. Jesus is made unto you wisdom. You have the ability to conquer, and you are a master. The sword of your recreated spirit is the Word of God, and you can conquer demons in the name of Jesus. You can deliver men and women our of his hand.

+ You can heal the sick. You can strengthen the weak. You can meet every need. You are more than conquerors through Him that loved us. (See Romans 8:37.)

HOW MUCH DO YOU REMEMBER?

1. When Jesus vanquished Satan, what kind of an act was it, and for whom?

2. What two Scriptures describe the victory of the Master before His resurrection?

3. Explain Revelation 1:18. How should we walk to show men that Satan is defeated?

4. a. From whom were we redeemed?

   b. Has Satan any right to reign over us?

5. When did Jesus sit down at the right hand of the Majesty on High?

6. a. Who is spoken of in 1 Corinthians 5:17–21?

   b. In John 8:44?

7. What kind of redemption have we? What kind of righteousness and fellowship has been given to us?

8. Who died and conquered Satan that man might be redeemed?

9. Who could make claim on us if we had been given only forgiveness of sins?

10. What stand can we take in regard to weakness and sickness after Christ has redeemed us?

LESSON 20 NOTES

_____

_____

_____

_____

_____

_____

_____

_____

_____

Lesson 21
JESUS DOES NOT NEED TO SUFFER AGAIN

The expression, "Sat down," occurs about twenty times in the New Testament.

Hebrews 8:1–2 is a good example: *"Now in the things which we are saying the chief point is this: We have such a high priest, who sat down on the right hand of the throne of the Majesty in the heavens, a minister of the sanctuary, and of the true tabernacle, which the Lord pitched, not man."*

Why did He sit down? Because His work was finished.

In John 17:4, He said, *"I glorified thee on the earth, having accomplished the work which thou hast given me to do."* And again, He said on the cross, *"It is finished"* (John 19:30).

What does He mean by that? His work of redemption was not finished until He sat down on the right hand of the Majesty on High. He had finished the work of a Son.

You remember that twice God says, *"This is my beloved Son, in whom I am well pleased"* (Matthew 3:17) and *"Thou art my beloved Son, in thee I am well pleased"* (Mark 1:11).

There never had been anyone on earth before who had perfectly pleased the Father, doing His will in love, and who was a great blessing and comfort to Him. (See John 6:38.)

The words that He uttered on the cross have a far deeper meaning. He had come as the Jew's Messiah; He had come as the Son of Abraham; He had come as a member or the Abrahamic covenant. He had been circumcised into it; and when He went to the cross, He had finished the work as a Son of Abraham—a Hebrew. He had fulfilled the covenant. He had satisfied every claim of the law, and of the covenant.

They are all fulfilled and now the old covenant can be laid aside with the old law of the covenant. Now a new covenant can take its place with a new law and a new creation people. (See Luke 22:20; 1 Corinthians 11:24.)

How few of our theologians have recognized this.

When Jesus arose from the dead, carried His blood into the heavenly Holy of holies, He had satisfied every claim of the Supreme Court of the universe, and He brought the red seal to put upon the document of that redemption. Hebrews 9:12: *"With His own blood."*

All things are now ready for a new covenant in His blood, a new law based upon the new kind of love that Jesus brought to the world and gives to men in the new creation.

That new kind of love is the nature of the Father, and on the basis of the finished work of Christ, God is able to legally give to man His nature, His love nature.

So, *"Wherefore if any man is in Christ, he is a new creature"* (2 Corinthians 5:17), and that new creation has the new nature in it.

Now we have a new covenant for the new creation, and we have a new law for the new creation. We have a new creation that is to keep the new covenant and walk in the new law.

JESUS HAS FINISHED THE WORK

+ Now we can understand how Jesus, after He had finished His work, could enter into His rest.
+ Hebrews 4:1: *"Let us fear, therefore, lest haply, a promise being left of entering into his rest, any one of you should seem to have come short of it."*

+ What does He mean by that? Well, Christ has entered into His rest. You remember that God finished the work of creation, and on the seventh day rested from all His work. Jesus came now for the new creation—has made provision for the new creation. He did that mighty work. He has conquered Satan. He has put sin away by the sacrifice of Himself. He has suffered everything that justice demanded that humanity should suffer for its union with Satan in Adam. Now having finished that work and satisfied the claims of justice, He sits down at the right hand of the Majesty on High.

+ Let us repeat Hebrews 1:3: *"Who being the effulgence [the shining] of his glory, and the very image of his substance, and upholding all things by the word [Logos] of his power, when he had made purification of sins, sat down on the right hand of the Majesty on high."*

+ Jesus is resting, then, from His work. Then it is my business to enter into that rest myself, and to stop all my works and my struggling. I rest in His finished work. I settle down in it.

+ But you say, "That doesn't agree with modern teaching. For instance, believers are struggling with their sin nature."

+ The new creation is the work of God. They have never recognized that they are translated from the kingdom of darkness into the kingdom of the Son of His love. They figure that they are one-half alive, one-half recreated, but that they are under the dominion of their old nature. They have never grown out of their childhood life.

+ First Corinthians 3:1–3 gives us a picture of them. *"And I, brethren, could not speak unto you as unto spiritual, but as unto carnal, as unto babes in Christ"* (verse 1). In other words, "I could not write unto you as spiritual, but as unto sense-ruled believers. *"I fed you with milk, not with meat; for ye were not yet able to bear it: nay, not even now are ye able; for ye are yet carnal: for whereas there is among you jealousy and strife, are ye not carnal, and do ye not walk after the manner of men?"* (verses 2–3).

+ These men were behaving as mere natural men, ruled by the adversary, governed by the defeated one, sense-ruled men.

+ He keeps your bodies full of disease. Perhaps he keeps your finances in a muddled condition. He robs you of your faith and quiet confidence in the Lord. You have never entered into your rest. You have never ceased from your old life habits of thinking that are governed by the adversary. You are governed by the defeated one.

+ "Yes," you say, "But what am I going to do? I do not have faith."

+ First Corinthians 3:21 illustrates this for us: *"Let no one glory in men. For all things are yours [in Christ]."*

+ You are rich. The very wealth of heaven belongs to you, but you have never taken advantage of it. You are living as though the Supreme Court of the universe had not granted you the riches unveiled in Christ. (See Ephesians 1:3.)

+ You know nothing about the unsearchable riches of Christ mentioned in Ephesians 3:8. You are not acquainted with the ability of His spirit in the inner man; that ye may be strengthened with power through his Spirit in the inward man;

> *That Christ may dwell in your hearts through faith; to the end that ye, being rooted and grounded in love, may be strong to apprehend with all the saints what is the breadth and length and height and depth, and to know the love of Christ which passeth knowledge, that ye may be filled unto all the fulness of God.* (Ephesians 3:17–19)

+ But you say, "Well, what about my diseases?"

+ Let us read Isaiah 53:3 (marginal rendering):

He was despised and rejected of men, a man of sickness and acquainted with pain: and as one from whom men hid their faces he was despised; and we esteemed him not. Surely he hath borne our sicknesses and carried our diseases; and we have come to esteem him as the one who was stricken, smitten of God, and afflicted.

- You say, "That settles it. He does not need to bear them again. He bore them once. He does not need to be sick with my sickness again. When I accepted Him as my Savior and confessed Him as my Lord, God gave to me eternal life, His very nature. He breathed into me His own substance and being. I partook of His love nature."

- Christ does not need to die again for you. His work is accepted, and if you are a new creation, Satan has no dominion over you.

- First John 4:8 declares that God is love, and it is His love nature that has become our new nature. He is a faith God, and we have become faith children and love children. He is righteous. We become healed and well children. (See Ephesians 4:24.)

DISEASE HAS BEEN BORNE

- He doesn't need to bear our diseases again.

- But you say, "How do you get rid of your diseases?"

- If Satan has been adroit enough to deceive us and to bring along a bundle of diseases and place them at our door and tell us that they are our disease, that they have our names on them, and we are unwise enough to sign up for them, that is unfortunate. Now we are instructed, however, and we know the truth.

- We say, "Satan, whose diseases are these?" He says, "They are yours." We say, "We beg your pardon. Our diseases were borne by Jesus. If you have any diseases, sir, they are your own; and in the name of Jesus I command you to take them away."

- We hold fast to our confession that *"Surely he hath borne our griefs, and carried our sorrows [diseases]"* (Isaiah 53:4); and because He did it, it is well done and perfectly done; so we hold fast to that confession.

- But you say, "Didn't James say,

  Is any among you sick? let him call for the elders of the church; and let them pray over him, anointing him with oil in the name of the Lord: and the prayer of faith shall save him that is sick, and the Lord shall raise him up; and if he have committed sins, it shall be forgiven him. Confess therefore your sins one to another, and pray one for another, that ye may be healed. The supplication of a righteous man availeth much in its working. (James 5:14–16)?

BABES VERSUS BELIEVERS

- Yes, I remember that, but to whom is James writing? He is writing to babes in Christ, people described to you in 1 Corinthians. You will find another picture of them in Hebrews 5:12–14:

  For when by reason of the time ye ought to be teachers, ye have need again that some one teach you the rudiments of the first principles of the oracles of God; and are become such as have need of milk, and not of solid food. For every one that partaketh of milk is without experience of the word of righteousness; for he is a babe. But solid food is for fullgrown men, even those who by reason of use have their senses exercised to discern good and evil.

- James 1:5–7. This is the babe in Christ.
- You go into our orthodox churches and you will hear these babes crying for faith, for wisdom, and praying for deliverance, for their healing, for this and for that. What is the matter with them? They have never read the Pauline Revelation. They do not know anything about it.
- Paul has received from God revelation of His Son and of His Sonship. It is a revelation of what God did in Jesus for man, and what the Holy Spirit throughout the word does in the man who accepts Christ as Savior.
- As babes, we have to have someone do our believing for us, our receiving. Someone else has to do all the work for us.
- Then, as we remain as babes, we have to have someone pray for us when we are sick.
- This babe in Christ is held under the dominion of the senses. He is sense-ruled. When the elders come into the room, he can see them. He can feel the oil upon his head; he can feel the hands upon his head. He does not have faith himself.
- The elders recognize their righteousness so that they pray for him and the Lord hears their prayer and the man is healed.
- This babe acts as though the Lord didn't do His work, so he has to be healed through the faith of some other person.

WISDOM, REDEMPTION, STRENGTH, AND REST

- First Corinthians 1:30 tells us that Jesus is made unto us wisdom from God.
- Colossians 1:9: "*That ye may be filled with the knowledge of his will in all spiritual wisdom and understanding.*"
- That belongs to the believer in order that he may "*walk worthily of the Lord unto all pleasing, bearing fruit in every good work, and increasing in the knowledge of God*" (verse 10).
- This is speaking of wisdom. There are two kinds of wisdom spoken of in James 3. One is the wisdom that comes down from above, and the other is the wisdom of the devil. But you have the wisdom that comes from God. You are trusting utterly in Him. Here is His living Word, which, in reality, is the wisdom of God that becomes a part of your very being. You rest in it.
- When anyone would rap at the door or call on the phone, I used to say, "Father, give me wisdom." Now I say, "Father, I thank Thee that Jesus is made wisdom."
- "I have been lifted out of the old life, from the old creation into the new creation. In my spirit is the nature of God." Every one of you can say this, for you have been made a new creation in Christ Jesus. Now you can understand this Scripture in Hebrews 1:3.
- I am not going to ask Him to get up to give me victory over my enemies, to deliver me out of the hands of my enemies, because I have been delivered. "*Who delivered us out of the power of darkness, and translated us into the kingdom of the Son of his love; in whom we have our redemption, the forgiveness of our sins*" (Colossians 1:13–14).
- He doesn't have to redeem you again. He doesn't have to do the work again. The work has been accepted.
- What do you do? You rest in His rest. You rest in the confidence that it is done.
- But you say, "Mr. Kenyon, it is so hard to recognize that it is done. It is so hard to grasp."
- Well, the Spirit that raised up Christ from the dead will give clearness to your mind if you will practice it. Begin to live the Word. Begin to take your place right now as a son or daughter in the family. You whisper, "Father, I am what You say I am. I can do what You say I can do in Christ. I can do all things in Him who strengthens me." (See Philippians 4:13.)

- God is the very strength of your being now. (See Psalm 27:1; Philippians 4:13.)
- Ephesians 3:20 shows us what we have studied so much in this course. Write out this verse:

_____

_____

_____

- You must not forget that you have Him inside you, the One who raised Jesus from the dead. He is actually there.
- Read the American Standard Version of Ephesians over and over again until it prevails in your life; then whisper, "God is working in me according to His ability (for that word *"power"* means ability). His grace, His love, His life is effectually working in me."
- May I give you another Scripture? *"I came that they may have life, and may have it abundantly* [or in abundance]" (John 10:10).
- The Father wants you to have the abundance of His nature. He wants your whole spirit and soul swallowed up in His life. (See 2 Corinthians 5:4.)
- He wants you so dominated by His nature that Satan can gain no advantage over you.
- You remember now that the work has all been accomplished for you, and it is all yours the moment you accept Christ. There is no struggle to get it. It is resting in His rest.

HOW MUCH DO YOU REMEMBER?

1. When was the work of redemption completed?
2. What does the new creation in Christ have in place of the old covenant?
3. Do Christians need to struggle with sin consciousness?
4. What is meant by "living and walking as natural men"?
5. What should be our attitude toward disease in the light of Christ's substitutionary sacrifice?
6. What type of Christian is always pleading, crying, and praying for faith?
7. What is Paul's revelation of Christ?
8. Explain the two kinds of wisdom.
9. Why can you rest with confidence in the finished work of Christ?
10. What can John 10:10 mean in your life today?

LESSON 21 NOTES

_____

_____

_____

_____

_____

_____

_____

_____

Lesson 22
ABUNDANCE OF LOVE

Man had an abundance of spiritual death. It reigned over him. It was his despotic master. All the sins and crimes and wars have grown out of that awful thing called spiritual death. It was the very nature of Satan.

Romans 5:12–21 is God's commentary on it. It is called a law of sin and of death. (See Romans 8:2–3.) Even the Ten Commandments are called the law of sin. This law of sin wrought in the human family.

John 10:10: *"I came that they may have life, and may have it abundantly."*

Eternal life is the nature of God (see 2 Peter 1:4), and spiritual death is the nature of Satan.

There is a combat between life and death, between God's nature and Satan's nature in man. Just as spiritual death swallowed the human race, so now God is going to give eternal life in such an abundance that it will swallow up death.

Second Corinthians 5:4: *"For indeed we that are in this tabernacle do groan, being burdened; not for that we would be unclothed, but that we would be clothed upon, that what is mortal may be swallowed up of life."* This word *"life"* is *zoe*. Way translates it "drowned in a sea of Life," showing the abundance of life.

There is in the world today an abundance of sickness. There is the very fullness of Satan. It is so apparent everywhere. Men are filled with the devil.

A new order is coming, however. Man is to be filled with God, filled with His nature, His life, His Being—to be like Him, swayed by Him, ruled by Him.

THE LOVE NATURE

+ God is love.
+ First John 4:8 shows us that man is to be filled with *agape*, the new kind of love. It has never been taught. The church has never majored it in its teachings or creeds.
+ Can you conceive of a body of believers filled with the life and nature of God?
+ We understand Colossians 2:9–10: *"For in him dwelleth all the fulness of the Godhead bodily, and in him ye are made full [or complete], who is the head of all principality and power."*
+ We are made full of the nature of God, full of God. That explains John 1:16: *"For of his fulness we all received, and grace for grace."*
+ Of His abundant nature, abundant life, have we all received. That means that we have received of His love life.
+ Write out 1 John 4:16:

_____

_____

_____

+ We abide, live in our daily walk, in the life and nature of God. The nature of God dominates us, rules us. We live in the realm of love. The love nature dominates our lives just as Jesus in His earth walk lived in the realm of love. (See 1 John 4:17–18.)

- Now, we have been *"delivered…out of the power of darkness, and translated…into the kingdom of the Son of his love"* (Colossians 1:13).

- That love nature of God has swallowed up, dominated us so that we act like lovers, we speak like lovers, and our course of conduct is governed by this nature of God, this new nature given to men.

- Can you visualize a man living in God, walking in God? Just as you walk in the early morning's dense and heavy fog, which saturates your clothes and drips from your hat, you are walking in God until you are saturated with love, until love drips out of your words. Your entire being is love-saturated.

- We can understand 1 John 4:6: *"We are of God: he that knoweth God heareth us; he who is not of God heareth us not. By this we know the spirit of truth, and the spirit of error."*

- We are love and he who knows love will listen to us. You see, *"love is of God; and every one that loveth is begotten of God, and knoweth God"* (1 John 4:7).

- The test of the new birth is the love life. How beautiful it would be if we were actually swallowed up of love. That is what it means—swallowed up of life, and life is love.

- It would solve the home problem, wouldn't it? There would be no quarreling or bitterness. What a heavenly atmosphere the children would grow up in; they would never hear an unkind word or a bitter criticism.

- You can read 1 John 5:13: *"These things have I written unto you, that ye may know that ye have eternal life, even unto you that believe on the name of the Son of God."* You could read it this way, "We know that we have received the nature of God, this love life. We know that we are in the love family. The abundance of His life dominates us. We are ruled by the abundance of God."

- From Hebrews 11:1–3 we understand that the worlds were framed by the word of God. Then God is not only a love God, but He is a faith God. We have in us this faith, God's nature, so that faith becomes an unconscious fact in our lives, just as it was in Jesus's life.

- Jesus had no consciousness of the need or lack of faith. He had no consciousness of the need or lack of love. He lived in the realm of life. He had this life in abundance. He had love and faith in abundance.

- That throws new light upon that sentences in James 1:22: *"But be ye doers of the word, and not hearers only, deluding your own selves."*

"BE YE DOERS"

- The Word is love expressed. Love has spoken, and we have a record of it.

- I become a doer of the Word, then I become a doer of love. I become a doer of faith. I become a doer of this abundant life that is in me. I am living it, letting it loose in me. It lives in me, and rules me.

- I am not receiving myself now with mere empty profession because I assent to a creed or the doctrines of a church. This means very little to the world and to the Father. But now that Word has become a part of my very being. It is building into me the love nature of the Father.

- You remember what Jesus said in Matthew 7:24: *"Every one therefore that heareth these words of mine, and doeth them, shall be likened unto a wise man, who built his house upon the rock."*

- And then He contrasts it with the foolish man in the twenty-sixth verse who didn't do the Word, and built his house upon the sand.

- It is the doer of love, the doer of faith, who is the doer of the Word.

- You remember 1 John 2:29. It is a staggering verse: *"If ye know that he is righteous, ye know that every one also that doeth righteousness is begotten of him."*

+ What is righteousness? Why, it is acting in the realm of love. It is doing love as Jesus did love. Love gives us a holy boldness as it is mentioned in 1 John 4:18: *"There is no fear in love: but perfect love casteth out fear."*

LOVE MAKES US MASTERS

+ Love lets us into the throne room in the very presence of the Father. (See Hebrews 4:16.)

+ Love makes us masters over disease and over lack, weakness, and failure. Love makes us conquerors.

+ Letting love loose in me is letting God loose in me, for God is love.

+ Ephesians 3:19 is a thrilling Scripture in this connection: *"And to know the love of Christ which passeth knowledge, that ye may be filled unto all the fulness of God."* Knowledge here is sense knowledge. This Christ love is the Father's love. It is the abundance of God unveiled in Christ Jesus.

+ The Scripture says, in essence, *"That we may know"* this love; that is, speaking it, entering into it. We are also to be filled unto all the fullness of God. (See 2 John 3:14–21.)

+ That belongs to us, is our inheritance. That is one of the things that Ephesians 1:3 brings to us. *"Blessed be the God and Father of our Lord Jesus Christ, who hath blessed us with every spiritual blessing in the heavenly places in Christ."*

+ How it thrills the heart! He has blessed us with the fullness of Himself. As the air is saturated with moisture, so your spirit and body are saturated with God. You have received the gift of grace, which means the unveiling of the Father's very purpose in you in such abundance that people are affected by what you say.

+ You are rooted and grounded in love. Men are affected by it; selfishness shrinks and shrivels in the presence of this love life in you.

+ You are the living Ephesians 4:13: *"Till we all attain unto the unity of the faith, and of the knowledge of the Son of God, unto a fullgrown man, unto the measure of the stature of the fulness of Christ."*

+ This is the substance of God. This is the abundance of life. This is being rooted and grounded in the love life, the love nature of the Father Himself.

+ This throws light on Ephesians 4:7: *"But unto each one of us was the grace given according to the measure of the gift of Christ."*

+ This abundant life has been given us according to the measure of the grace of God unveiled in Jesus.

+ Romans 15:1–2 now becomes intelligible to us: *"We that are strong ought to bear the infirmities of the weak, and not to please ourselves. Let each one of us please his neighbor for that which is good, unto edifying."*

+ Then He illustrates it, *"For Christ also pleased not himself"* (verse 3).

+ The new self that has come into us is a Jesus-self, a love-self. It is an eternal life-self, a God-ruled, God-dominated self.

+ We are taking over the overload of men around us. We are taking Jesus's place in the earth. (See Ephesians 6:2.) You are bearing men's infirmities instead of finding fault with them and criticizing them.

+ Jesus is thrilled by your conduct toward men, and I can hear Him whisper, "Father, aren't we glad that we made the sacrifice? See how they are responding to your love nature and your love call."

+ How wonderfully Ephesians 5:18–19 is fulfilled in this life: *"And be not drunken with wine, wherein is riot, but be filled with the Spirit [be filled in your recreated spirit with this love nature]; speaking one to another in psalms and hymns and spiritual songs, singing and making melody with your heart to the Lord."*

+ Your whole being is swinging out of the orbit of self-seeking into worship and praise and adoration.

- Then, verses 20–21 become a reality: *"Giving thanks always for all things in the name of our Lord Jesus Christ to God, even the Father; subjecting yourselves one to another in the fear of Christ."*

- Now we move up into the realm into which we have been translated, the kingdom of the Son of His love. (See Colossians 1:13.) We are living in that new realm.

BRANCHES OF THE VINE

- Men recognize us as branches of the Vine, and they say, "Notice the wonderful fruitage, the great clusters of ripened fruit that are in the lives of these men and women." (See John 15:5.)

- It is love fruit. It is the fruit of the abundant life. The master has gained the ascendancy now. Jesus is crowned as Lord of the heart just as we get it in 1 Peter 3:15: *"But sanctify in your hearts Christ as Lord."* Sanctify means to set apart. Then we read it, "But set apart Christ as Lord in your hearts."

- His Lordship is the Lordship of love.

- Colossians 2:6–7 makes it even more manifest: *"Therefore ye received Christ Jesus the Lord, so walk in him, rooted and builded up in him, and established in your faith, even as ye were taught, abounding in thanksgiving."*

- Here is full growth. Here is the abundant life taking us over, crowning Jesus as the very Lord of our being so that His heart is filled with joy over us.

- First Corinthians 12:24: *"But God tempered the body together, giving more abundant honor to that part which lacked."*

- Here is a demonstration of love. The Father knew there would be some members of the body who would never receive any special honor and glory from men, so He glorifies them Himself, *"that there should be no schism in the body; but that the members should have the same care one for another. And whether one member suffereth, all the members suffer with it; or one member is honored, all the members rejoice with it"* (verses 25–26).

- This is where love has actually gained the ascendancy. First Corinthians 10:24 has become a reality: *"Let no man seek his own, but each his neighbor's good."*

- In verse 33, Paul says, *"Even as I also please all men in all things, not seeking mine own profit, but the profit of the many, that they may be saved."*

- *"Be ye imitators of me, even as I also am of Christ"* (1 Corinthians 11:1).

- Here is love in practicable, everyday life. Here is living the Word, letting it dwell in us richly. (See Colossians 3:16.)

- Until the Word does live in us richly, in all wisdom, teaching and admonishing one another in spiritual songs and psalms and hymns, teaching and admonishing one another in the Lord, we will not glorify Him.

- Now our words are love-filled. The abundance of life flows from them. Our bodies are filled with life. Disease and sickness are driven out.

- The joy of the Lord fills us. This is life abundant. This is God actually being let loose in us.

HOW MUCH DO YOU REMEMBER?

1. Between what two natures is there combat?
2. What is God's nature? Satan's nature?
3. In 2 Corinthians 5:4, what is the meaning of "life"?
4. How do we live if we possess the life and nature of God?
5. What does 1 John 4:8 show us?
6. What are the meanings of Ephesians 3:19 and 4:13?
7. What is meant by "abundant life"?
8. What is the fruit of this life?
9. When will we practice 1 Corinthians 10:24?
10. When we are filled with abundant life, what happens to disease and sickness?

LESSON 22 NOTES

Lesson 23
ESTABLISHED

The Father has no pleasure in weak and feeble children. He loves them, will care for them, shield and protect them, but He has no joy in it. (See Ephesians 6:10.)

He never made anyone sick. He never has made one of His children sick or hurt him. He never oppresses them.

Every believer owes it to himself to be established in the Word, to be settled and fixed so that he will not be wafted about by every wind and storm. (See Ephesians 4:14–16.)

WHAT THE BELIEVER NEEDS TO KNOW

- He should know what he is in Christ, know it so thoroughly that no matter what happens he stands unruffled, unaffected. (See Ephesians 1:3–7.)

- He should know what Christ **is** to him, and what He **has done** for him, and what He **is doing** for him now. (See 1 Corinthians 1:30; Philippians 1:6; Hebrews 7:25.)

- This threefold knowledge should be a part of his daily equipment. He should know what belongs to him, what is really his. (See Philippians 1:9–11.)

- No matter what may happen, he stands quiet and restful in the consciousness that if God is for him, no one can successfully be his enemy. (See Romans 8:31–33.)

- He should know about the indwelling Spirit. He should become God-indwelt conscious. (See Philippians 2:13.)

- I know that He that is in me is going to breathe through my lips today the message that you need. You want to be God-inside conscious. (See 1 John 4:4.)

- The believer should know what the Word is to him, what it means to him, what the Father intended it should mean to him. (See Psalm 119:105.)

- The Word is the food of the recreated spirit. (See Matthew 4:4.) It is the mightiest thing in all the world. It slays and makes alive.

- The Word slew Ananias and Sapphira, and the same day made well hundreds of men and women. (See Acts 5:1–11.)

- Every believer should know what the name of Jesus can mean to him in his daily life, so that no matter what happens, he is a victor, a conqueror. (See John 16:24.)

- *"In my name ye shall cast out demons"* (Mark 16:17). You can cast out **all** demons if you cast out **a** demon, and you can cast out the work of a demon.

- Every believer should be established in this truth. So many are established in weakness; they live under the shadow of it. Others are established in sickness and infirmities. (See James 5:14–17.)

- Others are established in fear, in the sense of sin, the sense of lack and inability. (See Isaiah 41:10.)

- We want to learn to be established in the Word.

- Second Peter 1:12: *"Wherefore I shall be ready always to put you in remembrance of these things, though ye know them, and are established in the truth which is with you."*

- Romans 8:31–38 is God's photograph of the established believer. We haven't room to quote it, but I want you to read it with great care. Here is the first sentence: *"If God is for us, who is against us?"* (verse 31). We should be established in that.

- You know that Scripture is yours. You know that God is for you. You know that He is your Father and that He gave up His Son to die for us; and you know that He has given us His own nature, His own life. (See 1 John 5:12–13.)

- You know the next verse: *"He that spared not his own Son, but delivered him up for us all, how shall he not also with him freely give us all things?"* (verse 32). You are established in that. You are settled, fixed.

- Revel in the next sentence, *"Who shall lay anything to the charge of God's elect? It is God that justifieth; who is he that condemneth?"* (verses 33–34).

- No one can hinder you now. God has given you His own Son, His own righteousness. (See 2 Corinthians 5:21.)

- You swing down on through the remainder of these wonderful verses. Dig into that wonderful thirty-fifth verse, *"Who shall separate us from the love of Christ?"*

- Rest under the shadow of that great Rock in this weary land; and you hear someone saying, *"Nay, in all these things we are more than conquerors through him that loved us"* (verse 37).

- You know who you are, what you are. (See 1 John 3:2.) You know who is backing you up, who is protecting you. For it is God who is at work within you working and willing His own precious will. (See Philippians 2:13.)

- John 15:5: *"I am the vine and ye are the branches."* No one can touch a branch without hurting the vine. The vine and the branch are one. You are a part of him, and He is a part of you. He is taking care of you. You are established in this truth. All hell knows it, too. (See James 2:19.)

- Write out Philippians 4:19:

_____

_____

- You are so established in that truth that you never worry about your finances any more. Your Father is now meeting your obligations. You and He are laboring together. (See Matthew 6:27–34.)

- Second Corinthians 6:1 has become a reality to you. You are laboring together with Him. You are partners. You are fellowshipping each other. You are sharing with Him, He is sharing with you. What a wonderful life it is!

- Jeremiah 33:3 sings its song of confidence in your heart: *"Call unto me, and I will answer thee, and will show thee great things, and difficult [fenced in things, mighty things], which thou knowest not."*

- "You have sought Me and I will lead you in the realm of omnipotence; and I will lead you in the place where only those whose feet are shod with the gospel of peace have trod, where none can breathe the rarified atmosphere but those who are partakers of My grace and have received the abundance of My life." (See John 1:16; Colossians 2:9–10.)

- Why? He said, in essence, "You call unto Me and I will hear you. I listen to you all the time. You are my child. I am your Father, and this Jesus who is seated at My right hand is your intercessor and your advocate. I want you to walk in now and take your place."

- Can't you hear Him whisper, *"Fear thou not, for I am with thee; be not dismayed, for I am thy God; I will strengthen thee; yea, I will help thee; yea, I will uphold thee with the right hand of my righteousness"* (Isaiah 41:10). What more do you want?

- "I am thy God. I am your Father. I am your strength. I am your wisdom and your ability." (See 2 Corinthians 3:4–6.)

- When you are established in that, fixed and settled in it, you become a world-ruler in the spiritual realm. Men can feel the effect of your prayer life in Europe, Asia, and Africa. (See John 14:13–14.) The demons that rule the warring elements of Europe and Africa are afraid of you, and they are afraid that you will turn the mighty influence of your lips and prayers against them. (See John 15:7.) You are established at last in the very heart of God—established in love.

- Have you ever realized what that means? For years I was afraid of my Father although I was a preacher. I was afraid to trust Him. I didn't dare abandon myself to His Son. Then one day, 1 John 4:16 became unveiled to me. Let me give it to you: *"And we know and have believed the love which God hath in us. God is love; and he that abideth in love abideth in God, and God abideth in him."*

- *"We know and have believed the love which God hath in us."* That little preposition *"in"* belongs there. Now see what it means: *"I know and I have come to believe that my Father has love in my case. Why, He is love; and I abide in love, so I am abiding in Him and with Him. He and I are laboring together. I have come to believe in His love for me."* (See 1 John 4:7–8.)

- I was afraid once, but now I rest in it. I am established in His love. I know that I cannot fail. I know that He loved me enough to give His Son to die for me, and that He will freely give me all things. (See John 3:16.)

- Ephesians 3:17–19 must ever stand out among the great sentences of revelation:

  That Christ may dwell in your hearts through faith; to the end that ye, being rooted and grounded in love, may be strong to apprehend with all the saints what is the breadth and length and height and depth, and to know the love of Christ which passeth [sense] knowledge, that ye may be filled unto all the fulness of God [this love-God].

- I have sat by the side of this Scripture as I sat in my boyhood days by the side of a little stream that used to flow down through the pasture, and dreamed the dreams of a little boy. I have say by the side of this Scripture and dreamed of what it could mean to me to be rooted and grounded in God until the taproot of my being was saturated with this abundant life of God, until the very fullness of His great love nature came pouring into my whole being, filling me with Himself. What it could mean to be rooted, grounded, established in love! (See Ephesians 3:20.)

ESTABLISHED IN RIGHTEOUESNESS

- Isaiah 54:14: *"In righteousness shalt thou be established: thou shalt be far from oppression, for thou shalt not fear; and from terror, for it shall not come near thee."* And while your heart meditates in that, we will turn to Isaiah 32:17: *"And the work of righteousness shall be peace; and the effect of righteousness, quietness and confidence forever."*

- You are going to be established in the consciousness of the absolute reality of your being the righteousness of God in Christ. (See 2 Corinthians 5:21.)

- There is Romans 3:26: *"Or the showing, I say, of his righteousness at this present season: that he might himself be just, and the justifier of him that hath faith in Jesus."*

- You have faith in Jesus as your Savior and Lord. Now the Father has become your righteousness and by this new birth, this new creation, He has imparted unto you His very life and nature.

- Second Corinthians 5:17–18: *"Wherefore if any man is in Christ, he is a new creature: the old things are passed away; behold, they are become new. But all things are of God, who reconciled us to himself through Christ, and gave unto us the ministry of reconciliation."*

- You have the nature and life of God. You are a new creation. John 6:47: *"He that believeth hath eternal life."*

+ Eternal life is the nature and life of the Father. You have that now. You have become, by the new creation, by the impartation of God's very nature, the righteousness of God in Christ. Few people are established in that. Few appreciate or understand it, or have ever entered into its fullness.

+ It means that you can stand in the Father's presence, just as Jesus, without the sense of inferiority, that you can stand in the presence of Satan and all his works with the same fearless grace that Jesus had. (See 2 Corinthians 2:14–15.)

+ He didn't have any fear when He stood by the tomb of Lazarus and spoke. There wasn't any fear in His heart when He said, *"Lazarus, come forth"* (John 11:43). He was Master.

+ There wasn't any fear in Peter's heart when he said to Sapphira, *"Behold, the feet of them that have buried thy husband are at the door, and they shall carry thee out,"* (Acts 5:9), and she gave up the ghost there.

+ You see, it makes men masters of life and of death.

+ When Peter said to the dead Dorcas in Acts 9:40–43, in essence, "Dorcas, come back; they need you," she arose.

ESTABLISHED IN GRACE

+ Hebrews 13:9: *"Be not carried away by divers and strange teachings: for it is good that the heart be established by grace; not by meats, wherein they that occupied themselves were not profited."*

+ Think of it! We are being established in grace. What is grace? It is love pouring itself out upon the graceless and the unworthy.

+ The Spirit gave to us a marvelous interpretation of grace in Romans 4:4–5: *"Now to him that worketh, the reward is not reckoned as of grace, but as of debt. But to him that worketh not, but believeth on him that justifieth the ungodly, his faith is reckoned for righteousness."* Then, in Romans 5:6, we read, *"For while we were yet weak, in due season Christ died for the ungodly."*

+ You see, grace is love in operation, love in action.

+ I could never get it clear in my heart how Jesus could love the man who was putting the lash upon His back, or how He could love the man, and die for him, who put the nails through the palms of His hands and feet; but I imagine that if you had been back there near the sepulcher when Jesus arose from the dead, you would have heard Him say, "Where is the man who plaited the crown of thorns and placed them upon my brow? I want to tell him that I died for him, that I suffered the torments of the damned for him."

+ Don't you remember that He said, *"Go, tell [My] disciples and Peter"* (Mark 16:7)? That little conjunction there ties the heart of Peter with the Master in a way that moves my heart. "Go, tell Peter, who denied me; tell him that I love him." That is grace, indeed.

+ You notice that God put His love beyond a doubt: *"In that, while we were yet sinners, Christ died for us"* (Romans 5:8).

+ Then you notice the tenth verse: *"For if, while we were enemies, we were reconciled to God through the death of his Son."*

+ You remember John 3:16: *"For God so loved the world, that he gave his only begotten Son."* Jesus belongs to the world. He doesn't belong to you any more than He belongs to the despairing, wicked men who have murdered so many women and children in Europe. That is grace; and you are so established in grace that you don't criticize anyone.

+ Don't you know that the man you are "knocking" is the man Jesus died for?

+ Did you ever realize that you and I, before we can ever become soul-winners, before we can reach a lost world, have to be established in grace? We have to know the Master, and know the motives behind His love gift, His sacrifice. We have to be established in it so that we will be like John G. Paton was in the New Hebrides. He stood and watched a chieftain shoot his companion; and then—would you believe it—the day came when he baptized that chieftain and administered the Lord's Supper to him. He so loved that he gave his life to those desperate heathen men and women.

+ You who read this lesson, take God, by His grace, to establish you in love, to establish you in grace.

+ Do you know what that will mean? That will be establishing you in the perfect Word of grace. You will become a soul-winner when grace gains the ascendancy.

+ God so loved that He gave. I so love that I give. I so love that I give my time; I give my money; I give my ability. I lay it all upon the altar of grace.

+ He loves you now and He wants you to love Him as He loved you. He wants you to give as He gave. You can't give as much, but you can give with the same spirit of love that He gave, can't you?

+ One of my students from Central America could not speak much English, yet was attending our evangelistic meetings. He watched Miss Ridge, a returned missionary, pleading with a high school girl to yield to Christ. He politely said, "Teacher, tell her that if I could, I give her my heart. It would believe on Jesus." That is grace!

HOW MUCH DO YOU REMEMBER?

1–3. Give three descriptions of the daily life of one who is established in: love; righteousness; grace.

4. What is the importance of being established in the Word?

5. What threefold knowledge of Christ should we know?

6. Give the **contrast** of the established lives of a believer and an unbeliever.

7–10. **Quote** and **explain** four Scriptures in this lesson that have been the greatest revelation to you.

LESSON 23 NOTES

_____

_____

_____

_____

_____

_____

_____

_____

_____

_____

_____

_____

_____

_____

Lesson 24
THE HIDDEN MAN OF THE HEART

Man was created in the image and likeness of God. He is in the same class with God. (See Genesis 1:26–27; 1 Peter 3:4.) *"God is a Spirit: and they that worship him must worship in spirit and truth"* (John 4:24).

Psychology has called this inward man of the heart a subconscious mind. They have recognized that "conscience" was a voice from an inward personality.

The natural man does not understand the things of the spirit. (See 1 Corinthians 2:14.) The natural man cannot know himself or know God; consequently, the student of psychology, unless he has received eternal life, cannot understand himself.

THE THREEFOLD MAN

+ This subconscious mind is the real man. This real man, the spirit, is like God. It never grows old. It is neither mortal nor immortal. It is eternal.

+ The body is mortal and will become immortal at the coming of the Lord Jesus. The senses that convey all knowledge to the human reason belong to the body and they will grow old with the body.

+ The part that is recreated is the human spirit. Those who have received eternal life will receive immortality for their bodies when Jesus returns.

+ Second Timothy 1:10 declares that life and immortality came to light through Jesus Christ. Life here is *zoe*, the nature of God. No one knew anything about that until Jesus came and unveiled Himself to man.

+ First Thessalonians 5:23 is a glimpse of the threefold man. The spirit is the part that knows God. The soul is the intellect, or the sensibilities and will, that knows the sensuous things. The physical body is the house in which we live.

+ God says that this threefold man is to be preserved entire without blame at the coming of the Lord.

THE FALL OF MAN

+ It is evident that before man fell in the garden, his spirit dominated his reasoning faculties. After he fell, the senses gained the ascendency. Before he sinned, his body was eternal like his spirit; but when he sinned, his body became mortal and his spirit became a partaker of spiritual death.

+ Read very carefully Romans 5:12–17 and notice that death came to man at the fall, and that this death gained the ascendancy over his thinking faculties. He is described in 2 Corinthians 4:4. Man not only died spiritually, but his mind became darkened, subjected to the adversary.

+ Romans 1:20–22 gives us a graphic picture of the fall of man. Read these verses carefully: *"The invisible things of him since the creation of the world are clearly seen"* (verse 20).

+ Man lived in that realm before he fell, but in the twenty-first verse we read, *"Because that, knowing God, they glorified him not as God, neither gave thanks; but became vain in their reasonings."*

SENSES VERSUS SPIRIT

+ The word *"heart"* is used simultaneously with the word *"spirit."* Ephesians 1:17–18: *"That [He] may give unto you a spirit of wisdom and revelation in the knowledge of him; having the eyes of your heart enlightened."* The word *"enlightened"* means "illuminated." In essence, "That the eyes of your spirit shall be so illuminated that you may know the riches of the inheritance in Christ."

- He is speaking here of the new creation man, the man who has received eternal life into his spirit. Paul is praying that we may see and know the Father's will. You see, the senses have blinded man's reasoning faculties. (See Ephesians 4:17–19.) He is described in 1 Corinthians 3:1–3.

- These are children of God, but they walk in the senses. They have never developed a spiritual life.

- They are in the condition that is spoken of in Hebrews 5:12–13. Then in the fourteenth verse, we see that these babes in Christ may have been Christians for years, but they have never developed or grown. Sense knowledge governs them when their recreated spirits should have the ascendancy. (See Ephesians 3:14–19.)

- The new birth is the recreation of the spirit of man. That recreated spirit is to gain the ascendancy over the reasoning faculties and govern them. But in the undeveloped believer, the reasoning faculties govern the spirit instead.

- When by reason of time the recreated spirit should have gained the ascendancy, they are still living under the dominion of their bodies. (See Galatians 5:16–17.)

- Now you understand what he means in Romans 12:1–2. Here is a believer whose mind has never been renewed. His body is governing him. His mind cannot be renewed until he begins to practice and live the Word. He will not know the will of the Father. He will not know how to walk in the will of God. (See James 1:22–25.)

- His walk is described in 1 John 2:9–11. He has been recreated and is in the family of God, but he is walking according to the senses. He should walk in the light of love and of the Word, but he is walking in the light that Jesus describes in Luke 11:35.

- The light of sense knowledge is really darkness. He is not walking in the light of the Word.

- Write out Jesus's words in John 8:12:

_____

_____

_____

- This is not a light that comes to the human reason, but a light that comes to the human spirit, this hidden man of the heart.

- Romans 7:22 calls him the inner man: *"For I delight in the law of God after the inward man."* It is the natural human spirit that Paul is speaking of, not the recreated man.

- You understand that the human spirit can be developed as spiritualists have developed it; as it has been developed in many Christian scientists and teachers of the occult. The human spirit is capable of marvelous development before it is recreated as well as after.

- After we are recreated, the Holy Spirit through the Word can lead us into marvelous development.

- It is a strange fact that the church has never sought to develop the human spirit, the recreated human spirit. It has spent hundreds of millions of dollars on developing the mind that receives all its impulses and knowledge from the senses; and it has spent vast fortunes of money in developing the physical body; but the real man, this "hidden man of the heart," has never been developed.

CONSCIENCE

- First Peter 3:4: *"But let it be the hidden man of the heart, in the incorruptible apparel of a meek and quiet spirit, which is in the sight of God of great price."*

- This hidden man of the heart is as capable of development along spiritual lines as the reasoning faculties are along intellectual lines. What we call "conscience" is the voice of *"the hidden man of the heart."*

- Paul says some strong things about conscience in Acts 24:16: *"Herein I also exercise myself to have a conscience void of offence toward God and men always."* Here is a real spiritual development. He says, in essence, "I exercise myself to have a conscience that is always in harmony with the will of my Father."

- Acts 23:1: *"And Paul, looking steadfastly on the council, said, Brethren, I have lived before God in all good conscience until this day."*

- The conscience is the voice of the human spirit. It is governed by human reasonings and environment before it is recreated; but after it receives eternal life, it can become the voice of God.

- There is no limit to the development of the human spirit.

- Second Corinthians 1:12: *"For our glorying is this, the testimony of our conscience, that in holiness and sincerity of God, not in fleshly wisdom but in the grace of God, we behaved ourselves in the world, and more abundantly to you-ward."* The fleshly wisdom of which he speaks is sense knowledge. He says, "We have not exercised ourselves in sense knowledge, but in the grace of God and the testimony of our spirits, that in holiness and sincerity toward God we have behaved ourselves in your presence." This is a remarkable testimony.

- Second Timothy 1:3: *"I thank God, whom I serve from my forefathers in a pure conscience, how unceasing is my remembrance of thee in my supplications, night and day."*

- We have not only to obey our conscience, but we must develop our recreated spirits and let them govern us. I have found this true, that a believer can so develop his spirit that in every crisis of his life his spirit can get the will of the Father instantly; and if he follows the leading of his spirit instead of the reasoning faculties, he never makes a mistake in the investment of his money or in the choosing of his companions. He would practically never step out of the love walk and the love realm.

WAR BETWEEN THE SENSES AND THE RECREATED SPIRIT

- In Galatians 5:16–18, the word *"spirit"* is referring to our recreated spirit, and the word *"flesh"* refers to our senses. The war is between our senses and our recreated human spirit.

- John 14:6 can become a living reality. *"I am the way, and the truth, and the life: no one cometh unto the Father, but by me."*

- If a man develops his spirit, he can walk in this reality of truth, and he can enjoy all the fruits of eternal life. Galatians 5:22 gives the fruits of the recreated spirit.

- Now we are sick of our friends, and of the law, and of doctrine, because our spirits have been kept in bondage, kept in ignorance.

- Second Corinthians 4:16: *"Wherefore we faint not; but though our outward man is decaying, yet our inward man is renewed day by day."*

- The physical decays, grows old and feeble; but the inner man can receive continual strength and health, from eternal life, the nature of God, so that it is renewed day by day. This inward man never grows old; and if we learn to take advantage of our rights in Christ there is no doubt that we would live to a great age.

- Second Corinthians 5:4 suggests this: *"For indeed we that are in this tabernacle do groan, being burdened; not for that we would be unclothed, but that we would be clothed upon, that what is mortal may be swallowed up of life."* The physical body is mortal, subject to death. Here is the suggestion that this mortal body be swallowed up of *zoe*, the nature of God.

- The fifth verse is striking: *"Now he that wrought us for this very thing is God, who gave unto us the earnest of the Spirit."* The earnest of the Spirit is the recreation; and He has given to us this taste, this sample of the life of God in our spirits. Now He said, "I want your bodies swallowed up of this life." Way translates it, "drowned in a sea of life."

- Jesus said, *"I came that they may have life, and may have it abundantly"* (John 10:10). There is offered to us an abundance of the nature of God imparted to our spirits so that they will utterly dominate our mortal bodies.

- That would suggest a perfect physical body with no disease, Satan's power and influence over it eliminated. What a wonderful thing it would be if there could be groups of believers who would develop this hidden man of the heart until it actually dominated the physical, that mortality would be swallowed up of life, God's life.

- We would be spirit-ruled. Then this hidden man of the heart would govern the reasoning faculties. The senses would be under dominion of the spirit. The new creation would rule the physical body.

- You see, the name of Jesus would become a living reality: its authority over diseases and over demons, a part of our daily walk just as eating and drinking are a part of our daily experience. Our dominion over demoniacal forces can also become a daily reality. We have never become God-inside minded.

- First John 4:4 is almost an unknown fact: *"Ye are of God, my little children, and have overcome them: because greater is he that is in you than he that is in the world."* We have never given place to that fact, never considered it seriously.

- Second Corinthians 10:3 reads, *"For though we walk in the flesh, we do not war according to the flesh."* Let us read it like this, *"For though we walk in the senses, our warfare is not according to the senses; for the weapons of our warfare are not of the senses, but they are of the spirit; and they are mighty before God to the casting down of strongholds. Casting down imaginations (or reasonings born of the senses) and every high thing that the senses have erected."*

- The senses have suggested these through our false teachers, and have exalted them against the Word of God; but we are bringing every thought into captivity to the obedience of Christ.

- I am sure that this translation is correct. It is what God wants us to do; that our spirits should cast down reasonings born of the senses or born of the physical body and bring them all into captivity to the Lordship of Christ.

SOME FACTS THAT WE SHOULD MASTER

- Man is in God's class of being. His spirit is capable of receiving God's nature so that he may be dominated by God's revelation.

- The spirit of the natural man is in union with Satan. His is ruled by his physical body. The senses dominate him. His reasoning faculties cannot know God or understand God. They can't know *"the hidden man of the heart"* (1 Peter 3:4)—the hidden man that lives in the physical body. He is a total stranger to sense knowledge; so only the psychologist who is born again, who has given place to his own spirit, can know himself in his own nature. (See 2 Corinthians 5:17.)

- Then He renews the mind, brings it into subjection to the recreated spirit through obedience to the Word. There can be no renewing of the mind without practicing, living, doing the Word.

- The natural human spirit has been governed and ruled by the senses, so it will be a difficult thing for the recreated spirit to gain the ascendancy over the sense-ruled mind; but this must be done.

- We have never recognized that faith is a product of the recreated human spirit—that dominating faith means a dominating recreated spirit.

- Love is a fruit of the recreated human spirit; consequently, natural man cannot love in the New Testament sense. His love is dominated by his senses.

- The recreated human spirit's love gains the ascendancy over the senses. Love is not a product of the reasoning faculties. The spirit alone can love, can develop faith and the other beautiful fruits spoken of in Galatians 5:22–23. This comes by a study in this new realm of revelation as unveiled to us in the Pauline Epistles. We would suggest that the student go beyond this, as we can continue no further on it in this lesson.

+ Due to limited space, many of our important Scripture references in this lesson are not quoted. We are depending upon you to look up each one, so that you can receive a clearer conception of this lesson.

HOW MUCH DO YOU REMEMBER?

SUMMARY TEST QUESTION

From the material contained in this lesson, and that derived from the study of the Scripture references given in this lesson, prepare a complete **descriptive summary of a spirit-ruled Christian**—and another **summary of a sense-ruled Christian**, which will show the contrast between the two.

LESSON 24 NOTES

Lesson 25
STUDIES IN THE BOOK OF ACTS

Acts was written by Luke between 63 and 65 A.D. It is a history of the first thirty-three years of Christ at the right hand of God. It is a revelation of the hidden drama of redemption through the Holy Spirit.

It is not man. No men but Stephen or Barnabas received a word of eulogy. Paul is seen working quietly as a common man.

All greatly used men in the New Testament are roots out of dry ground. Their weakness is never covered. They are there, God-used, but ever falling into the reason realm. Neither Peter nor Paul have an apology. They are seen without a halo. Their faults and failings are written down, but are used of God. They are common men used for the most uncommon work.

The three key instruments unveiled in the book of Acts are: The **Word**, the **name**, and the **Holy Spirit**. We will study the Word in this lesson, followed by the name and the Holy Spirit in proceeding lessons.

THE WORD IN THE BOOK OF ACTS

- The Word holds a unique place in the first thirty-three years of church history. It is a suggestion of the place the Word should hold in the church through the entire dispensation.
- Acts 2:41: "*They then that received his word were baptized: and there were added unto them in that day about three thousand souls.*" This is unique. They that received the Word—not the doctrines, nor the teachings, nor a creed—but the **Logos**.
- Acts 4:4 has another suggestion, "*But many of them that heard the word believed; and the number of the men came to be about five thousand.*" It doesn't say that they heard the apostles, but that they heard the Word.
- Acts 6:2: "*And the twelve called the multitude of the disciples unto them, and said, It is not fit that we should forsake the word of God, and serve tables.*"
- How early they learned the place of the Word!
- Acts 6:4: "*But we will continue steadfastly in prayer, and in the ministry of the word.*"
- These were untaught men, fishermen. The Spirit had unveiled to them the place and dignity of the Word.
- The seventh verse staggers one: "*And the word of God increased; and the number of the disciples multiplied in Jerusalem exceedingly; and a great company of the priests were obedient to the faith.*" Here is another striking sentence: "*The word...increased.*"
- The Pauline Revelation had not yet been written; the four Gospels had not yet been written. All they had was the Old Testament. The Word that is increasing and growing upon the hearts of the people is the new truth about Jesus.
- Did you notice the last clause? "*And a great company of the priests were obedient to the faith.*" Christianity was called "the faith" as early as that.
- Acts 8:4 tells us that there had been a great persecution. Stephen had been stoned to death. Saul of Tarsus was laying waste the church, entering into every house and dragging men and women out and committing them to prison.
- In the first of this fearful persecution, Acts 8:4 declares, "*They therefore that were scattered abroad went about preaching the word.*"

+ I heard an outstanding evangelist the other night, and he only quoted two passages of Scripture in his entire address. He told experiences, anecdotes, and kept the audience intensely interested, but God had no place in it.

+ *"Now when the apostles that were at Jerusalem heard that Samaria had received the word of God, they sent unto them Peter and John"* (Acts 8:14).

+ Philip had gone down to Samaria, and a revival had taken place. There is not a word of eulogy about Philip; only some men at Jerusalem had heard that Samaria had received the Word of God. Then it tells how they baptized the converts and laid their hands upon them and they received the Holy Spirit.

+ Write out verse 25:

_____

_____

_____

+ The Word holds a new position.

+ Acts 10:44 is the story of the Gentiles receiving Christ. Up to this time, only Jews and Samaritans had accepted Christ. God appeared to Peter in a dream and unveiled to him that he was going to give the glad tidings to the Gentiles: *"While Peter yet spake these words, the Holy Spirit fell on all them that heard the word."*

+ Then the Jews had to acknowledge that the Gentiles had received the Holy Spirit in the same manner that they did when they first believed on the day of Pentecost. But the Spirit came upon them that heard the Word. That did the work.

+ Acts 11:1–4, 15:

> Now the apostles and the brethren that were in Judaea heard that the Gentiles also had received the word of God. And when Peter was come up to Jerusalem, they that were of the circumcision contended with him, saying, Thou wentest in to men uncircumcised, and didst eat with them. But Peter began, and expounded the matter unto them in order.... And as I began to speak, the Holy Spirit fell on them, even as on us at the beginning.

+ You see two elements at work. Peter had preached the Word, the Gentiles had accepted Christ, and the Holy Spirit fell on them.

+ The Jewish believers in Judea were still governed by sense knowledge, were ruled by the old covenant with its law, priesthood, and sacrifices.

+ You can see in the nineteenth verse how they took the Word abroad: *"They therefore that were scattered abroad upon the tribulation that arose about Stephen travelled as far as Phoenicia, and Cyprus, and Antioch, speaking the word to none save only to Jews."*

+ What a struggle there was between the men who wanted to adapt Christianity to Judaism and those who saw that Christianity was a new covenant and a new relationship with God.

+ The Pauline Revelation had not yet been given. They knew nothing about the new creation, the new covenant teaching, the substitutionary work of Jesus, the body of Christ, and Christ's marvelous ministry at the right hand of the Father. The believers were living in the realm of the senses very largely. They witnessed the marvelous miracles and they believed because of them.

+ Acts 13:5–7 is the story of the Bible school at Antioch. They had several teachers: Barnabas, Symeon who was called Niger, Lucius of Cyrene, Manaen the foster brother of Herod the tetrarch, and Saul. I have often wished that I might have had an opportunity to sit under those teachers.

- The Spirit had separated Saul and Barnabas to send them out into evangelistic work.

- The seventh verse has a striking message. The proconsul had been entertained by a sorcerer, a prophet whose name was Bar-Jesus. "*The same called unto him Barnabas and Saul, and sought to hear the word of God.*"

- You notice that he did not desire to hear Barnabas and Saul, but the Work of God. Then came one of Paul's great miracles. Read carefully the next paragraph.

- In the twenty-sixth verse, at the conclusion of Paul's address at Antioch of Pisidia, he said, "*Brethren, children of the stock of Abraham, and those among you that fear God, to us is the word of this salvation sent forth.*" You can see how they honored the Word above everything.

- In the forty-fourth verse it says, "*And the next sabbath almost the whole city was gathered together to hear the word of God.*" That stirred mighty persecution on the part of the Jews, as described in these verses. Read on to the fifty-second verse, which is striking: "*And the disciples were filled with joy and with the Holy Spirit.*"

- In the midst of persecution, often in hunger, they went from village to village, to preach the Word.

- Acts 14:3. For the first time the Word is called the "*word of grace.*" It makes us almost jealous as we read the story of their mighty ministry. How we would like to see it again!

- Read carefully the rest of this chapter down to the twenty-fifth verse. This is Paul's first missionary journey, and all the equipment that he had was the Word.

- In the fifteen chapter, we have the council in Jerusalem. Paul and Barnabas had gone up to Jerusalem to tell the story of what God had done through them among the Gentiles as well as among the Jews.

- Acts 15:6–7. What confidence those men had in that "*word of the gospel*" (verse 7)!

- Acts 15:35–36. This is Paul's second ministry journey. They are going back over the towns where they have preached to comfort and strengthen the converts. They left an assembly in every community.

- It takes us almost a generation in a heathen country before a church is established. It is not that the disciples were brighter, smarter men. It wasn't because the crucifixion and resurrection were only a few years past. It was because the Word held a place in their ministry, the name of Jesus held a place we have never given it, and the Holy Spirit held a place of Guide and Director that He has never been given since that day.

- The Word brought conviction; the name gave them their credentials in miracles; and the Holy Spirit unveiled Jesus to the listeners as the Word was expounded.

- Acts 16:6. You notice who governed the disciples—the Holy Spirit. It wasn't the time to go into Asia. Things were not ready. They had an opportunity to unveil the Word in the towns where the Spirit guided them.

- How it thrills the heart to realize that there was a superintendent guiding the men. He is still in the earth. This is His day of ministration.

- In the thirty-second verse is a story of Paul in Philippi. He had cast a demon out of a girl, thus causing trouble. He and Silas had been arrested and locked in prison. Their backs had been scourged. Their hands and feet were in stocks, yet they had been singing and praising the Lord. The prisoners had been listening to them. Suddenly, there was a great earthquake so that the foundations of the prison house were broken, "*and immediately all the doors were opened; and every one's bands were loosed*" (verse 26). The jailer awakened out of sleep, saw the gates open, and thought the prisoners had escaped. He was going to kill himself rather than be killed by the Roman authorities, but Paul and Silas spoke to him and told him that none had escaped.

- He said unto them, *"What must I do to be saved?"* (verse 30). *"And they spake the word of the Lord unto him, with all that were in his house"* (verse 32). The caretakers and the prisoners all heard the Word, and in that jail a church was organized.

- Acts 17:11 is a beautiful Scripture. This was a Jewish audience that held the Old Testament; and instead of treating them as the people in Thessalonica, they accepted the Word. What tremendous effect God's Word had!

- Acts 18:11 is an account of Paul at Corinth. He taught the Word there a year and six months.

- Acts 19:10–20 tells us of Paul at Ephesus, one of the greatest ministries of his life. The ninth and tenth verses say that he had been reasoning daily in the school of Tyrannus, and that this had been going on for two years.

- Verses 17–20 give us a picture of the prevailing Word:

  And fear fell upon them all, and the name of the Lord Jesus was magnified. Many also of them that had believed came, confessing, and declaring their deeds. And not a few of them that practiced magical arts brought their books together and burned them in the sight of all; and they counted the price of them, and found it fifty thousand pieces of silver. So mightily grew the word of the Lord and prevailed.

- In Acts 6:7 we saw the Word increase. In 12:24, the Word grew and multiplied. But here, the Word so mightily grew that it prevailed over the great city of Ephesus.

- When the Word is given its place today in the assemblies and churches, it will produce the same kind of results. You understand that up to this time, the Pauline Revelation had not yet been written. First and Second Corinthians had not yet been written. Ephesians, Philippians, and Colossians—the great body of truth—had not yet been written to the church,

- There are three phases of the Word. We have the Word incarnate in the flesh. (See John 1:14.) Next, we have the spoken Word in the book of Acts. Then we have the written Word that takes in the entire New Testament, but especially the Pauline Revelation.

- So, we have the "incarnate," the "spoken," and the "written" Word. But the Word in the lips of Jesus was the Father's Word that was given to men through His Son. It was the healing Word, the miracle-performing word.

- The Word preached by the apostles was the living Word, the live-giving Word, the recreating Word, the miracle-performing Word.

- The Word given to us by the Holy Spirit through the apostles' lips (this would include the epistles) is not only a written Word, but it is a living Word; it is a life-giving Word; it is a healing Word; it is a prevailing Word; it is a God-indwelt Word.

- In the lips of men of faith, the Word is filled with faith, filled with love, filled with grace, filled with the very nature and life of God.

- What a privilege it is to have in our lips this living Word, this life-giving Word.

- God is love and God is light; but God is also a faith God; so when He gives us His nature in the new birth, there comes with that a measure of faith to every one of us.

- However, that life has to dominate us. It has to be sustained and fed with the Word; and as we act on the Word and live in the Word, faith grows in us.

- Believing, you understand, is acting on the Word. Faith is having acted on the Word.

HOW MUCH DO YOU REMEMBER?

1. Who wrote the book of Acts? During what years was it written?

2. What three spiritual instruments are unveiled in this book of Acts?

3. What is the difference between the Word as expressed by the original "Logos," and mere doctrines, teachings, or creeds?

4. What should be the place of the Word in our churches today?

5. Give five references in Acts showing the Word working through the apostles.

6. Why were the Jewish believers against the expounding of the Scriptures to the Gentiles?

7. Give a brief summary of Paul's first and second missionary journeys.

8. What did Paul and Silas speak unto the jailer who wanted salvation?

9. What are the three phases of the Word? Explain.

10. Choose the chapter or episode in Acts that reveals the most to you from this lesson, and write a few paragraphs of explanation or personal thought on it.

LESSON 25 NOTES

_____

_____

_____

_____

_____

_____

_____

_____

_____

_____

_____

_____

_____

_____

_____

_____

_____

_____

_____

Lesson 26
THE NAME OF JESUS IN THE BOOK OF ACTS

POWER OF ATTORNEY

- Jesus gave to the church the power of attorney to use His name. In the gospel of John, we have the record of this legal act on the part of the Master.

- John 15:16: *"Ye did not choose me, but I chose you, and appointed you, that ye should go and bear fruit, and that your fruit should abide: that whatsoever ye shall ask of the Father in my name, he may give it you."*

- The disciples are commissioned to go and bear fruit; and they are given a legal right to use the name of Jesus and to have the same authority that Jesus exercised in His earth walk.

- John 16:23–24: *"And in that day ye shall ask me no question. Verily, verily, I say unto you, If ye shall ask anything of the Father, he will give it you in my name. Hitherto have ye asked nothing in my name: ask, and ye shall receive, that your joy may be made full."*

- And in verses 26–27: *"In that day ye shall ask in my name: and I say not unto you, that I will pray the Father for you; for the Father himself loveth you, because ye have loved me, and have believed that I came forth from the Father."*

- First, the Master says that we are not to pray to Him. He is the mediator between us and the Father. He is our advocate and our intercessor; but whatsoever we ask of the Father in His name, the Father will give to us.

- Jesus says that up to this time we have never asked anything in His name, but that now He is giving His disciples the right to use His name. He uses this strange expression, *"that your joy may be made full"* (John 15:11).

- Happiness comes from circumstances. Joy alone comes from the Lord. There is to come to us a joy through the miraculous use of the name of Jesus.

- He told us that in that day it would not be necessary for Him to pray to the Father for us; *"for the Father himself loveth you"* (John 16:27). We have access into His presence. Now we can come boldly into His presence any time. As Jesus's representatives we are doing business for the Father in Jesus's name.

- In John 14:13–15, we see the name introduced. This is not prayer; it is something different. *"And whatsoever ye shall ask in my name, that will I do, that the Father may be glorified in the Son"* (verse 13).

- This is not prayer. That word *"ask"* here can be translated "demand." In essence, "And whatsoever ye shall demand in my name that will I do." Jesus says that He will make that good.

- What does He mean? In Acts 16:18, we read the story of Paul casting the demon out of a girl that had a spirit of divination: *"But Paul, being sore troubled, turned and said to the spirit, I charge thee in the name of Jesus Christ to come out of her. And it came out that very hour."* Paul is casting a demon out of a girl in the name of Jesus.

- Acts 3:1–6 tells us the story of Peter and John healing the man at the Beautiful Gate.

    And Peter, fastening his eyes upon him, with John, said, Look on us. And he gave heed unto them, expecting to receive something from them. But Peter said, Silver and gold have I none; but what I have, that give I thee. In the name of Jesus Christ of Nazareth, walk.

    (verses 4–6)

+ The man was instantly healed. Ankle bones that had never sustained his body were suddenly made normal. When the people gathered around them, Peter said,

> *Ye men of Israel, why marvel ye at this man? or why fasten ye your eyes on us, as though by our own power or godliness we had made him to walk? The God of Abraham, and of Isaac, and of Jacob, the God of our fathers, hath glorified his Servant Jesus; whom ye delivered up, and denied before the face of Pilate, when he had determined to release him. But ye denied the Holy and Righteous One, and asked for a murderer to be granted unto you, and killed the Prince of life; whom God raised from the dead; whereof we are witnesses. And by faith in his name hath his name made this man strong, whom ye behold and know: yea, the faith which is through him hath given him this perfect soundness in the presence of you all.*
>
> (verses 12–16)

+ Peter is using his legal right to use the name of Jesus.
+ In John 14:14 we read, *"If ye shall ask anything in my name, that will I do."*
+ In the previous verse, verse 13, we see, *"that the Father may be glorified in the Son."* The Father is going to get glory from our use of the name of Jesus to heal the sick and cast out demons, and in the working of miracles.
+ Mark 16:17–20:

> *And these signs shall accompany them that believe: in my name shall they cast out demons; they shall speak with new tongues; they shall take up serpents, and if they drink any deadly thing, it shall in no wise hurt them; they shall lay hands on the sick, and they shall recover. So then the Lord Jesus, after he had spoken unto them, was received up into heaven, and sat down at the right hand of God. And they went forth, and preached everywhere, the Lord working with them, and confirming the word by the signs that followed.*

+ Here is the place of the name of Jesus in the daily ministry of the church. You see, it has the same authority treasured up in it that Jesus has.
+ Matthew 28:18–20:

> *And Jesus came to them and spake unto them, saying, All authority hath been given unto me in heaven and on earth. Go ye therefore, and make disciples of all the nations, baptizing them into the name of the Father and of the Son and of the Holy Spirit, teaching them to observe all things whatsoever I commanded you: and lo, I am with you always, even unto the end of the world.*

+ Jesus is going to accompany the church in its earth walk in the power and might of His name. You mark that Jesus has all authority given to Him in heaven and on earth. That authority is in His name.
+ Philippians 2:5–11. (Read this carefully.) We will use the ninth to eleventh verses,

> *Wherefore also God highly exalted him, and gave unto him the name which is above every name; that in the name of Jesus every knee should bow, of things in heaven and things on earth and things under the earth, and that every tongue should confess that Jesus Christ is Lord, to the glory of God the Father.*

- Jesus is given the highest position in the universe. He has the name that is above every name, with all the authority of God in it. That name has been given to the church, to us common folks, to use. In that name we are masters of demons and of their works.
- Ephesians 1:19–32. Here is Paul's prayer for us that the eyes of our hearts may be opened that we may know the exceeding greatness of His ability on our behalf; it is to us who believe.

> [That ability] *according to that working of the strength of his might which he wrought in Christ, when he raised him from the dead, and made him to sit at his right hand in the heavenly places, far above all rule, and authority, and power, and dominion, and every name that is named, not only in this world, but also in that which is to come: and he put all things in subjection under his feet, and gave him to be head over all things to the church, which is his body, the fulness of him that filleth all in all.*

- This is almost literal, but it unveils to us the very heart of this revelation.
- Now notice that God has lifted Jesus above every name and every authority in the universe; He has put all things in subjection under His feet. The church is His feet.
- And He gave Him to be the Head over all things to the benefit of the church, which is His body; and His body is the fullness of Him that fills all things in all.
- We have never recognized what we are in Christ in the mind of the father. We are the absolute masters of demons and their forces in the earth.

THE BOOK OF ACTS

- The first reference is Acts 2:38. On the day of Pentecost, when the mighty outpouring of the Spirit was in the room, and the disciples received eternal life, Peter began to preach; and the men cried out afterward and said unto Peter and the rest of the apostles, *"Brethren, what shall we do?"* (Acts 2:37) Write out what Peter said in verse 38:

_____

_____

_____

- They were Jews that knew nothing of what He is doing now at the right hand of the Father on high.
- Peter told them to be baptized in that name. Three thousand Jews responded that day to that call he gave.
- *"And it came to pass on the morrow, that their rulers and elders and scribes were gathered together in Jerusalem; and Annas the high priest was there, and Caiaphas, and John, and Alexander, and as many as were of the kindred of the high priest"* (Acts 4:5–6). This was the same crowd that had murdered Jesus.

> *And when they had set them in the midst, they inquired, By what power, or in what name, have ye done this? Then Peter, filled with the Holy Spirit, said unto them, Ye rulers of the people, and elders, if we this day are examined concerning a good deed done to an impotent man, by what means this man is made whole.* (verses 7–9)

- Then here Peter's voice rings out:

> *He is the stone which was set at nought of you the builders, which was made the head of the corner. And in none other is there salvation: for neither is there any other name under heaven, that is given among men, wherein we must be saved. Now when they beheld the*

boldness of Peter and John, and had perceived that they were unlearned and ignorant men, they marvelled; and they took knowledge of them, that they had been with Jesus. And seeing the man that was healed standing with them, they could say nothing against it.

(verses 11–14)

+ They marveled. They had to admit that a notable miracle had been wrought through them.
+ But notice this:

   But that it spread no further among the people, let us threaten them, that they speak henceforth to no man in this name. And they called them, and charged them not to speak at all nor teach in the name of Jesus. But Peter and John answered and said unto them, Whether it is right in the sight of God to hearken unto you rather than unto God, judge ye: for we cannot but speak the things which we saw and heard. (verses 17–20)

+ The name of Jesus had created greater consternation in the city than Jesus had in His earth walk.
+ The disciples went to their room where they were gathered and had a prayer meeting; and in their prayer they said this:

   And now, Lord, look upon their threatenings: and grant unto thy servants to speak thy word with all boldness, while thou stretchest forth thy hand to heal; and that signs and wonders may be done through the name of thy holy Servant Jesus. And when they had prayed, the place was shaken wherein they were gathered together. (Acts 4:29–31)

+ The thirty-third verse tells us, "And with great power gave the apostles their witness of the resurrection of the Lord Jesus: and great grace was upon them all."
+ You must read this book with great care. Begin with the first chapter and read it through, marking every place where the name is used; mark how it was used and the circumstances surrounding it.
+ Notice Acts 5:27–28. Fear had fallen upon the leaders of Israel. They were combating a force that they had never met before. Jesus, they had crucified, but His name was more powerful than the Man Himself.
+ *"And to him they agreed: and when they had called the apostles unto them, they beat them and charged them not to speak in the name of Jesus, and let them go"* (Acts 5:40).
+ Verse 41: *"They therefore departed from the presence of the council, rejoicing that they were counted worthy to suffer dishonor for the Name."*
+ The church has never been persecuted since then for the name of Jesus. You will find that as we go through the book of Acts, that the name of Jesus was their method of advertising; they had miracles everywhere.
+ Acts 8:12–6. *"But when they believed Philip preaching good tidings concerning the kingdom of God and the name of Jesus Christ, they were baptized, both men and women"* (verse 12).
+ You notice that Philip not only preached Jesus as a Savior, but he also preached about the name.
+ The sixteenth verse tells how they were baptized into the name of the Lord Jesus. Read that chapter carefully, notice the miracles that followed the use of that name.
+ Acts 9:14–16 gives us the conversion of Paul. Read this section very carefully and notice the place of the name.
+ The sixteenth verse, *"For I will show him how many things he must suffer for my name's sake."* Jesus is talking to Ananias. Paul is to suffer for the name.

- About the only suffering we have today in the church is that for our eccentricities and our sense knowledge teaching.
- Paul begins to preach at once. In the twenty-first verse we read, *"And all that heard him were amazed, and said, Is not this he that in Jerusalem made havoc of them that called on this name?"*
- Then Barnabas takes Paul back to Jerusalem; and in the twenty-seventh verse: *"And declared unto them how he had seen the Lord in the way, and that he had spoken to him, and how at Damascus he had preached boldly in the name of Jesus."*
- I wonder if you are grasping the significance of the name. We have preaching everything but the name.
- Acts 10:43–48. (Read this whole chapter over carefully.) *"To him bear all the prophets witness, that through his name every one that believeth on him shall receive remission of sins"* (verse 43).
- Read and study carefully the following: Acts 15:25–26; 16:18; 19:5, 17; 21:13; 22:16; 26:9.
- We have seen the authority of the name of Jesus and the results that followed its use in the book of Acts.

HOW MUCH DO YOU REMEMBER?

1. What is meant by the term "power of attorney"?
2. Explain how the disciples are commissioned to go and bear fruit.
3. Explain John 14:13–15.
4. a. In what authority was the commission in Mark 16:17–20 given?

   b. To whom?

   c. For how long?
5. What place does the name of Jesus hold in the daily ministry of the church?
6. What is a disciple? Explain how disciples are made.
7. Explain Philippians 2:5–10.
8. How does the fact that Jesus has a name above every other name affect the church today?
9. What significance has the name of Jesus as used in Acts 10:43–48?
10. Give and explain at least three Scriptures showing the use of the name of Jesus in the book of Acts.

LESSON 26 NOTES

_____

_____

_____

_____

_____

_____

_____

_____

Lesson 27
THE WORD IN THE BOOK OF ACTS

Acts was written by Luke between 63 and 65 A.D. It is a history of the first thirty-three years of Christ at the right hand of the Father. It is a sample of the supernatural life of the sons of God carrying out the will of their seated Lord. It is the only unfinished book in the New Testament.

Not a man is seen in it. The Holy Spirit is given His place as the governing, ruling personality of the new creation.

Luke was led to Christ by Paul and had lived with him for fifteen or eighteen years. He knew the revelation that the Father had given to him of Jesus and of His finished work; and yet you cannot see either in the gospel of Luke or in this book a single indication of it. Luke wrote as he was moved by the Holy Spirit. If he had written as a man, as a historian, he would have eulogized Paul.

But Paul moves through the book of Acts as a common man. His weaknesses, his strength, his failings, and his successes are recorded without any apology.

Jesus's name has its place. It isn't the first place. It has a place all its own. It has within it the authority that Adam lost in the garden.

There isn't a thing that Jesus did in His earth walk that the name will not do today in the lips of the new creation.

This book is a revelation.

Demons yield to the authority of the name. The dead are raised; men are baptized into it; the sick are healed by it. Men preached it. The Sanhedrin feared it. The name took the place of the risen Christ just as the Word took the place of the risen Christ.

SOME FACTS ABOUT THE WORD THESE MEN PREACHED

+ It ruled their private lives.
+ It was magnified.
+ It increased; it grew, a living power.
+ It multiplied.
+ Men were mastered by the Word.
+ Men proclaimed the Word.
+ Men gathered to hear the Word.
+ The Word grew mightily and prevailed in heathen cities.
+ The Word of grace is the revelation of the ability of God to build Himself into the lives of men.

THE WORD PERTAINING TO THE BOOK OF ACTS

+ In the book of Acts no one is using the New Testament as we use it today. (It was in course of making.) The Pauline Epistles were written between the period of 54 and 65 A.D. They were not in circulation until the second century. They were not bound together until even later than that, so the Word that we have in the book of Acts is the spoken Word.
+ Jesus was the Word Incarnate. The four Gospels are what the Holy Spirit has to say about the incarnate Word; and they have the record of the word spoken by the incarnate One.

- The book of Acts is a record of the Holy Spirit taking Jesus's place on the earth for the thirty-three years. It is a revelation of God in the infant body of the new creation. It is a record of the effect of eternal life upon the heathen world, upon the apostate Jewish nation.

- God's people of the old covenant had repudiated the God of the covenant. There was no substitute for the Word in that day.

- During those thirty-three years there was no organization of the body of Christ as we see it today. The Word held the first place.

- Mary, the mother of Jesus, drops out of sight. John, who leaned on Jesus's bosom, is but one of the witnesses. Peter stands in the foreground for a bit, but the Word is greater than Peter.

- The Holy Spirit takes the precedence over any of the apostles. The Word alone gave faith. The Word alone gave the new birth. The Word alone gave healing. The Word alone bound the disciples together. One might almost say the Word is Christianity.

- That spoken Word that we see in the book of Acts was the manna of God for the recreated human spirit. It still is.

- You can't find in the book of Acts or in the book of Luke even a suggestion of the finished work of Christ, of His great substitutionary battle—except in that first sermon that Peter preached, and in Acts 13:33 where Paul says, "*That God hath fulfilled the same unto our children, in that he raised up Jesus; as also it is written in the second psalm, Thou art my Son, this day have I begotten thee.*"

- Here he is speaking of Jesus's being born again and His resurrection after He had been made sin.

- It is very important that we recognize the power of this spoken Word and the written Word.

- Acts 6:2, 4: "*And the twelve called the multitude of the disciples unto them, and said, It is not fit that we should forsake the word of God, and serve tables. …But we will continue steadfastly in prayer, and in the ministry of the word.*"

- In the seventh verse: "*And the word of God increased; and the number of the disciples multiplied in Jerusalem exceedingly; and a great company of the priests were obedient to the faith.*"

- They were not speaking of the Old Testament, but of the Word of God that came to the apostles by revelation. It tells how this Word increased and dominated the people.

- Acts 8:4: "*They therefore that were scattered abroad went about preaching the word.*"

- In the fourteenth verse, we read, "*Now when the apostles that were at Jerusalem heard that Samaria had received the word of God, they sent unto them Peter and John.*"

- Our hearts must grasp the significance of this: that the Word had taken Jesus's place; and it was the Word that was being born in the hearts of those early Christians.

- Acts 11:1: "*Now the apostles and the brethren that were in Judaea heard that the Gentiles also had received the word of God.*"

- They had not received a creed or doctrine but just this unwritten Word.

- Acts 12:24: "*But the word of God grew and multiplied.*"

- In the sixth chapter, it had increased. Now, it multiplied. It was gaining the ascendancy rapidly. It was having a tremendous influence upon men.

- Acts 14:3: "*Long time therefore they tarried there speaking boldly in the Lord, who bare witness unto the word of his grace, granting signs and wonders to be done by their hands.*"

- It was the "*word of His grace,*" of His love. It was the Word of the ability of the unseen God.

- It is what we get in Ephesians 3:20: "*Now unto him that is able to do exceeding abundantly above all that we ask or think, according to the power [or ability] that worketh in us.*"

- It is according to the ability of the Word that is at work within us.

- That early church lived in the Word. The Word lived in them. The Word was a revelation of what they were in Christ; but the "in Christ" truth had not yet gripped them. If it was preached, there was no record of it in the book of Acts.

- You see, preaching the Word was preaching Jesus. It is preaching what Christ was to them and what He meant in their lips and in their lives. They lived in the Word. The Word lived in them, so they grew to be like the Author of the Word.

- It is important to know that the real Word preacher is the one in whom the Word has made good. His testimony is what the living, saving, healing Word has done in him and through him. It is the real Word of faith. It is the faith-God's Word.

- Paul said, *"For to me to live is Christ, and to die is gain"* (Philippians 1:21). In essence, "For me to preach is for Christ to preach through me; to live is for Christ to be reproduced among men." Strong language, wasn't it? He says that Christ lives in him. "I live because He lives in me. Christ's life and my life are one life. I am a branch of the living Vine." That is the language of Paul.

- Today, doctrines have taken the place of the Word. Sense knowledge rules the body of Christ.

- Acts 19:20: *"So mightily grew the word of the Lord and prevailed."*

- And yet, it wasn't written. It was the living, spoken Word. Today, Christ may absorb one, and one may so absorb the Word, that what one says will be the living Word. One can be so dominated by the Word that the words of one's mouth, and the meditation of his heart, will be pleasing to the Father.

- In Ephesus, the Word had gained such authority that we read in Acts 19:17–18: *"And this became known to all, both Jews and Greeks, that dwelt at Ephesus; and fear fell upon them all, and the name of the Lord Jesus was magnified. Many also of them that had believed came, confessing, and declaring their deeds."*

- Mind you, they didn't confess their deeds until after they had accepted Christ. Many of them were spiritualists, and many of them that had done this brought their books and burned them. They counted the cost and it was thirty thousand pieces of silver. The Word had prevailed.

- Paul's personality hadn't prevailed. Paul's philosophy hadn't prevailed; but the Word had prevailed.

- That Word is the Logos; the Logos is Christ. You can't separate this living Logos from the living Christ. It heals the sick; it breaks the power of demons over lives, and fills those lives with fearless confidence so that persecution, even death, did not daunt them.

- In Acts 20:32, Paul is saying goodbye to the church at Ephesus: *"And now I commend you to God, and to the word of his grace, which is able to build you up, and to give you the inheritance among all them that are sanctified."*

- He said to those elders,

  I coveted no man's silver, or gold, or apparel. Ye yourselves know that these hands ministered unto my necessities, and to them that were with me. In all things I gave you an example, that so laboring ye ought to help the weak, and to remember the words of the Lord Jesus, that he himself said, It is more blessed to give than to receive. (Acts 20:33–35.)

- He lived the Word. His preaching would have little effect had not the Word governed his life.

- The church will never exercise the divine authority that belongs to it until the Word becomes a part of our daily lives.

- That unwritten Word had more authority over the lives of these men than the written, living Word has today. That is wrong. This Word should govern us today. Our lips should be filled with it.

+ We have substituted sense evidences for the Word. We have substituted education and organization for the Word. They are all of them failures.

+ The Word in the lips of faith, filled with love, filled with the very life of God, has as great authority and ability as it ever had in the history of the church.

+ We must realize that He and His Word are one; that man's word is a dying word; and that God's Word is a living, abiding Word. The most cultured and beautiful sermon is dead as soon as it is given unless it is filled with the Word.

+ The Word is the sword of the spirit. That is, the Word is the sword of the recreated, human spirit. The Word in the lips of the man that is filled with love will be as effectual today as the Word was in the lips of Jesus, or Stephen, or Peter, or Paul. These words become a healing, saving, present-tense reality.

+ The Word is actually Christ. Write out Jesus's words in John 6:63:

_____

_____

+ We were made alive by the Word. We are kept spiritually alive by the Word. We have fed on the Word; and the words of Jesus in John 6:53 become a reality: *"Except ye eat the flesh of the Son of man and drink his blood, ye have not life in yourselves."*

+ The body and the blood of the Lord are in His Word. It is not the bread and wine. That is but a symbol. It is in this living Word.

+ The Word is a dead word in the Bible on the table. It only takes on life as we begin to act it, as we give it place, as we practice it in our daily conduct.

+ The word *"righteousness,"* as the Pauline Revelation gives it, is hardly mentioned in the book of Acts, yet they lived in the reality of it. Nothing is said about the Holy Spirit in them, but the whole book breathes of the indwelling presence of the One who came on the day of Pentecost. They knew nothing about the new creation as the Pauline Revelation gives it to us, but the new creation was the living fact that was overturning the Roman government.

+ They preached the name and saw it demonstrate the reality that Jesus had declared was in it. They knew nothing about the Lordship of Jesus as we see it unveiled in the Pauline message, but they recognized it; they lived it.

+ The first fifteen years of the early church was lived in the sense realm altogether. They didn't have the written Word. They only had what was spoken by the apostles on the day of Pentecost.

+ They heard the sound of that rushing wind. They saw the tongues of fire on the heads of those 120 men and women. They heard them speak in those strange tongues. They saw the mighty miracles take place.

+ The Jewish nation was shaken by the physical evidences of the resurrection of Jesus. The Word slowly but surely gained the ascendancy over the senses; but God dealt with them as only a wise parent could deal with His children. There came a constant unveiling through the spoken word, the living Word that unveiled Jesus to them.

+ The contrast between God's truth and God's Word and man's truth and man's word startles us. Man's word is a dying word. His Word, spoken two thousand years ago, is living, life-giving, a mighty thing. The reason is that the Word is a part of God Himself, just as man's word is a part of himself. God's Word is like its Author. My word is like me.

+ God's Word is full of love, for God is love. It is full of divine ability. It is full of creative ability.

- We have the Word, the sure Word, this living Word; and our hearts can depend on that. The new convert must feed upon this recreating Word. The old believer must feed upon this life-sustaining and strength-giving Word.
- It is the prevailing Word that is needed today. It is needed to prevail over our thinking, to prevail over our diseases, to prevail over our weakness, to prevail over our fears, to prevail over our doubts. It is the prevailing, living Word of our Master.

HOW MUCH DO YOU REMEMBER?

1. Why is man not mentioned in the book of Acts?
2. Give at least three facts about the Word as it was preached in the book of Acts.
3. Explain the statement, *"And the word of God increased."*
4. In what form did the Word exist in the book of Acts?
5. Explain Acts 14:3.
6. What is the difference between speaking the Word and giving an experience?
7. What gives the Word authority and ability today?
8. What is revealed in John 6:53?
9. Explain the difference between God's truth and man's truth.
10. a. What place must the Word be given in the life of the babe in Christ?

    b. In the old believer?

LESSON 27 NOTES

_____

_____

_____

_____

_____

_____

_____

_____

_____

_____

_____

_____

_____

_____

_____

_____

Lesson 28
THE HOLY SPIRIT IN THE BOOK OF ACTS, PART 1

There are three great personalities standing out in the book of Acts: The Holy Spirit, the living Word, and the name of Jesus.

You remember that the Word and Jesus are often identical. *"In the beginning was the Word, and the Word was with God, and the Word was God"* (John 1:1).

You cannot separate the name from the Man. It is a part of Him.

There is no great preacher. There is no great man overshadowing others in this wonder book. I sometimes think of the book of Acts as "the book of the seated Christ at the right hand of the Father"—the first twenty-three years of His ministry there. Then I think of it as the book of the Comforter, the Paraclete, the Superintendent of the church, the One who took Jesus's place after He sat down at the right hand of the Father.

JESUS'S PROMISES REGARDING THE HOLY SPIRIT

+ Let us first look at the promises that Jesus made in regard to the Holy Spirit before He left.
+ John 7:37–38: *"Now on the last day, the great day of the feast, Jesus stood and cried, saying, If any man thirst, let him come unto me and drink. He that believeth on me, as the scripture hath said, from within him shall flow rivers of living water."*
+ One translator says, "From within him shall gush forth torrents of living water."

JESUS GIVES THE COMFORTER

+ *"But this spake he of the Spirit, which they that believed on him were to receive: for the Spirit was not yet given; because Jesus was not yet glorified"* (verse 39).
+ Jesus was not glorified until He took His seat at the right hand of the Majesty on High. His work of redemption was not available unto man unto He was glorified.
+ The living water spoken of was eternal life; and Jesus said, *"I came that they may have life, and may have it abundantly"* (John 10:10).
+ From one angle it would seem as though the reason for Jesus's coming was that man might receive eternal life; from another, that man might be redeemed. But they are all blended one into the other. So, Jesus said, in essence, "They that believe on Me are to receive."
+ They were not to receive the Holy Spirit until they had believed on Him. What did that mean by "believing on Him"? It was not believing that He had died for their sins according to the Scriptures, and that the third day He had been raised because the sin problem had been settled.
+ Redemption was a fact. The new creation was available.
+ You understand that no one believed on Jesus in this sense until after the day of Pentecost. No one believed that He had risen from the dead. The disciples ridiculed the testimony of the woman when they told them that Jesus had risen.
+ Luke 24:11: *"And these words appeared in their sight as idle talk; and they disbelieved them."*
+ I suppose that there was no one in all Palestine more staggered by the resurrection of Jesus than were those who had been with Him for three years, His chosen disciples.

- John 14:16: *"And I will pray the Father, and he shall give you another Comforter."* This is a *helper*, an *advocate*. It is the Greek word *paraclete*. Notice that Jesus is to give this comforter, *"that he may be with you forever."*

- *"Even the Spirit of truth: whom the world cannot receive; for it beholdeth him not, neither knoweth him: ye know him; for he abideth with you, and shall be in you"* (verse 17). Notice that He is to be a comforter and a helper. He is called the *"Spirit of truth,"* or literally, the Spirit of reality. The world cannot receive Him, for it cannot behold Him. The natural man cannot receive the Holy Spirit.

- The Spirit may convict him. The Spirit may operate in him and speak through him as He did the men in the old covenant; but He could not make His home in the bodies of men until they were recreated, until they had received eternal life.

- *"For [the world] beholdeth him not, neither knoweth him."* The world knows nothing about the Holy Spirit. The world can know Jesus. That is why Jesus said in John 16:13, *"Howbeit when he, the Spirit of truth, is come, he shall guide you into all the truth: for he shall not speak from himself [or, literally, 'about Himself']."*

- Notice once more: *"For he abideth with you, and shall be in you."* How was the Holy Spirit with the disciples before He could come into them? Why, He was with them in the person of Jesus. Jesus and the Holy Spirit were working together; so Jesus could say, in essence, "He is with you in My presence."

- Then, John 14:26: *"But the Comforter, even the Holy Spirit, whom the Father will send in my name, he shall teach you all things, and bring to your remembrance all that I said unto you."*

- Jesus said that He would send the Comforter. Now He says that the Father will send Him *"in my name"*; and He is going to be a teacher. He is going to teach the disciples all things, and is going to bring to their remembrance all the things that Jesus had told them.

- You see, the disciples didn't understand the Master any more than natural man today can understand deeply spiritual things. Spiritual things are revealed to those who have received eternal life.

- In John 15:26, He takes a step in advance: *"But when the Comforter is come, whom I will send unto you from the Father, even the Spirit of truth, which proceedeth from the Father, he shall bear witness of me."*

- He is not only going to be their teacher, but He is going to bear witness of the Master. His primal business in the church is the office of Teacher about Jesus—the unveiler of what Jesus actually did in His substitution, what Jesus's nature and life does to the believer in the new creation, and how the spirit can take the things of Christ and bring them into the believer's life until the believer will live and walk as Jesus did in His earth walk.

BAPTISM OF THE HOLY SPIRIT

- But there is a further development of the Holy Spirit in John 16:7–15. Write out this verse:

_____

_____

_____

- That is striking. He was there with Jesus, but He was not functioning. He was not their teacher, yet. He was not their re-creator. He had not given birth to them, for they had to be born of the Spirit.

- You remember that John the Baptist said, *"Nevertheless I tell you the truth: It is expedient for you that I go away; for if I go not away, the Comforter will not come unto you; but if I go, I will send him unto you"* (Luke 3:16).

- Baptism is immersion. One is put into water, and when they are raised out of the water, they are born out of the water just as a child is born of its mother.
- But you notice that baptism didn't mean filling with the Holy Spirit. It simply meant that some other act was taking place.
- It was receiving the nature and life of God. That is what Jesus was going to do. He was going to baptize into His body. That had not yet come into being. That was prophecy.
- Let us go on from there.

> And he, when he is come, will convict the world in respect of sin, and of righteousness, and of judgment: of sin, because they believe not on me; of righteousness, because I go to the Father, and ye behold me no more; of judgment, because the prince of this world hath been judged.
> (John 16:8–11.)

- Note it carefully, that there is a threefold conviction that is coming to the world. We will reverse the order.
- He said that the world is going to come to judgment because Satan has been judged; and I wondered what that meant. What relation did Satan sustain toward man? And then I remembered John 8:44–45:

> Ye are of your father the devil, and the lusts of your father it is your will to do. He was a murderer from the beginning, and standeth not in the truth, because there is no truth in him. When he speaketh a lie, he speaketh of his own: for he is a liar, and the father thereof.

- Then I remembered 1 John 3:10: "In this the children of God are manifest, and the children of the devil."
- Then I saw that there are to be two families—the family of God and the family of Satan. Satan is not only the god of this world and the prince of this world (see John 12:31 and 2 Corinthians 4:4) but he is the father of the spiritually dead.
- Now I can understand what it is going to mean for Satan to be judged. His family is judged in him just as the believer was judged in Christ when God put our sin upon Him and He became our Substitute. Then if Satan is judged, every one of his children is judged with him.
- Then I saw the awfulness of the judgment. The sinner is not judged for what he has done, but he is judged because of what he is, spiritually in union with the devil. A second thing the Holy Spirit is going to convict men of is righteousness, because Jesus had made that available in His substitutionary sacrifice; and he has gone unto the Father and sat down at the Father's right hand.
- What does righteousness mean? It means the ability to stand in the Father's presence without the sense of guilt, or of condemnation, or of judgment. Jesus has wrought such a perfect redemption that the unsaved man has a legal right to eternal life and righteousness.
- God so loved the world that He gave Jesus to the world; and the substitutionary sacrifice of Christ makes that gift a legal thing.
- Now, what is the sin that the Holy Spirit is going to convict men of? It is the sin of the rejection of eternal life, of rejection of His finished work on their behalf.
- That is the only sin that has judgment for the sinner. He has committed other sins, but this is the sin that shuts him out of the new heaven. He has rejected Jesus Christ as his own Lord and Savior.
- In John 16:12–13, Jesus said, "I have yet many things to say unto you, but ye cannot bear them now. Howbeit when he, the Spirit of truth, is come, he shall guide you into all the truth: for he shall not speak from himself; but what things soever he shall hear, these shall he speak."

+ He shall guide you into the reality of this substitutionary sacrifice. In other words, He is going to use Paul as an instrument to give to the new creation, this body of Christ, a revelation of this great substitutionary work of Christ.

STRIKING TRUTHS OF THE HOLY SPIRIT

+ Now we come to some striking things. This Holy Spirit that is coming is going to be in the body of every believer. We can't understand it. We don't have to. It is beyond sense knowledge, but it is a spiritual reality.

+ He is going to be the Teacher of every one of us. Some of us will have the special gift of teaching, but every one of us will have Him in us to guide us in the study of the Word. *"For he shall not speak from himself; but what things soever he shall hear, these shall he speak."*

+ He shall speak and shall declare unto you the things that are to come. This is not only prophetic knowledge, but He is speaking unto you about the work that the Father has wrought in Christ; for God was in Christ reconciling the world unto Himself. The Spirit is going to take this hidden truth and is going to reveal it to the spirit consciousness of the new creation.

+ *"He shall glorify me: for he shall take of mine, and shall declare it unto you. All things whatsoever the Father hath are mine: therefore said I, that he taketh of mine, and shall declare it unto you"* (John 16:14–15). You see how deeply important it is that the Holy Spirit have an opportunity to unveil these mighty things to us.

+ The book of Acts was a mystery to me for a long time. You can find almost nothing taught about the new creation, the indwelling presence of the Holy Spirit, the body of Christ, the headship of Jesus over the body, or of the new kind of love that came through Jesus. Very little is taught about the new creation, but they are always practicing it.

THE UPPER ROOM

+ A group of men and women gathered in that upper room that knew nothing about what was going to happen. No one knew about the new birth. No one knew about indwelling. No one knew about speaking in tongues. No faith was demanded on the part of Jesus.

+ First Corinthians 2:14 describes absolutely the men and women in that upper room: *"Now the natural man receiveth not the things of the Spirit of God: for they are foolishness unto him; and he cannot know them, because they are spiritually judged."*

+ Can that be true about them? Yes, you see what they did. They cast lots about who should take Judah' place. Jesus had already planned that Saul of Tarsus should take his place. They asked Jesus, *"Lord, dost thou at this time restore the kingdom to Israel?"* (Acts 1:6)

+ They knew nothing about what was going to happen. Oh, the grace of our Father to take a crowd of men and women, just like the Jews of today, and perform the staggering miracle of the upper room.

+ These men were all in the sense realm. The Father came down to their level. Four mighty things happened in that upper room that morning.

+ First, the Holy Spirit came with the sound of a mighty rushing wind (see Acts 2:1–4); and when He filled that room, He recreated that one hundred twenty, and they didn't know what it meant. No one had had such an experience before. (See 1 Corinthians 12:13.)

+ A second thing that happened was that a tongue of fire sat upon the brow of each one of them. They looked in amazement at those torches that didn't burn or injure—a lambent flame touching them. But they didn't understand it—that the good news was to be proclaimed with tongues of fire, that the message was to burn the very hearts of the world until men who were hating it, fighting it, thinking that the only way to get rid of it was to kill as they did Stephen, would be born again.

- The third thing that happened was that those folks were all born again. The Spirit filled them now, entered into their bodies, took possession of them and spoke through them with other tongues. They spoke as the Spirit gave them utterance. (See Acts 2:4.)
- Second Corinthians 5:17 becomes a reality: *"Wherefore if any man is in Christ, he is a new creature* [or a new species].*"* This was something that had never been before. Then, *"old things are passed away; behold, they are become new. But all things are of God, who reconciled* [those men and women] *to himself"* (verses 17–18) by a new creation.
- Read carefully the tenth chapter. Notice how the Holy Spirit is guiding Peter to come into a Gentile's home where he had no right to come as a Jew. He went in and began to speak the Word: and as he did so, the Spirit fell on them identically as He did in the upper room. The Gentiles are recreated, and the Holy Spirit indwells them.

HOW MUCH DO YOU REMEMBER?

1. What three personalities do we find in the book of Acts?
2. Who took Jesus's place after He sat down at the right hand of the Father?
3. a. When were those who believed to receive the Spirit?

    b. What were they to believe?
4. How long was the Comforter to be with us? Can He live in us before we have eternal life?
5. In John 15:26, where was the Comforter to come from, and what was His mission?
6. a. Is the sinner judged for what he has done?

    b. What is the judgment?

    c. What is the result of rejecting the work of Christ?
7. Who received the revelation of the substitutionary work of Christ?
8. What does 1 Corinthians 2:14 describe?
9. What four things happened in the upper room?

LESSON 28 NOTES

_____

_____

_____

_____

_____

_____

_____

_____

_____

_____

_____

Lesson 29
THE HOLY SPIRIT IN THE BOOK OF ACTS, PART 2

'BELIEVERS' BEFORE AND AFTER THE DAY OF PENTECOST

+ I always believed that the disciples were Christians before the day of Pentecost; but one day this question came: Did anyone believe before the day of Pentecost that Jesus was going to die for their sins and rise again after God had justified them?

+ I turned to Matthew 16:16 and read Peter's confession: *"And Simon Peter answered and said, Thou art the Christ, the Son of the living God."*

+ Then I turned to John 11:27 where Martha makes her confession. *"She saith unto him, Yea, Lord: I have believed that thou art the Christ, the Son of God, even he that cometh into the world."*

+ And then there is John 20:26–29, Thomas's confession. Thomas had said that he wouldn't believe that Christ had risen from the dead except *"I shall see in his hands the print of the nails, and put my finger into the print of the nails, and put my hand into his side"* (verse 25).

+ Eight days later, Jesus appeared before them, and said, *"Thomas, Reach hither thy finger, and see my hands; and reach hither thy hand, and put it into my side: and be not faithless, but believing"* (verse 27).

+ And Thomas said, *"My Lord and my God. Jesus saith unto him, Because thou hast seen me, thou hast believed: blessed are they that have not seen, and yet have believed"* (verses 28–29).

+ I saw then that the disciples had believed that Jesus was the Son of God, that He was the Messiah, but no one believed according to Romans 10:9–10: *"Because if thou shalt confess with thy mouth Jesus as Lord, and shalt believe in thy heart that God raised him from the dead, thou shalt be saved: for with the heart man believeth unto righteousness; and with the mouth confession is made unto salvation."*

+ And the Scripture says that *"Whosoever believeth on him shall not be put to shame"* (verse 11).

+ Or you might read from 1 Corinthians 15:3–4: *"For I delivered unto you first of all that which also I received: that Christ died for our sins according to the scriptures; and that he was buried; and that he hath been raised on the third day according to the scriptures."*

+ You see, none of the disciples knew that Christ was going to die for their sins, and was going to suffer as their substitute, that He was going to put sin away; and that God was going to lay upon Him the iniquity of us all. They did not know that *"Him who knew no sin he made to be sin on our behalf; that we might become the righteousness of God in him."*

+ No one knew that Jesus was going down to the dark regions and conquer Satan and strip him of his authority, and paralyze his death-dealing power so that men who had been held in bondage all of their lives could be set free by confessing Jesus as their Lord and Savior.

+ No one knew that. No one knew about righteousness—what it meant.

+ They confronted me, and at first, I wondered why we had never seen it before.

+ The disciples were Jews under the first covenant. They were under the blood of bulls and of goats. They had obeyed the law in regard to sacrifice, in regard to the keeping of the Sabbath and everything else regarding the law. They had a limited righteousness under the law as servants. But they knew nothing better than that.

+ They knew that a Messiah was going to come, but they thought it was purely national. They thought that He would free them from the Roman law and give them back the kingdom that was established by David.

- None of them believed in Christ as we believe in Him today, because they had no teaching. Jesus hadn't opened that up to them. He had left it to Paul to open up—the part of His finished work.

- You remember Galatians 1:8–12: *"But though we, or an angel from heaven, should preach unto you any gospel other than that which we preached unto you, let him be anathema [or accursed]"* (verse 8). That is strong language, isn't it?

- Verses 11–12 are significant: *"For I make known to you, brethren, as touching the gospel which was preached by me, that it is not after man. For neither did I receive it from man, nor was I taught it, but it came to me through revelation of Jesus Christ."*

- To Paul was given the revelation of the substitutionary sacrifice of Jesus Christ; to Paul was given the revelation of the body of Christ of which Jesus is the Head; to him was given the revelation of the union of the believer with Christ; and to him was given the revelation of the ministry of the Holy Spirit in the body of Christ.

- How much was taught by the "spoken Word" we don't know. It isn't recorded in the book of Acts. You understand that none of the churches had more than two or three of Paul's epistles until after the beginning of the second century. John's gospel wasn't written until after 110 A.D., so that all the revelation that John had was not known until after the gospel of John had been written.

- You remember that Paul was not sent to the Jewish people, but was sent to the Gentiles.

- You remember the church teaching in 1 and 2 Corinthians, in Ephesians, Philippians, and in Colossians was only locally known. It is true that some of them had parts of the Old Testament, but there was no printing at that time. Copies had to be made by slaves and poor men; and most of the converts were poor. They had no access to the Hebrew Scriptures; and, if they had, they could not have read them. So you see, that on the day of Pentecost, there was very little known.

- The things that amazed me and made me think was that when Peter preached, he did not say, "Repent and believe." In fact, the words *faith* or *believe* were not used on the day of Pentecost.

- God didn't demand faith of the disciples in the upper room. He didn't demand anything of them, only that they tarry for the Holy Spirit.

BAPTISM OF THE HOLY SPIRIT

- We notice some significant things in the four Gospels where it speaks about the Baptism of the Holy Spirit.

- Beginning with Matthew 3:11, we read, *"I indeed baptize you in water unto repentance: but he that cometh after me is mightier than I, whose shoes I am not worthy to bear: he shall baptize you in the Holy Spirit and in fire."* (The preposition *in* is not in the Greek.)

- Now notice this carefully, "I am going to immerse you in water, but Jesus is coming and he is going to immerse you in the Holy Spirit."

- The immersion in the water was for their bodies. The immersion in the Holy Spirit was for their spirits. But what did it do to their spirits? It recreated them.

- When they were immersed in the Spirit, they received eternal life. They were born again. Then the phenomenon of fire was manifest in a tongue that sat on their heads.

- The disciples must have looked in amazement. They did not understand what it meant. But we know that this message of the substitutionary sacrifice of Jesus, of the body of Christ, of the church, was going to be proclaimed with tongues of fire, a resistless message just as fire is resistless.

- That is the reason for the great persecutions that come upon the church. I question if there has ever been a persecution of a dead, formal church.

- After the tongues of fire were manifested, then it says: *"And they were all filled with the Holy Spirit, and began to speak with other tongues"* (Acts 2:4).

- He had recreated them. He had made their bodies a temple, a sanctuary. Now He enters into this new home. He had dwelt in the Holy of holies and in the tabernacle, and in the temple. Now He is going to dwell in their bodies.

- You understand Romans 12:1–2: *"I beseech you therefore, brethren, by the mercies of God, to present your bodies"*—a temple of God. I want you to present it to God for His use.

- This is just as we have in 1 Corinthians 6:19–20: *"Or know ye not that your body is a temple of the Holy Spirit which is in you, which ye have from God? and ye are not your own; for ye were bought with a price: glorify God therefore in your body."*

- *"Glorify God…in your body."* That is a striking sentence. The body is not only a temple, but I want you to glorify God with your body.

- Now I can see why the body would need be perfectly well, healthy, and strong; and that it be free from all unclean habits—because it is the temple of God.

- Philippians 1:20–21 throws a little more light on it: *"So now also Christ shall be magnified in my body, whether by life, or by death. For to me to live is Christ, and to die is gain."*

- And you might think of Galatians 2:20: *"I have been crucified with Christ; and it is no longer I that live, but Christ liveth in me: and that life which I now live in the flesh I live in faith, the faith which is in the Son of God, who loved me, and gave himself up for me."*

- The great truth of indwelling was only hinted by Christ in John 7:38–39, in which Jesus said, *"From within him shall flow rivers of living water. But this spake he of the Spirit, which they that believed on him were to receive."*

- But you say, "What about that sentence in John where Jesus breathed on them and said, *"Receive ye the Holy Spirit"* (John 20:22)? That is the instance that is recorded in the gospel of Luke 24:45: *"Then opened he their mind, that they might understand the scriptures."* When He breathed on them, he touched their minds, just as they did under the first covenant. It was not in any sense their receiving the Holy Spirit as you and I receive Him today, or as they received Him on the day of Pentecost.

KNOWLEDGE BEFORE AND AFTER THE DAY OF PENTECOST

- Perhaps it might be good for us to think of just a few things that the disciples and others did not know on that wonder day.

- No one had ever been redeemed, so they knew nothing about redemption except the redemption out of Egypt. That was a national redemption.

- No one knew anything about eternal life. John's gospel had not yet been written. What Jesus said, John recorded. John 10:10: *"I came that they may have life, and may have it abundantly."* That was a new kind of life. The very word, *zoe*, was new to the ears of most of the hearers.

- No one had ever been recreated. The new birth was unknown to them. The little talk that Jesus had with Nicodemus when He told him that he must be born again hadn't recreated Nicodemus. Nicodemus didn't understand what it meant. He said, *"How can a man be born when he is old?"* (John 3:4). Jesus said, *"That which is born of the flesh is flesh; and that which is born of the Spirit is spirit. Marvel not that I said unto thee, Ye must be born anew"* (verses 6–7).

- Man's physical body is not born again. Man's spirit is the real man. It is the part that is born again. One should study this very carefully. Read John 3:3–8 as though you had never read it before. Don't read it with any preconceived notions. Eliminate everything from your mind; and you will discover this fact: that it was a prophecy of the birth of the church.

- They were to be born of the Holy Spirit. The thing that took place on the day of Pentecost was the birthday of the body of Christ.
- Nicodemus didn't understand it. No one else understood it until it was revealed to Paul.
- You see, no one had ever talked about a new creation, a new kind of man. It was utterly new to them.
- Second Corinthians 5:17 would have fallen upon dead ears.
- No one had ever been made righteous. The only righteousness they knew was the reckoned righteousness that Abraham had, and the law righteousness that those who kept that law had.
- But here is a new kind of righteousness. A phenomenon had taken place at the death of Jesus. The curtain that had shut men out of the Holy of holies had been rent from the top to the bottom. There is no longer any secret place where men meet God under the blood of bulls and goats.
- Now a new thing has taken place. Man can enter the presence of God without the sense of guilt or condemnation. Hebrews 4:16 becomes a reality. Write out this verse:

_____

_____

_____

- The tenth chapter of Hebrews, the second verse, is effective. He said that the sacrifices that they made continuously did not make them perfect.

  > _The same sacrifices year by year, which they offer continually, make perfect them that draw nigh. Else would they not have ceased to be offered? because the worshippers, having been once cleansed, would have had no more consciousness of sins. But in those sacrifices there is a remembrance made of sins year by year._ (Hebrews 10:1–3)

- In the twelfth and thirteenth verses it shows how Christ, by one sacrifice, has perfected forever them that are sanctified. When a man is cleansed by the blood of Christ, he can stand in the Father's presence as though sin had never been.
- Then there is 1 Corinthians 1:30. Every believer should know this Scripture: _"But of him are ye in Christ Jesus, who was made unto us wisdom from God, and righteousness and sanctification, and redemption."_
- Read Romans 3:26, the marginal rendering. Jesus becomes the righteousness of the man who has faith in Jesus.
- No one had ever known anything about indwelling. Jesus said, _"For he abideth with you, and shall be in you"_ (John 14:17).
- No one had ever had real friendship with the Father under the first covenant. That was practically impossible. No one had ever used the name of Jesus. No one had ever called God, Father. They crucified Jesus for doing it. No one knew of the new covenant. No one knew of the new kind of love.
- All this came by revelation knowledge after the day of Pentecost, after men had received eternal life and had received into their bodies the great, mighty Holy Spirit.

HOW MUCH DO YOU REMEMBER?

1. Did the disciples believe Jesus was Christ before the day of Pentecost? What it according to Romans 10:9–10?

2. Who was Paul sent to with his revelation of the substitutionary sacrifice?

3. Were the words *faith* or *believe* used on the day of Pentecost? What were the disciples to do?

4. a. What was the immersion of water for?

   b. What did immersion in the Holy Spirit do to them?

5. Explain 1 Corinthians 6:19–20.

6. Had anyone ever been redeemed? Had any eternal life? Were there any new creations?

7. How did Jesus answer Nicodemus?

8. Did anyone understand that the body of Christ had been born until Paul had his revelation?

9. a. Had any been made righteous?

   b. What does righteousness mean?

   c. Could the law make anyone righteous?

10. a. Explain 1 Corinthians 1:30.

    b. What came by revelation knowledge after the day of Pentecost?

LESSON 29 NOTES

_____

_____

_____

_____

_____

_____

_____

_____

_____

_____

_____

_____

_____

_____

_____

_____

_____

Lesson 30
HOW LONG CAN OTHERS CARRY YOU?

There are so many who refuse to take their place in the family of God. This family may be like a family that I once knew. There was one girl and one boy in it who never did their share of the work or bore their share of the responsibility. Others had to deny themselves to do their work for them.

For many years I have recognized that the same thing was true in the Father's family. Here are a man and a woman who have been Christians for thirty or forty years. They apparently have not grown any in the last thirty-five years. When they are sick, others have to exercise faith for them. When they are in a hard place, others bear their burdens. They are always seeking for help, yet they have ability that has never been exercised or developed.

YOUR PLACE IN THE FAMILY

+ You know your place in the family. You know your rights and privileges.

+ First John 3:2: *"Beloved, now are we children of God."*

+ This one has never taken a son's place, never assumed a son's responsibility, or enjoyed a son's privileges. The Father is a stranger to him. He enjoys preaching very much, and helps support the church; but he does not appreciate his righteousness in Christ, neither does he take advantage of it in helping himself or others.

+ You understand that righteousness means the ability to stand in the Father's presence without the sense of guilt or inferiority. Romans 8:1: *"There is therefore now no condemnation to them that are in Christ Jesus."*

+ They are in Christ. They have access to the throne. They have heard the invitation of Hebrews 4:16 to come boldly to the throne of grace to make their requests known that they may receive mercy and find grace to help in time of need.

+ In their time of need they go to others. It would seem as though they were ashamed to go into their Father's presence. A sense of inferiority has gained the ascendancy in them.

+ Hebrews 4:1 has never had any effect upon them: *"Let us fear therefore, lest haply, a promise being left of entering into his rest, any one of you should seem to have come short of it."*

+ This is the rest of faith, the rest of righteousness. I am no longer anxious. I am in His family. My Father is caring for me.

+ John 10:29: *"My Father, who hath given them unto me, is greater than all; and no one is able to snatch them out of the Father's hand."*

+ This man has never yet recognized that his Father is greater than all circumstances. They are his masters. Demons and their work hold him in bondage. He is afraid of sickness and afraid of want; yet his Father is greater than all.

+ He knows nothing about this quiet rest where he no longer fears anything.

+ He knows that his Father cares for him. He knows that Hebrews 7:25 is absolutely true: *"Wherefore also he is able to save to the uttermost them that draw near unto God through him, seeing he ever liveth to make intercession for them."*

+ They have never enjoyed His intercession. They have never taken advantage of it. They have never quietly said, "He ever liveth to pray for me. He is holding me."

- They have never enjoyed their rest. They are like the one spoken of in Hebrews 4:11, *"Let us therefore give diligence to enter into that rest, that no man fall after the same example of disobedience."*

- He is talking about those who failed to enter into His rest, and they did not enter because they were not able to enter into the rest God had provided. Today so many are unable to act upon the Word. They cannot be persuaded to enter into the rest of Christ.

- They do not have the fruits of righteousness. Do you know what they are? Why, the first fruit of righteousness is rest in the Word. It is that quiet confidence in the Word. Write out Isaiah 32:7:

_____

_____

_____

- That is a fore gleam of the effect of righteousness in the new creation. It is peace. It is quietness. It is assurance. This is the highest type of faith. There is no irritation. There is no anxiety or restlessness. (See Psalm 23:1–2.)

- *"I know him whom I have believed, and I am persuaded that he is able to guard that which I have committed unto him against that day"* (2 Timothy 1:12).

- There was no fear of demons, of circumstances, or of lack. He knows the Father cares for him.

- Jesus said, *"Your heavenly Father knoweth that ye have need of all these things"* (Matthew 6:32). Seek first His kingdom and His righteousness, and all of these things shall be added unto you. (See Matthew 6:33.)

- The believer has sought and found the kingdom of God. He is a new creation. He is a possessor of the very nature of the Father, and that nature has given him righteousness, so he lives and walks in fearless quietness.

- Hebrews 5:12–14:

  > For when by reason of the time ye ought to be teachers, ye have need again that some one teach you the rudiments of the first principles of the oracles of God; and are become such as have need of milk, and not of solid food. For every one that partaketh of milk is without experience of the word of righteousness; for he is a babe. But solid food is for fullgrown men, even those who by reason of use have their senses exercised to discern good and evil.

- Notice carefully: *"by reason of the time."* How long have you been a Christian? How long have you had eternal life? Directly after you received eternal life you should have begun a careful study of the word, for you never can tell when a crisis will come and you will desperately need faith in the Word. You also need the Word every day. You need that quiet, restful spirit.

- You know what the Word says, *is.* You know that every statement of fact that is made, either through Jesus or through Paul or James or Peter or John, is worth its face value.

- Paul says, *"By reason of the time ye ought to be teachers."* Every believer was supposed to be an evangel—not an evangelist, but in his own circle he was to be a soul-winner. They were to be praying for sick folks, carrying other people's burdens.

- But Paul says that though they ought to be teachers, instead they haven't learned anything. They aren't able to teach themselves or to guide themselves from day to day. They need someone to teach them the first principles of the Word of God. They can't eat the solid food of the Word. They can't understand it. They are babes, and must be fed on milk.

- Had they acted it, had they practiced it, it would be become a part of them.

- Instead, James describes them in James 1:22: *"But be ye doers of the word, and not hearers only, deluding your own selves."*

- What an army they are, these self-deluded Christians. They think that because they go to church and likely have been baptized, or may have had some wonderful experience back yonder, that they are all right. But when a crisis comes, they utterly collapse.

- In essence, "When by reason of time ye ought to have known the Word." Yet we are babes in Christ. We have never exercised ourselves in the Word, never exercised our faith, never put love to the test, never tried to live the Word. We have just floated.

- Second Corinthians 3:4–6: *"And such confidence have we through Christ to God-ward: not that we are sufficient of ourselves, to account anything as from ourselves; but our sufficiency is from God; who also made us sufficient as ministers of a new covenant."*

- Notice first, *"And such confidence have we through Christ to God-ward."* I want you to be able to say that in the face of every difficulty, "Such confidence have I in the Word, that nothing can overwhelm me. I stand here a master in the midst of the failures of others."

- You are conscious of the reality of the Word. He can't fail you. He is with you. He is with you in the written Word; He is with you in the name of Jesus; He is with you in the presence of the Holy Spirit.

- That sufficiency of God is your sufficiency. His ability is your ability.

- Second Corinthians 9:8–10 is a challenge from the very heart of the Master: *"And God is able to make all grace abound unto you; that ye, having always all sufficiency in everything, may abound unto every good work"* (verse 8). Here is the sufficiency of God at our disposal. Here is the fullness of God spoken of in John 1:16: *"For of his fulness we all received, and grace for grace."*

- This fullness or sufficiency, or ability of God, belongs to every believer; and He has made it to abound to us that we, having "all sufficiency in everything, may abound unto every good work."

- But let us go back to 2 Corinthians 9:7, and see what he says, *"Let each man do according as he hath purposed in his heart: not grudgingly, or of necessity: for God loveth a cheerful giver."* This is not a giver only of money, but a giver of his time, a giver of his ability, a giver of his wisdom.

- *"When by reason of the time"* you ought to have much to give the church…you ought to be able to open the Word up to hungry hearts that come into your home.

- Notice this tenth verse: *"He that supplieth seed to the sower and bread for food, shall supply and multiply your seed for sowing, and increase the fruits of your righteousness."*

- Do you know what the fruits of your righteousness are? You have become the righteousness of God in Christ. That means that you have ability to stand in the presence of Satan and all his works with utmost freedom, without a sense of inferiority. You can stand in the presence of other men's failures, a victor. You can walk into the Father's presence any time with boldness. The Father has invited you to come with freedom of speech to the throne of grace and make your requests known. (See Hebrews 4:16.) It may be for yourself, or it may be for others. You have a right here.

- You know Philippians 1:11 is a marvelous sentence: *"Being filled with the fruits of righteousness, which are through Jesus Christ, unto the glory and praise of God."*

- You are filled with the fruits of your righteousness in Christ, of your ability to know the Word, your ability to heal the sick. You strengthen the weak to bear the burdens of the overloaded. You have ability to teach the Word and have it become a living thing in your lips. Why? John 6:63 has become a reality to you: *"The words that I have spoken unto you are spirit, and are life."*

- They will become spirit. They will become life. They will become healing. They will become strength in your lips. Have you ever thought of it?

- Philippians 1:20. Paul said, *"In nothing shall I be put to shame, but that with all boldness, as always, so now also Christ shall be magnified in my body."* What does that mean? He will be seen as a victor.

- Second Corinthians 2:14: *"Thanks be unto God, who always leadeth us in triumph in Christ."*

- That should be the song on the lips of every believer. There isn't any reason for your being a weakling. There is no reason for it whatsoever. The strength and ability of God are yours.

FIRST STEPS

- The first step in this wonder life is recognizing the Lordship of Jesus. You do that. That leads you into your rights. Now that you have confessed the Lordship of the Master, it means that you have confessed the Lordship of His Word. It governs your life.

- You confess the Lordship of love, that new kind of love, which has been shed abroad in your hearts by the Holy Spirit. (See Romans 5:5.)

- You see, when you receive eternal life, you receive the nature of the Father; and the nature of the Father is love. You receive the love nature. Now you let that love nature dominate and rule you.

- You who are studying this lesson, I want you to think: This is what I must give to the world. This is what I must give to the church. I am learning what must be given to the people. You are like a mother who eats in order to produce milk to feed her babe. You are feeding on the Word so that you will have ability to minister to the others, so they will no longer be in the class of those who must be carried as an infant.

- Ephesians 4:11–13 has become a reality to you:

  > *And he gave some to be apostles; and some, prophets; and some, evangelists; and some, pastors and teachers; for the perfecting of the saints, unto the work of ministering, unto the building up of the body of Christ: till we all attain unto the unity of the faith, and of the knowledge of the Son of God, unto a fullgrown man, unto the measure of the stature of the fulness of Christ.*

- We are all to study to show ourselves approved unto the Father. (See 2 Timothy 2:15.) We must satisfy His heart. He has no pleasure in ignorant or sickly children, for He has made provision for their education and perfect healing.

- He never intended that His children should be dependent in their old age upon the world for their care. *"And my God shall supply every need of yours"* (Philippians 4:19).

- You want to learn to trust that absolutely. You want to trust Philippians 4:13: *"I can do all things in him that strengtheneth me."* That must become a part of your very being.

- Philippians 4:11: *"For I have learned, in whatsoever state I am, therein to be content."*

- First Corinthians 1:30. Jesus is made unto us wisdom.

- You know that wisdom is the ability to use knowledge that you have gathered from experience, or from books, or from the Bible. Now you know what to do with that. Wisdom leads you out into victory.

- It is a wonderful thing—this divine life. This life is an unsolved life. From day to day there is an unveiling of the riches of His grace, riches of His love, riches of His wisdom, the riches of His ability that has become ours.

HOW MUCH DO YOU REMEMBER?

1. When 1 John 3:2 becomes real to us, how are we to take our place?
2. What are the fruits of righteousness?
3. Explain Hebrews 5:12–14.
4. When we have confidence in the Word, what are we to confess?
5. Explain 2 Corinthians 9:7.
6. What leads you into your rights?
7. If Ephesians 4:11–13 has become a reality to you, what should you do?
8. Explain Philippians 4:11.

LESSON 30 NOTES

_____

_____

_____

_____

_____

_____

_____

_____

_____

_____

_____

_____

_____

_____

_____

_____

_____

_____

_____

_____

_____

_____

_____

_____

Lesson 31
THE FATHER FACT

No body of believers since the Reformation has majored the Father fact, and yet it is one of the most outstanding features of Jesus's teaching. It was always a sort of undercurrent of desire on the part of Jesus to go back and be with His Father.

John 16:28 illustrates this: *"I came out from the Father, and am come into the world: again, I leave the world, and go unto the Father."*

Here are four striking facts:

JESUS HAD A PRE-EXISTENCE

+ That is, He remembered who He was before He became a man.
+ In John 17:4–5, Jesus said, *"I glorified thee on the earth, having accomplished the work which thou hast given me to do. And now, Father, glorify thou me with thine own self with the glory which I had with thee before the world was."*
+ You can see that He remembered what the glory had been before the world was ever made; and He wanted to go back to His Father.
+ John 1:18: *"No man hath seen God at any time; the only begotten Son, who is in the bosom of the Father, he hath declared him."* Or, as Rotherham translates it: *"He hath introduced him."*

JESUS INTRODUCED GOD AS HIS FATHER

+ Jesus introduced the God of the Jews, Elohim, as His Father; and He called Him His Father so often that the Jews considered it blasphemy.
+ John 5:17–18: *"Jesus answered them, My Father worketh even until now, and I work. For this cause therefore the Jews sought the more to kill him, because he not only brake the sabbath, but also called God his own Father, making himself equal with God."*
+ John 19:7 shows us that Jesus was crucified because He had called God His Father. Then, the unveiling of the Father to the world cost Jesus His life. *"The Jews answered him, We have a law, and by that law he ought to die, because he made himself the Son of God."*
+ John 5:19–20 shows the intimacy of the Father and Jesus:

    The Son can do nothing of himself, but what he seeth the Father doing: for what things soever he doeth, these the Son also doeth in like manner. For the Father loveth the Son, and showeth him all things that himself doeth: and greater works than these will he show him, that ye may marvel.

+ Here He is, the intimate companion and assistant and fellow worker with the Father. We might carry it a step further and take the next three verses, *"For as the Father raiseth the dead and giveth them life, even so the Son also giveth life to whom he will. For neither doth the Father judge any man, but he hath given all judgment unto the Son that all may honor the Son, even as they honor the Father"* (verses 21–23). Here is not only the deity of Jesus confessed, but a divine oneness between Jesus and the Father.
+ Perhaps it will be clearer to us in John 14:8–9: *"Philip saith unto him, Lord, show us the Father, and it sufficeth us. Jesus saith unto him, Have I been so long time with you, and dost thou not know me, Philip? he that hath seen me hath seen the Father; how sayest thou, Show us the Father?"*

- You can see that the entire ministry of Jesus is interwoven with this Father fact. He came to introduce the Father. He came to do his Father's will. Perhaps that would help us to grasp the significance of His position as a Son.

- John 5:30: *"I can of myself do nothing: as I hear, I judge: and my judgment is righteous; because I seek not mine own will, but the will of him that sent me."* Whose will is it that He is to do? Verses 36–37 show us,

  > But the witness which I have is greater than that of John [the Baptist]; *for the works which the Father hath given me to accomplish, the very works that I do, bear witness of me, that the Father hath sent me. And the Father that sent me, he hath borne witness of me."*

JESUS CAME DOING HIS FATHER'S WILL

- He came not doing His own will. He came doing His Father's will.

- Perhaps John 6:37–38 makes it a bit clearer: *"All that which the Father giveth me shall come unto me; and him that cometh to me I will in no wise cast out. For I am come down from heaven, not to do mine own will, but the will of him that sent me."*

- Here is a clear declaration that He came down from heaven, that He came down from the Father, and He came into the world with but one purpose: to do His Father's will.

- Perhaps the strongest verse that we have thought of is John 6:57: *"As the living Father sent me, and I live because of the Father."* Notice, *"I live because of the Father."*

- But then, in John 7:29, Jesus said, *"I know him; because I am from him, and he sent me."* That has always been so precious to my heart. Jesus says, in essence, "I know my Father because I am from Him. I came out from heaven. I have lived with Him through the ages. He sent me, and I am doing His will here on earth."

- One of my students once asked, "What is the outstanding feature of Jesus's life?" It was His continual confession of what He was to the Father and what the Father was to Him. There are many other striking things about Jesus, but there is nothing like this.

- John 8:26–29 is like the lifting of a curtain on a stage that is already set. He had just told them, *"I am from above: ye are of this world; I am not of this world"* (verse 23). That forced His listeners to find out who He was. He said,

  > He that sent me is true; and the things which I heard from him, these speak I unto the world. They perceived not that he spake to them of the Father. Jesus therefore said, When ye have lifted up the Son of man, then shall ye know that I am he, and that I do nothing of myself, but as the Father taught me, I speak these things. (verses 26–28)

- Then He said one of the most beautiful things that ever fell from His lips: *"He that sent me is with me; he hath not left me alone; for I do always the things that are pleasing to him"* (verse 29).

- Notice: *"I do nothing of myself,"* from verse 28. I teach nothing of myself. I teach what the Father taught me. The Father is with me. He hath not left me alone. Why? Because He was the Father-pleaser. Do you know that every one of us can be that? What change it would make in life, wouldn't it? Almost all of us are hindered and imprisoned in the things we want that He is not pleased with. We are struggling with things that shut us away from the sweetest fellowship with Him.

- *"For I am come down from heaven, not to do mine own will, but the will of him that sent me"* (John 6:38).

- Now you can understand the power and the authority of that Man. The singleness of purpose is one of the keys that unlocks the miracle power of the Man. He had nothing to seek for.

- Hear this confession in John 8:42: *"If God were your Father, ye would love me: for I came forth and am come from God; for neither have I come of myself, but he sent me."*

- And, in John 8:54, we read, *"If I glorify myself, my glory is nothing: it is my Father that glorifieth me; of whom ye say, that he is your God."*

- Do you notice the difference? The Jews called Him God, and Jesus called Him Father. The church today calls Him God. How few ever intelligently call Him Father. How lonesome He must be. He is a Father God with a Father heart, and His people call Him God—just "Mr. God," like they should speak of a neighbor. Let us learn the secret of His Father heart.

- John 10:25–29:

  > *Jesus answered them, I told you, and ye believe not: the works that I do in my Father's name, these bear witness of me. But ye believe not, because ye are not of my sheep. My sheep hear my voice, and I know them, and they follow me: and I give unto them eternal life; and they shall never perish, and no one shall snatch them out of my hand. My Father, who hath given them unto me, is greater than all; and no one is able to snatch them out of the Father's hand.*

- Then, the great sentence: *"I and the Father are one"* (verse 30).

- Now we can see the Man in His majesty and greatness. You see, He has been magnifying the Father. He has been lifting the Father up before our hearts; and now He pushes aside the curtain and lets us look at Him as He really is: *"I and [my] Father are one."*

- John 10:37: *"If I do not the works of my Father, believe me not."*

- Then there is a marvelous closing. Write out John 10:38:

_____

_____

_____

YOU ARE IN THE FATHER, AND THE FATHER IS IN YOU

- This is the very relationship of the church to the Father now. This is your relationship as a child of God. You are in the Father, and the Father is in you. That is, He has imparted His life to you. His very nature has been given to you. You are as much His child as Jesus was.

- When you heart can take this in, He will become more to you, and you will realize someone of what we are to Him.

- John 12:45–50 has some real nuggets that you ought to study carefully. *"He that beholdeth me beholdeth him that sent me"* (verse 45).

- We ought to be able to say, "You that see me are looking upon a branch of the Vine. I am the part of Jesus that is bearing fruit. Jesus and I are one." Jesus and the Father are one, so you see what your relationship is to Him.

- *"I am come a light into the world, that whosoever believeth on me may not abide in the darkness"* (John 12:46). We ought to say, "I have been born again that I might be a light in the world."

- Philippians 2:15: *"Ye are seen as lights in the world."* John 12:47: *"I came not to judge the world, but to save the world."*

- I wish that the Christian workers would learn to say, "I came not to judge. I am not to criticize you because you walk in sin and do not know the Father. I am here to bring you the glad message that God so loved that He gave His Son to die for you."

- Why, Jesus said, in essence, "I came not to condemn the world, but that the world through me might be saved." He that believes on Him is not judged.

- Notice the forty-eighth verse of John 12: *"He that rejecteth me, and receiveth not my sayings, hath one that judgeth him: the word that I spake, the same shall judge him in the last day."*

- Why is the Word so vital? *"For I spake not from myself; but the Father that sent me, he hath given me a commandment, what I should say, and what I should speak"* (John 12:49). Here you see the vital issue before the heart: Is it the Word of God? What is my attitude toward the living Word?

- In John 14:10–11, Jesus says, *"Believest thou not that I am in the Father, and the Father in me? the words that I say unto you I speak not from myself: but the Father abiding in me doeth his works. Believe me that I am in the Father, and the Father in me."*

- I believe that our ministry would be much stronger and more effective if we knew in our hearts, "The words that I speak are not mine. They are my Father's words. I am an ambassador. I have received instructions from my government. This is what my King says to me, and I am repeating His words."

- Did you notice that He gave us a legal right to the use of His name in the thirteenth and fourteenth verses? Why? *"That the Father may be glorified in the Son"* (John 14:13).

- You see the sons are going to use the name of the Son to bless, heal, convert, and deliver men from the bondage of the enemy. It is through the name of that first-begotten One, and it is going to bring glory to the Father. It is going to be a great joy to the Father to hear us cast out demons and heal the sick through His Son's name.

- How proud I am to see my children do meritorious things. How much more does my heavenly Father glory in my doing things through Jesus's name.

- Read very carefully chapters 14–17 of John. We haven't time to go into them as we would like. We can just call your attention to a few things.

- John 14:20: *"In that day ye shall know that I am in my Father, and ye in me, and I in you."* Here is a holy union, a God-created union, between your heart and the Father's and Jesus's hearts.

- In the twenty-first verse: *"He that hath my commandments, and keepeth them, he it is that loveth me: and he that loveth me shall be loved of my Father, and I will love him, and will manifest myself unto him."*

- I look upon this as one of the great privileges that belongs to us as sons of God—to have Jesus manifest Himself to us individually.

- The twenty-third verse has a sweet fragrance all its own: *"If a man love me, he will keep my word: and my Father will love him, and we will come unto him, and make our abode with him."*

- Then I want to know Him. I want to please Him. I want to make His heart glad as that first Son did. What a beautiful life it is. It is not struggling to be righteous. It is just struggling to make His heart glad.

- The sixteenth chapter is very beautiful. Begin reading from the eighth verse down to the sixteenth, and notice how the Father is going to send the Comforter; and that Comforter is going to be a Convicter of the world.

- A comforter is a gentle person, a tender person. And it is going to be a gentle, tender person who is going to convict the world of their sin, of righteousness, and of judgment that is going to come upon them.

- You see, the judgment is because they are in the family of Satan, and the judgment is upon the head of that family. Satan is judged. The Spirit is going to convict this unsaved world that a righteousness awaits every one of them, that every human being has a right to stand in His presence free from guilt and condemnation: that righteousness is the reason for redemption.

- He wanted children. And He wanted children who could stand in His presence without the sense of guilt or inferiority. Then He says that the Spirit is going to convict the world of sin.
- There is just one sin that is important. That is the fact that they have not accepted Jesus as Savior and Lord. That is all. All the other sins are just the by-products of their spiritual condition. But here is one thing they can do: they can confess Jesus as Savior and Lord and receive eternal life.

HOW MUCH DO YOU REMEMBER?

1. Give four facts and Scriptures showing Jesus's teaching about God as His Father.

2. What two Scriptures show us Jesus came to do the Father's will?

3. a. What was Jesus's continual confession?

    b. Did Jesus acknowledge that He did anything of Himself?

4. What would happen in our lives if we pleased the Father?

5. Tell what you can about the difference in Jesus calling God "Father," and the Jews calling Him "God."

6. John 10:38 shows that Jesus is in the Father. How does this compare with the relationship existing between the church and God?

7. a. Are we to judge those who sin?

    b. What did Jesus say He came to do?

8. Explain John 14:10.

9. Having a legal right to the use of His name, what are we to do?

10. a. What is the important sin?

    b. How can they accept Jesus?

LESSON 31 NOTES

_____

_____

_____

_____

_____

_____

_____

_____

_____

_____

_____

_____

_____

_____

Lesson 32
PAUL'S NATURAL MAN

A KEY TO THE PAULINE REVELATION

How few of us appreciate the vast field of new material that we find in the Pauline Epistles.

John, Peter, and James give practically no new material. They all grew out of the teachings of Jesus in His earth walk. You can feel that John leaned on the breast of his Master. As you read his epistle, you can feel love throbbing through him.

But as we read the Pauline Revelation, we get no such consciousness of that. We are wading into new material—revelation knowledge.

We are going to study now the reason for the incarnation and the substitutionary work of Christ. We are going to look at man in the raw, just as he appeared before the Father.

You want to keep John 3:16 before your mind always in thinking of lost men. You must understand that man is not lost because of what he does. He is lost because of what he is.

THE NATURAL MAN: SPIRITUALLY DEAD

+ Ephesians 2:1–3: "*And you did he make alive, when ye were dead through your trespasses and sins*" (verse 2). Notice this first verse, that it says that this man, this natural man, is spiritually dead.

+ Romans 5:12: "*Therefore, as through one man sin entered into the world, and death through sin; and so death passed unto all men* [that was Adam's transgression]." He is not talking of physical death. He is talking of the nature of Satan.

+ God's nature is life. Its first manifestations are love, joy, and peace.

+ Satan's nature is spiritual death. Its first manifestations are hatred, murder, and deceit. His whole realm is called darkness.

+ Colossians 1:13: "*Who delivered us out of the power of darkness, and translated us into the kingdom of the Son of his love.*"

+ Notice the contrast. You have come out of the realm of Satan (spiritual death, hatred, and murder) into the realm of life, of light, and joy.

+ Jesus is describing natural man in John 8:44–45. He says what is hard for us even to repeat:

   > *Ye are of your father the devil, and the lusts of your father it is your will to do. He was a murderer from the beginning, and standeth not in the truth, because there is no truth in him. When he speaketh a lie, he speaketh of his own: for he is a liar, and the father thereof.*

+ In those two awful sentences, Jesus describes natural man.

+ This awful insurrection covering the whole world is another instance. Think of the men and women who have been murdered in order to give one man or a few men glory and power and riches. The inhuman, devilish atrocities that have taken place in the last few decades, in so-called civilized countries, prove beyond any shadow of a doubt that natural man is a partaker of the very nature of the devil, who was a murderer and a liar. There is no truth in him.

+ Don't expect natural men to give us a Christian government. They may be refined, cultured, highly educated children, but they are children of the devil.

- This is the reason that natural man needs eternal life, the nature of God.
- First Corinthians 2:14: *"Now the natural man receiveth not the things of the Spirit of God: for they are foolishness unto him; and he cannot know them, because they are spiritually judged [or understood]."* The marginal reading is: *"The natural man [or the unspiritual man] receiveth not the things of God."*
- The Greek word means "the psychical man," the man that is absolutely under the dominion of Satan.
- We must realize that the natural man is as much under the dominion of Satan as the recreated man is under the dominion of Jesus Christ.
- When the mothers and fathers realize that their boy must receive eternal life or else he is going to walk in the way of Satan-ruled men, they will become anxious about their children.
- Second Corinthians 4:3–4: *"And even if our gospel is veiled, it is veiled in them that perish: in whom the god of this world hath blinded the minds of the unbelieving, that the light of the gospel of the glory of Christ, who is the image of God, should not dawn upon them."*
- Notice now that the gospel is veiled by the god of this world. He has made the gospel to seem a sort of tyranny, and men shrink from it. The unsaved man doesn't want to hear it. You see, his mind is enmity against God; he is not subject to the law of God.
- Romans 8:7 is a description of the natural man though the epistle is dealing with the undeveloped believer who is under the dominion of the senses. This natural man's mind is blinded. His thoughts are twisted by the adversary. He cannot see nor understand the things that belong to him in Christ.
- Romans 1:21–22: *"Because that, knowing God, they glorified him not as God, neither gave thanks; but became vain in their reasonings, and their senseless heart was darkened. Professing themselves to be wise, they became fools."*
- The twenty-eighth verse is perhaps the most awful: *"And even as they refused to have God in their knowledge, God gave them up unto a reprobate mind, to do those things which are not fitting."*
- You see, the natural man's mind receives all those impulses and knowledges from the five senses: seeing, hearing, tasting, smelling, and feeling. They are all connected with his body, and his body is mortal, Satan-ruled. Now it is easy to understand that all the knowledge that the natural man would have would be biased by the adversary, cultivated by the adversary, so that the natural man would not understand the things of God. They are foolishness to him. His mind is blinded. He is living in the realm of darkness, spiritual darkness—the worst kind of the darkness.
- You can turn an electric light on and illumine a room, but nothing will illumine that dark spirit but the life of God.

THE INDICTMENTS AGAINST NATURAL MAN

- Romans 3:10–18 is the great indictment of the "supreme court" against natural man; and in that indictment there are fourteen charges. Every one of those charges is enough to destroy him, shut him out from heaven.
  1. The first one: *"There is none righteous, no not one"* (verse 10).
     - He is not talking to Christians. He is talking to men outside of Christ.
     - There is no one that has a standing with God. They are all under condemnation.
  2. *"There is none that understandeth"* (verse 11).
     - Their minds have been darkened. Their spirits are filled with the nature of the adversary; and their minds receive all their impressions and knowledge from the five senses.
     - That knowledge is distorted by Satan.

3. The third awful charge is, *"There is none that seeketh after God"* (verse 11).

    + They are all seeking for the gratification of the five senses; and through that sense knowledge they are acquiring dominion and authority over weaker men and women.

4. Next: *"They have all turned aside, they are together become unprofitable [unto God]"* (verse 12).

    + They have lost all their value. How this Scripture hurt me—that the whole unsaved world is unprofitable. Whatever they do will be the work of a spiritually dead man.

    + Their good works are the works of spiritual convicts, men who are living in rebellion against the knowledge of God and the will of God.

5. Notice the rest: *"There is none that doeth good, no, not so much as one"* (verse 12).

    + I can remember when convicts in state prisons used to manufacture shoes; and I remember, as boy, I didn't want to wear a pair of shoes made by a convict. I think that feeling is common among most people.

    + Now you can understand why the good works of a child of the devil would not satisfy God. It is the work of a man under the indictment of being in union with Satan.

    + The Holy Spirit was sent by the Father to convict the unsaved man of his union with the devil.

6. This indictment is awful, *"Their throat is an open sepulcher"* (verse 13).

    + Can you understand it? Their throat is full of death. They are murderers.

    + The whole war atmosphere is described by this: *"Their throat is an open sepulcher."* How it describes natural man as he really is.

7. But notice the next sentence, *"With their tongues they have used deceit"* (verse 13).

    + I asked a class in a Bible school, "What badge should natural man wear—one single word?" A bright young man said, "The word, liar." Think of wearing that on the lapel of your coat! Think of women wearing that badge!

    + Jesus said of Satan that he was a liar and the father thereof. When he speaks a lie, he speaks of his own. His own are natural men. (See John 8:44.)

8. Notice the next indictment, *"The poison of asps is under their lips"* (verse 13).

    + It makes us think of Pearl Harbor, doesn't it? It makes us think of the dark, awful crimes planned under the shadow of a free flag. It has been done.

    + The poison of asps is a deadly poison. The sting of an asp is death; and the sting of these men is death.

9. *"Whose mouth is full of cursing and bitterness"* (verse 14).

    + Here is the noisy, rough, thoughtless man whose mouth is the most dangerous part of him. Words have no sanctity nor beauty. He just uses words as children quarreling throw mud at each other.

    + How few men realize that the most sacred bonds of life are sealed with words. The tongue is the most beautiful element of man. And yet, this mouth that can speak love words and woo hearts, is full of cursing and bitterness.

10. This next indictment hurts: *"Their feet are swift to shed blood"* (verse 15).

    + Notice the steps we travel down. There is none righteous; none can appreciate God; none can understand; none seek after God; all are seeking after things that gratify their senses; they are turned aside and together unprofitable.

- They never help anyone to be better.
- Nietzsche made Germany a nation of murderers—robbed them of their respect as a great nation.

11. *"Their throat is an open sepulcher."*
    - The dead are there. *"Their tongues are filled with deceit. The poison of asps is under their lips. Their mouth is full of cursing and bitterness. Their feet are swift to shed blood"*—to commit wholesale murder.
    - It is not the stealthy thief that is stealing in order to get food to eat, but it is the swift, fearless tread of an army led by a bloodthirsty general.

12. Notice: *"Destruction and misery are in their ways"* (verse 16).

13. *"The way of peace have they not known"* (verse 17).
    - All that they have lived for and struggled for is to gain the ascendancy over the weak.
    - There is no peace in the homes of the people in those nations.

14. *"There is no fear of God before their eyes"* (verse 18).

- That is the end. This great indictment by the supreme court of the universe is the most awful document ever penned. It is descriptive. These charges are self-evident. They require no prosecuting attorney. The conscience of every man answers back that it is true.

TWO FAMILIES, TWO TYPES OF LOVE

- First John 3:10 is a picture of the two families: *"In this the children of God are manifest, and the children of the devil: whosoever doeth not righteousness is not of God, neither he that loveth not his brother."*

- First John 3:14: *"We know that we have passed out of death into life, because we love the brethren. He that loveth not abideth in death."* Or, we know that we have passed out of death into life; that is, out of the family of Satan into the realm of life, the family of God. Why? *"Because we love the brethren." "He that loveth not abideth in death."* "Oh," you say, "that man loves his family."

- Professor Henry Drummond, looked upon as one of the world's greatest scientists, makes this remark, backed up by the testimony of every investigator in this realm: "No primitive people have love. All they have is sex attraction. The mother will fight for her child as the mother lioness will fight for her cub; but that same mother will offer that child to the crocodiles to appease her religious convictions. Mothers barter their children for immoral purposes."

- No, there is no love like the love that is spoken of in the new covenant. You know, we have never realized this fact: that there are two kinds of love in the world—natural, human love, described by the Greek word *phileo*, which means the love of natural man based upon selfishness; and the divine love, which is from God.

- Natural love will turn to jealousy, bitterness, and hatred. The modern divorce court is the goddess of natural, human love; yet this human love is the best that the world has today.

- But natural man hasn't anything that commends him except to the heart that has been moved by the love nature of God. God so loved that He gave His Son to this world, this natural, demon-ruled, Satan-controlled human race. (See John 3:16.)

- These people, dominated purely by sense knowledge, without any convictions that come from Christianity, are covenant breakers. Their word has no value. They are in union with Satan. They have the wisdom and cunning of the devil.

- You see, they live in the sense realm. Here is a bitter fact: they cannot know God, neither can they know themselves. No psychologist today who denies the Lordship of Jesus, who doesn't have eternal life, knows himself. Not knowing himself, he cannot know another.
- This natural man doesn't know the reason for creation. He doesn't know the reason for man. He doesn't know how man became what he is today; and he doesn't know why heathen nations cannot produce inventors and great chemists. He can't understand why that is.
- We know that when a man receives the nature of God, he receives the nature of the Creator of the universe.

HOW MUCH DO YOU REMEMBER?

1. Explain fully the reason for the incarnation and the substitutionary work of Christ.
2. Explain Romans 5:12.
3. How does Jesus describe natural man?
4. Explain 1 Corinthians 2:14.
5. To whom are the fourteen charges of Romans 3:10–18 directed?
6. Explain why the unsaved man does not want to hear the gospel?
7. Explain why the good works of a child of Satan cannot satisfy God.
8. Give Scriptures, and contrast the two families.
9. Why is it that natural man does not know the reason for creation?

LESSON 32 NOTES

_____

_____

_____

_____

_____

_____

_____

_____

_____

_____

_____

_____

_____

_____

_____

_____

Lesson 33
FELLOWSHIP AND RELATIONSHIP

This is another of the lost teachings of the Word. For years I wondered why the largest percentage of those who have accepted Christ and have joined the church were failures. I used to ask myself, "Has Satan more ability than God? Has he outwitted God in the fight?"

I didn't believe it. Then one day, a man listening to me said, "I see you make a distinction between *union* and *communion*."

I said, "Thank you." Then as he turned to go away, it flashed through my mind that I had been teaching beyond my classified knowledge.

The Spirit had unveiled to me something that I didn't recognize, the difference between union and communion.

Our union with Christ in the new creation, and our communion with Him, are based on two other words, "fellowship" and "relationship."

I had been very strong on relationship. I had been magnifying the new birth. Let us study it for a moment.

THE NEW CREATION

+ John 10:10: "*I came that they may have life, and may have it abundantly.*"
+ What was this life? It was the nature of God.
+ Who was to have it? The man for whom Christ died. John 3:16: "*For God so loved the world, that he gave his only begotten Son, that whosoever believeth on him should not perish, but have eternal life.*"
+ But the question is, how are we going to get that eternal life?
+ Jesus illustrated it in His talk with Nicodemus in John 3. He said, "*Except one be born anew, he cannot see the kingdom of God. …That which is born of the flesh is flesh; and that which is born of the Spirit is spirit. Marvel not that I said unto thee, Ye must be born anew*" (verses 3, 6–7).
+ Now, if we haven't Paul's revelation, we don't understand that, for we have nothing in Jesus's teaching that explains the nature of the new birth. Jesus merely tells us that He is bringing us eternal life and that we must be born again.
+ Second Corinthians 5:17–18: "*Wherefore if any man is in Christ* [or if a man has accepted Christ and confessed him as his Lord], *he is a new creature: the old things* [of sin, of spiritual death, and of union with Satan] *are passed away; behold, they are become new. But all things are of God, who reconciled us to himself through Christ.*"
+ That is tremendous! The Father has reconciled us unto Himself. The things that stood between us and the Father have been eliminated. A new creation has come into us. The old nature is driven out, and we are new creations in spirit, just as Adam was a physical new creation in the garden.
+ That spiritual new creation has come into being, imparted to us in eternal life that Jesus said He was bringing to the world.
+ You remember that the word "*life*" is *zoe*, the nature of God. Then the new creation is built out of the nature of God.

+ Write out Ephesians 4:23–24:

_____

_____

_____

+ That new creation is the product of God Himself. He, through the Spirit, has given birth to a new nature in us.

+ The old nature of failure, of sin consciousness, that was ruled by the adversary and was a part of the adversary, has stopped being. A new nature has taken its place. We are not the very sons and daughters of God Almighty.

+ Romans 8:14 is a reality: _"For as many as are led by the Spirit of God, these are sons of God."_

+ As many as are willing to let the Spirit guide them, will be led into the new creation.

> _For ye received not the spirit of bondage again unto fear; but ye received the spirit of adoption, whereby we cry, Abba, Father. The Spirit himself beareth witness with our spirit, that we are children of God: and if children, then heirs; heirs of God, and joint-heirs with Christ."_
>
> (Romans 8:15–17)

+ That is a fact of our relationship.

THE NEW CREATION'S STANDING WITH GOD

+ Now the next fact is that we have not only become new creations, but we are new creations with a God-given standing with Himself.

+ Romans 3:26: _"For the showing, I say, of his righteousness at this present season: that he might himself be just, and the justifier of him that hath faith in Jesus."_

+ You see, you haven't only become a son, but a son with a standing with the Father that He gives you Himself.

+ That is perfectly natural—that if the Father has sons, He will give them a standing with Himself so that they can approach Him with the uttermost freedom and liberty. He becomes their righteousness.

+ You know that righteousness means the ability to stand in the Father's presence without the sense of guilt or inferiority, to stand in the presence of Satan without any inferiority, to stand in the presence of anything Satan has done without any sense of inferiority. You stand in his presence as his master. You are taking Jesus's place in the world, and you are Satan's master because you do it.

+ Now you may have righteousness; you may have eternal life. You may have the consciousness of sonship. You may have the great, mighty Spirit come and make His home in your body, because that is the ultimate of the new creation.

+ You see, you are recreated so that your body might become the home of God.

+ You remember 1 Corinthians 6:19–20: _"Know ye not that your body is a temple of the Holy Spirit which is in you, which ye have from God? and ye are not your own; for ye were bought with a price: glorify God therefore in your body."_

THE SECRET OF JOY AND THE LAW OF LOVE

+ All this may be true, but you may never have learned the secret of joy.

+ You say, "What do you mean by joy?" John 15:10: _"If ye keep my commandments, ye shall abide in my love; even as I have kept my Father's commandments, and abide in his love."_

- Then we see in the ninth verse another secret: *"Even as the Father hath loved me, I also have loved you: abide ye in my love."*

- We are to walk in love and live love, and to keep His commandments.

- John 13:34–35 shows us that the law of the new creation, the law that governs the new creation, is the love law. We are to love one another even as He has loved us.

- Jesus said, *"Even as I have kept my Father's commandments, and abide in his love. These things have I spoken unto you, that my joy may be in you, and that your joy may be made full"* (John 15:10–11).

- For years that did not mean anything to my spirit until one day I saw that the secret of Christianity, the secret of evangelism, was that we were to have joy in our spirits.

- You remember Acts 13:52: *"And the disciples were filled with joy and with the Holy Spirit."*

- First Peter 1:8 tells us that it is joy unspeakable and full of glory. That didn't mean much to me until the Spirit unveiled it to me. Then I saw the secret of this new thing that was to come with the new creation.

- In essence, *"My joy I give unto you."* This is something that the world can't take away from me. It is something indescribable that fills our spirits.

- What does joy grow out of? What is the secret? First Corinthians 1:9: *"God is faithful, through whom ye were called into the fellowship of his Son Jesus Christ our Lord."*

- Fellowship is the secret; it is the thing that gives joy. When the fellowship is broken, the joy dies.

- The happiness of marriage is the fellowship between those two hearts. Misery comes to full tide when that fellowship is broken.

- You may be a child of God, and have all the knowledge and riches that belong to that marvelous relationship; but if you have no fellowship with the Father there is no joy in your life. It is an empty, dry thing. The power of our ministry lies in our fellowship.

- First John 1:3–4: *"That which we have seen and heard declare we unto you also, that ye also may have fellowship with us."* Why? *"Our fellowship is with the Father, and with his Son Jesus Christ: and these things we write, that our joy may be made full."*

FELLOWSHIP: THE MEANING; HOW IT IS BROKEN AND RESTORED

- There it is. Now what is that fellowship? It is that sweet communion between your spirit and the Father. It is that glad richness that comes through the unveiling of the Word to your spirit. It is the quiet assurance that fills your heart with an unspeakable, irrepressible joy.

- Faith cannot grow without rich fellowship with the Father. I don't care how much knowledge one has of the Word, if his fellowship is broken, his faith is crippled. The adversary takes advantage of him and holds him in bondage.

- Most people who have chronic physical trouble have an unsatisfactory fellowship with the Father and with the Word. They develop a petulant spirit. They begin to challenge the faithfulness and the love of the Father. "Well, if God loves me, why has He afflicted me like this?"

- You understand that the Father hasn't afflicted them. The adversary has afflicted them and they have submitted to the adversary's affliction, and have lived in misery and bondage.

- If they had known what held them, they would turn to 1 John 1:5–6: *"And this is the message which we have heard from him and announce unto you, that God is light, and in him is no darkness at all. If we say that we have fellowship with him and walk in the darkness, we lie, and do not the truth."*

- Notice now, if we say we have fellowship and don't know His will, it is evident that we are in darkness.

- First John 2:10–11: *"He that loveth his brother abideth in the light, and there is no occasion of stumbling in him. But he that hateth his brother is in the darkness, and walketh in the darkness, and knoweth not whither he goeth, because the darkness hath blinded his eyes."*

- That darkness may come from a hundred reasons. One may have failed in his finances. He hasn't given the Lord His share of his income. He may have failed in speaking to men and women about their souls. It can come from a million different sources.

- Fellowship can be broken because I willfully fail to do His will. I step out of light into darkness. I stop practicing love; and when I do that, I step over into darkness, want—into Satan's territory. I am filled with restlessness.

- Joy is gone. My fellowship with the Father is gone.

- If I say that I have fellowship with Him and walk in darkness, I lie and do not tell the truth.

- *"But if we walk in the light, as he is in the light, we have fellowship one with another [and with the Father], and the blood of Jesus his Son cleanseth us from all sin"* (1 John 1:7).

- When we break fellowship with the Father by refusing to do His will, and step out of love, we walk in darkness. That minute the Bible stops being a living message to us.

- No one ever criticizes another believer as long as he is walking in fellowship. All bitterness and criticism and unkindness are the products of broken fellowship.

- If we walk in the light, as He is in the light, we have fellowship one with another; but if we walk in darkness, we have no fellowship with one another. We have no knowledge of His will.

- *"And the blood of Jesus his Son cleanseth us from all sin."* That is effective as long as we are in fellowship.

- The correct meaning of the word *"sin"* is "missing the mark."

- As long as I am in fellowship with Him, I may miss the mark again and again, but His blood avails for me. Then I deliberately refuse to do His will, and darkness overwhelms me. If I deny that I've sinned, I deceive myself and the reality is not in me.

- How true that is! The truth is not in me. There is no sense of reality. The Word is no longer a thing of comfort and inspiration.

- But He says, *"If we confess our sins, he is faithful and righteous to forgive us our sins, and to cleanse us from all unrighteousness"* (1 John 1:9).

- In other words, if we say we have not sinned, and yet are out of fellowship, we do not have the reality of the life in us. But, if we confess our sins, He is just and righteous to wipe out all our sins, or the thing that stood in the way.

- Now we go to the next chapter of 1 John: *"My little children, these things write I unto you that ye may not sin. And if any man sin, we have an Advocate with the Father, Jesus Christ the righteous"* (1 John 2:1).

- I think that that is one of the most marvelous statements in the whole of the epistles. Seated at the Father's right hand is our righteous Advocate; and the minute that I break fellowship, He is there in fellowship with the Father. I lose my sense of righteousness. He is the righteous One. He is there, in the presence of my Father, to plead my case.

- I look up to the Father and say, "Father, forgive me for doing that thing." And the moment I do, He forgives me. It is wiped out as though it had never been. The instant that I confess it and tell the Father of it, Jesus says, "Lay that to My account."

- Notice that the Father has no memory of your past mistakes and failures. You must forget them too.

- Second Corinthians 13:14: *"The grace of the Lord Jesus Christ, and the love of God, and the communion of the Holy Spirit, be with you all."*

- Romans 8:38–39 will help our hearts just now. This is the climax of His great redemption teaching: *"For I am persuaded, that neither death, nor life, nor angels, nor principalities, nor things present, nor things to come, nor powers, nor height, nor depth, nor any other creature, shall be able to separate us from the love of God, which is in Christ Jesus our Lord."*
- He enumerates everything that can come to a man or a woman, every calamity that can possibly come in our earth walk, and tells us that none can separate us from the love of our Father.
- In the thirty-fifth verse we read, *"Who shall separate us from the love of Christ?"* Nothing can separate us from the love of Christ nor from the Father's love. Nothing can do it. Know this. Let this be the background of your faith.

HOW MUCH DO YOU REMEMBER?

1. What other words the difference between union and communion?
2. What is the nature of the new birth?
3. How do we acquire eternal life? Give Scripture.
4. What law governs the new creation?
5. Why does joy die? What makes faith grow?
6. Explain 1 John 1:5–9.
7. When does the Bible stop being a living message to us?
8. What are some reasons for darkness coming from broken fellowship?
9. What happens when we say, "Father, forgive me for doing that thing?"

LESSON 33 NOTES

_____

_____

_____

_____

_____

_____

_____

_____

_____

_____

_____

_____

_____

_____

_____

Lesson 34
JESUS THE HEALER

There are two views of healing held by different bodies of believers.

HEALING: A PART OF REDEMPTION

+ First, there are those who believe that healing is a part of the plan of redemption: that in the substitutionary sacrifice of Christ, God actually laid our diseases on Jesus and that He bore them with our sins, that when He put our sins away, He also put off our diseases.

+ Hebrews 9:26, *"But now once at the end of the ages hath he been manifested to put away sin by the sacrifice of himself."* This not only means sin in the spirit and soul, but sin in the flesh. Romans 8:2–3 uses sin in the sense of breaking of harmony in the flesh. That is disease.

+ They also hold Isaiah 53:3–5:

    He was despised, and rejected of men; a man of sorrows, and acquainted with grief: and as one from whom men hide their face he was despised; and we esteemed him not. Surely he hath borne our griefs, and carried our sorrows; yet we did esteem him stricken, smitten of God, and afflicted. But he was wounded for our transgressions, he was bruised for our iniquities; the chastisement of our peace was upon him; and with his stripes we are healed.

+ Then we have verses 10–11:

    Yet it pleased Jehovah to bruise him; he hath put him to grief: when thou shalt make his soul an offering for sin, he shall see his seed, he shall prolong his days, and the pleasure of Jehovah shall prosper in his hand. He shall see of the travail of his soul, and shall be satisfied.

+ Notice that in this, healing of the body comes before the dealing with the sin problem in both of these Scriptures. Then we confidently believe that there is no such thing as separating sin from the disease problem.

+ If He dealt with the disease, He dealt with the sin. If He dealt with the sin, He dealt with disease; for they are akin to each other.

+ There was no disease until sin came, and sin is breaking of a law. If it is a law of the body, it culminates in disease. If it is a law of the spirit, it culminates in sin.

HEALING: AN ACT OF GRACE

+ The other school holds that God heals by a special act of grace. They also hold that only those are healed who have faith, and that faith is the gift of God—that no man can get faith of his own accord. For healing, God must in His sovereign grace give them faith.

+ So, in the final analysis, God only heals those to whom He gives faith. Those who don't have faith are not to blame for it, because God didn't give it to them.

+ Most of them hold that disease comes as a judgment from the Lord for disciplinary purposes, and if that discipline hasn't wrought the desired effect, of course God couldn't give them faith for their healing. That makes God the Author of disease. Also, He doesn't heal unless they have faith, and they can't get faith unless He gives it to them.

- To me, the whole scheme is unthinkable. It is a sense knowledge effort to explain the reason why prayer isn't answered and why the sick do not get their deliverance.
- Psalm 107:20: *"He sendeth his word, and healeth them."*
- This is taken with John 1:1–4:

  In the beginning was the Word, and the Word was with God, and the Word was God. The same was in the beginning with God. All things were made through him; and without him was not anything made that hath been made. In him was life; and the life was the light of men.

- The fourteenth verse, *"And the Word became flesh, and dwelt among us* [and we beheld his glory, glory as of the only begotten from the Father], *full of grace and truth."*
- This Word is Jesus—the eternal Logos (you understand that the word *Logos* is the Greek word that is translated *"Word"*). All during Jesus's public ministry His love drove Him to heal the sick everywhere.
- He was God manifest in the flesh. He was love manifest in the flesh. He was the will of the Father unveiled to us.
- You remember that in John 4:31–34, Jesus said,

  In the mean while the disciples prayed him, saying, Rabbi, eat. But he said unto them, I have meat to eat that ye know not. The disciples therefore said one to another, Hath any man brought him aught to eat? Jesus saith unto them, My meat is to do the will of him that sent me, and to accomplish his work.

- Write out John 5:30:

  _____

  _____

  _____

- Then Jesus's healing the sick was the will of the Father, being accomplished. Jesus Christ is the same yesterday, today, and forever. (See Hebrews 13:8.)
- There is no change in the will of the Father. If it was His will to heal the sick while Jesus was here, it is His will to heal them today. But someone says, "Didn't Jesus heal the sick to prove His deity?" No, He healed the sick because He was love, because He was God manifest in the flesh. It was love that drove Jesus, just as it is love that drives every man and woman who is in fellowship with the Father, carrying out His will here on the earth, to heal the sick today.
- You cannot look upon the sick, if you are in fellowship with Jesus, but what you will long to do is what Jesus did for the sick.

THE CONDITION OF HEALING

- We might ask, "Well, if healing is in redemption, why doesn't Paul speak of it more often in his epistles? We will notice Romans 10:8–11:

  But what saith it? The word is nigh thee, in thy mouth, and in thy heart: that is, the word of faith, which we preach: because if thou shalt confess with thy mouth Jesus as Lord, and shalt believe in thy heart that God raised him from the dead, thou shalt be saved: for with the heart man believeth unto righteousness; and with the mouth confession is made unto salvation. For the scripture saith, Whosoever believeth on him shall not be put to shame.

- Notice: "*if thou shalt confess why thy mouth Jesus as Lord.*" The Lordship of Jesus is the first step in salvation and deliverance from Satan's dominion and authority over us, because the new creation is under the Lordship of Jesus. The old creation is under the lordship of Satan.

- The Word says, "*And shalt believe in thy heart that God raised him from the dead, thou shalt be saved* [healed]." That word "*saved,*" in the Greek, is *sozo*, which is translated "healed" throughout the Gospels and ought to have been translated "healed" here. But the translators were evidently prejudiced against healing.

- Now notice carefully the condition of healing. It is that "*thou shalt confess why thy mouth Jesus as Lord.*" Second, "*thou shalt believe in thy heart* [this recreated heart of yours] *that God raised Him from the dead,*" for He did raise Him from the dead.

- It is evident that Satan had been conquered and that disease had been put away, that Satan's dominion had been broken. And if you believe this you are healed.

- "*For with the heart man believeth unto righteousness.*" Now, he makes confession of his salvation. Salvation means deliverance from a state or condition. The state was first as a sinner. Second, as one that was sick. Whatever Satan has wrought in the spirit, in the soul, or in the body, has been healed.

- Let us get it clearly. Your confession of your healing is imperative; for notice carefully: "*If thou shalt confess with thy mouth.*" Then, "*With the mouth confession is made unto salvation* [from your sickness]."

- And then it is whosoever does this shall not be put to shame. Then it is imperative that a twofold confession be made. First, we are to confess the Lordship of Jesus, and, second, the confession of salvation or deliverance from the dominion of Satan.

- Hebrews 7:25: "*Wherefore also he is able to save to the uttermost them that draw near unto God through him, seeing he ever liveth to make intercession for them.*" The word "*saved*" here is *sozo*. So, it reads, "He is able to heal to the uttermost them that draw near unto God through Him.

- The sinner doesn't draw near to God through Jesus. The sinner accepts Christ as a Savior, and God gives him a new life. This, then, applies to the believer who has been out of fellowship with the Father, and who has had disease put upon him by Satan. Now he comes back into fellowship and Jesus makes intercession for him.

- This agrees perfectly with 1 John 2:1: "*I unto you that ye may not sin. And if any man sin, we have an Advocate with the Father, Jesus Christ the righteous.*"

- Sickness has come to the believer because of his lack of appreciation of what God has wrought for him in Christ.

THREE CLASSES OF PEOPLE HEALED

- In Mark 16:17–20, Jesus is just ready now to ascend to heaven and sit down at the right hand of the Father. He had told them,

  All authority hath been given unto me in heaven and on earth. Go ye therefore, and make disciples [or students] of all the nations, baptizing them into the name of the Father and of the Son and of the Holy Spirit: teaching them to observe all things whatsoever I commanded you: and lo, I am with you always, even unto the end of the world. (Matthew 28:18–20)

- He didn't send them to convert men. He sent them to make disciples, or students, of all men. As soon as a man was recreated and received the Holy Spirit, he was to become a student of the Word.

+ You understand that when Jesus spoke this, none of the New Testament had been written. But it was written for our admonition, so read it: *"These signs shall for them that believe"* (Mark 16:17). That doesn't mean some special faith, but every believer was to have these signs to accompany him.

+ *"In my name shall they cast out demons; they shall speak with new tongues; they shall take up serpents, and if they drink any deadly thing, it shall in no wise hurt them; they shall lay hands on the sick, and they shall recover"* (Mark 16:17–18). The people spoken of here, to be healed, are not Christians. They are the unsaved. It is a part of the evangelist's work to heal the sick. That is God's testimony, God's means of advertising.

+ Notice the twentieth verse: *"And they went forth, and preached everywhere, the Lord working with them, and confirming the word by the signs that followed."*

+ These signs were not for believers, but to the unbelieving. The first sign of healing was to the saved. If you will carefully read the book of Acts there are no believers healed with the exception of the young man who fell out of the window and broke his neck. All the other people healed were Jews under the old covenant, or Gentiles. That was God's method of advertising His message of grace that had come to all men.

+ The second class of people that were healed are spoken of in James 5:14–16:

> Is any among you sick? let him call for the elders of the church; and let them pray over him, anointing him with oil in the name of the Lord: and the prayer of faith shall save him that is sick, and the Lord shall raise him up; and if he have committed sins, it shall be forgiven him. Confess therefore your sins one to another, and pray one for another, that ye may be healed. The supplication of a righteous man availeth much in its working.

+ Notice: *"Is there any among you sick?"* The implication is that there should be no sick among us. Why? If you are a child of God and are walking in the light of the Word, you know that by His stripes you are healed. (Second Peter 2:24 makes it very clear.)

+ Paul tells us, in 1 Corinthians 3:1, *"And I, brethren, could not speak unto you as unto spiritual, but as unto carnal, as unto babes in Christ."*

+ Here is a believer that has never grown up. He doesn't feed on the Word. He has received eternal life, but he has never taken advantage of his privileges. For Paul says, *"I fed you with milk, not with meat; for ye were not yet able to bear it: nay, not even now are ye able, for ye are yet carnal [sense-ruled]: for whereas there is among you jealousy and strife, are ye not carnal, and do ye not walk after the manner of men?"* (verse 2–3).

+ There is no spiritual growth, no Word-filled lives. These are the people to whom James is writing. They have sense-ruled faith. They have faith like Thomas. He had said, *"Except I shall see in his hands the print of the nails, and put my finger into the print of the nails, and put my hand into his side, I will not believe"* (John 20:25).

+ And Jesus said, *"Blessed are they that have not seen, and yet have believed"* (verse 29).

+ That is revelation faith. The other is the faith in things. We see, hear, and feel—and then believe.

+ Notice the picture, then. The elder comes into the sick man's room. The sick man sees him. He hears him pray over him. He feels the anointing oil upon his head. The prayer of faith is not his; it is the prayer of the elder; and it has saved him that is sick, and the Lord has raised him up.

+ The whole picture is one of a sense-ruled believer, who has no faith himself in the living Word, but does trust in faith of others.

+ Hebrews 5:12 describes him: *"For when by reason of the time ye ought to be teachers, ye have need again that some one teach you the rudiments of the first principles of the oracles of God."*

- The third class of those healed is the full-grown believer. When sickness comes, he remembers that disease was laid on Jesus. "Surely he has borne my sickness and carried my diseases…and by His stripes I am healed" is the prayer of this believer. (See Isaiah 53:4–5.)
- He does not ask anyone to pray for him. He knows that if he should ask anyone to pray for him, he is repudiating the Word that Christ wrought for him. He knows that he is repudiating the Word, *"Surely he hath borne [my] griefs, and carried [my] sorrows… and with his stripes [I am] healed."*
- So he looks up quietly and says, "Father, I thank you that my sicknesses were laid on Jesus and that He bore them."
- First Corinthians 6:19–20 tells us that we are to glorify God in our bodies.

HOW MUCH DO YOU REMEMBER?

1. What are the two views of healing held by bodies of believers today?
2. What is revealed in John 5:30?
3. Did Jesus heal the sick during His earth walk to prove His deity?
4. What is the first step in salvation and deliverance form Satan's dominion?
5. Discuss the condition a believer must meet before healing becomes a reality?
6. Why is it imperative that a twofold confession be made?
7. To whom was Hebrews 7:25 written? Explain.
8. Give and explain the three classes of people healed.
9. Explain 1 Corinthians 3:1–3.
10. Give a description of a full-grown believer.

LESSON 34 NOTES

_____

_____

_____

_____

_____

_____

_____

_____

_____

_____

_____

_____

_____

_____

Lesson 35
FAITH'S REAL TEST

There are three great words that describe the condition of the believer who is taking advantage of his privileges in Christ—rest, peace and joy. These three words are the fruit of the full-grown faith.

REST

+ John 14:27: *"Peace I leave with you; my peace I give unto you: not as the world giveth, give I unto you. Let not your heart be troubled, neither let it be fearful."*

+ This peace didn't belong to the Jew under the first covenant. The only peace he knew would be national peace. But, with the new creation, it is a peace of heart, a peace of mind, a peace in his physical body.

+ Sickness is called disease, broken peace, broken rest, broken joy.

+ *"My peace I give unto you."*

+ It is not the world's peace. It is not the peace of mind, but it is the peace of heart. It is a heart peace.

+ Isaiah 26:3 is a prophecy of the church: *"Thou wilt keep him in perfect peace, whose mind is stayed on thee; because he trusteth in thee."*

+ This was to come to man on what is called *"in that day."*

+ You will find these words again and again.

+ Isaiah 27:2–5:

> In that day: A vineyard of wine, sing ye unto it. I Jehovah am its keeper; I will water it every moment: lest any hurt it, I will keep it night and day. Wrath is not in me: would that the briers and thorns were against me in battle! I would march upon them, I would burn them together. Or else let him take hold of my strength, that he may make peace with me; yea, let him make peace with me.

+ That is a prophecy of the church. It is the vine of which the Father is the husbandman, of which we are the branches. And He waters it every day. He is its keeper. He keeps it night and day.

+ Can't you see a picture of peace? The heart has come to recognize its perfect safety.

+ *"Lest any hurt it, I will keep it night and day."* Then He says the strangest words: *"Wrath is not in me."* Why? All that wrath was poured out on Jesus. That wrath dealt with sin.

+ Then the picture changes: *"Would that the briers and thorns were against me in battle! I would march upon them!"* Then He says that He wishes that all the trials and the briers and thorns in your contact with men were against Him. He would march upon them. He says, in essence, "I am sitting at the Father's right hand. I am ever interceding for you, and I am your strength and wisdom to meet every problem."

+ Now He says, "You take hold of My strength, and you drink in the nature of My Spirit, My peace."

+ Some of you have been in doubts and difficulty. This is the promise for my heart life: *"My peace I give unto you"* (John 14:27).

+ I breathed in the quietness and restfulness of my Lord. *"Great peace have they that love thy law; And they have no occasion of stumbling"* (Psalm 119:165).

+ John 16:33: *"These things have I spoken unto you, that in me ye may have peace."*

- The second word is *joy*. Joy is something that only believers have. The world may have happiness. They find that in their surroundings, their environment. But joy is a fruit of faith. It is a fruit that comes from a recreated spirit.

- But the fruit of this recreated spirit is love, joy, peace; not the fruit of the Holy Spirit. It is a product of the Holy Spirit who has recreated us, brought us into fellowship with Himself.

- Write out John 16:24:

_____

_____

- This is one of the miraculous things connected with the name of Jesus. In your prayer life you have been fellowshipping with the Father; you have been carrying out His precious will; you have been taking Jesus's place.

- You have seen your prayers answered. You have seen the mighty things of God wrought, and your heart is filled with joy that is unspeakable and full of glory. (See 1 Peter 1:8.)

- John 15:5, 7 tells us here about fruit:

    I am the vine, ye are the branches: He that abideth in me, and I in him, the same beareth much fruit.… If ye abide in me, and my words abide in you, ask whatsoever ye will, and it shall be done unto you. Herein is my Father glorified, that ye bear much fruit.

- And then in the eleventh verse: *"These things have I spoken unto you, that my joy may be in you, and that your joy may be made full."*

- Whenever our joy seeps out and leaves us barren and empty, it proves that we are out of fellowship, out of contact with Him.

- You remember that John the Baptist said in John 3:29: *"He that hath the bride is the bridegroom: but the friend of the bridegroom, that standeth and heareth him, rejoiceth greatly because of the bridegroom's voice."*

- Then he says these words: *"This my joy therefore is made full. He must increase, but I must decrease"* (verses 29–30).

- Jesus's joy is made full in us; our joy is made full in Him.

- This is one of the sweetest, most beautiful things Jesus ever prayed for us. The believer should never allow anything to rob him of his joy.

- The conquering power of the church is not knowledge of the miraculous, but joy. A joyful congregation is an attractive congregation. A joyful believer is attractive.

- Peter says in 1 Peter 1:8: *"Whom not having seen ye love; on whom, though now ye see him not, yet believing, ye rejoice greatly with joy unspeakable and full of glory."*

- In Philippians 4:1, Paul says to them, *"Wherefore, my brethren beloved and longed for, my joy and crown, so stand fast in the Lord."*

- In the fourth verse, he states, *"Rejoice in the Lord always: again I will say, Rejoice."*

- In 2 Corinthians 2:14: *"Thanks be unto God, who always leadeth us in triumph in Christ."*

- It is the triumphant, joyful spirit that makes one an attractive evangelist. The somber, discouraged face is not a good advertisement for the new creation. It is the triumphant, victorious spirit, filled with joy unspeakable and full of glory that is the evangel of grace.

REST

- The third great word is *rest;* the rest of redemption is the thing that every believer should know and enjoy.

- Hebrews 4:1: *"Let us fear therefore, lest haply, a promise being left of entering into his rest, any one of you should seem to have come short of it."*

- Every believer should read this Scripture over and ask himself, "Have I come short of this rest?"

- What kind of rest is it? It is not the rest of one who is climbing a hill with a heavy load, and then sits down for a moment and holds the load in his arms. It is the rest of one who has no burden, who has cast every burden upon the Lord.

- First Peter 5:7: *"Casting all your anxiety upon him, because he careth for you."*

- Every burden has been put over on the Master. You have come to recognize in Jesus and in the Father your perfect strength, your perfect rest, the place where nothing can disturb you.

- Philippians 4:6–7: *"In nothing be anxious; but in everything by prayer and supplication with thanksgiving let your requests be made known unto God. And the peace of God, which passeth all understanding, shall guard your hearts and your thoughts in Christ Jesus."*

- In nothing be fearful or anxious. Every anxiety has been committed to Him. This is God's formula for a life of victory.

- *"But in everything by prayer and supplication…."* With prayer and thanksgiving you have let your requests be made known unto Him.

- Then He says these mighty words: *"And the peace of God, which passeth all understanding, shall guard your hearts and your thoughts in Christ Jesus."*

- The rest of God has become your rest. The strange, beautiful quietness of Jesus seen in His earth walk has become yours. You are resting in Him. His quietness and peacefulness are yours.

- You can understand now the eleventh verse of this chapter: *"Not that I speak in respect of want: for I have learned, in whatsoever state I am, therein to be content."*

- That is rest. That is entering into His rest.

- Hebrews 4:3: *"For we who have believed do enter into that rest; even as he hath said."* What does He mean?

- We have believed. We have come to know the Word that has described the position of the believer. We have become new creations. The old things have passed away that disturbed us and kept us in bondage.

- We have no fear of the Father any more. He loves us. We love Him. We are living and walking in fellowship with Him.

- He called us into fellowship with His Son. The Son is in His rest. He has rested from His work that He wrought for us in our redemption. We have entered into that rest without works.

- We didn't have to do anything, so we are resting now in His rest. We are quiet with His quietness. We are fellowshipping Him. We have linked arms, as it were, with Him. He is our protection. He is the strength of our lives.

- Psalm 23:1–2 is a perfect illustration: *"Jehovah is my shepherd; I shall not want. He maketh me to lie down in green pastures."*

- He makes me to lie down in the quiet place, in the shadow of that great Rock. He leadeth me beside the waters of stillness. I have camped by the river of life. I am drinking deeply of its quietness, of its peace, of its love.

- You see, we are partakers of the divine nature. (See 2 Peter 1:4, 1 John 5:13.)

- That love nature is the eternal life, the nature of the Father; and the perfect love is perfect rest. It has cast out fear. Fear is the enemy of rest.

- First John 4:17: *"Herein is love made perfect with us, that we may have boldness in the day of judgment; because as he is, even so are we in this world."*

- As He is before the Father, so are we. As He is in His rest, so are we. As He is the Vine, so we are the branches.

- We have been called into fellowship with Him. We are walking in the light with Him. We live in love with Him.

- So there is no fear in love. Perfect love casts out fear. (See 1 John 4:18.)

- We have been made perfect in this love life because He has taken us over, and that love nature is in our spirits. It has the rest of heaven in it.

ENTERING INTO REAL REST

- You can see, mother, what this would mean to you in your family life. You have become tired physically, and the children nag until your spirit becomes restless and your voice is filled with irritation. You speak harshly. You are not in the place of rest.

- But you say, "How can one come into a place like that?" You remember that Scripture in Isaiah: *"Let him take hold of my strength"* (Isaiah 27:5).

- We are to take advantage of the indwelling One. You see, you asked Him to come in and dwell in you. Now, 1 John 4:4 is yours: *"Ye are of God, my little children, and have overcome them: because greater is he that is in you than he that is in the world."*

- You always remember that you are of God, and you remember that you are an overcomer.

- The irritations and vexations that come to you are nothing unless you are overwrought and are physically tired. You have allowed circumstances to get the ascendancy.

- Now the great One inside is called upon and He rises in His grace and love to meet your problem. He heals your nerves that are ragged, and irons out your difficulty. He makes you a victor over the circumstances. You have learned now the secret. In the midst of want, or poverty, or in the midst of confusion or lack, you are a conqueror.

- Right there, you are full of rest and quietness.

- A man said to his wife who had lived for a long time in the realm of rest, "How did you do it?" A fearful thing had happened. One of the neighbor's children had been accidentally injured, grievously, and she was binding up the wound. The mother was distracted; so, apparently, was everyone else. They were waiting for the ambulance to come. She was as quiet and calm as though she were caring for her own baby just dropping into slumber. She replied, "I didn't do it. *'Greater is he that is in me'* (1 John 4:4). That greater One in me gave me wisdom. Did you hear that the doctor said that I had saved the child's life? I have never studied nursing, and I knew nothing about it, but *'greater is he that is in me'* than the need that confronted me."

- Can't you see that if you give Him your life, He will give you peace? You may have the Holy Spirit in you and never give Him His place.

- The majority of people who have received the Holy Spirit, and have come in contact with my ministry, have never given Him a place in their lives.

- They have told me how great He was when He came in, but they have ignored Him and have tried to bear life's burdens alone. They have acted as though He weren't there.

- "Ye...have overcome them: because greater is he that is in you than he that is in the world" (1 John 4:4). He is greater than the world influences around you. The influence has broken upon you as a flood, but you stand as a rock and cannot be moved.
- Philippians 2:13 is becoming a living reality: *"For it is God who worketh in you both to will and to work, for his good pleasure."*
- It is God who is at work within me, building into me the Jesus-quietness and the Jesus-rest, and the Jesus-sense of the Father's presence. He is willing and working His own good pleasure in me and through me.
- It is so important that we remember 1 John 5:11–12: *"And the witness is this, that God gave unto us eternal life, and this life is in his Son. He that hath the Son hath the life; he that hath not the Son of God hath not the life."*
- You are begotten into the realm of faith. You are born into the realm of love. You were born into the realm of God, into the supernatural, victorious realm.
- Your faith becomes a part of you. As you feed and live in the Word, and the Word lives in you, there comes into you an unconscious rest, and an unconscious quietness.

HOW MUCH DO YOU REMEMBER?

1. What is the fruit of full-grown faith?
2. What is revealed in Isaiah 26:3?
3. Explain John 16:24.
4. Discuss the source of joy and of happiness.
5. What is revealed in Hebrews 4:1?
6. Explain how the rest of God becomes our rest.
7. According to 2 Peter 1:4, show how one becomes a partaker of the divine nature.
8. Explain what being independent of circumstances means.
9. Before Philippians 2:13 can become a reality to him, what condition must a believer meet?
10. Discuss fully the realm into which a babe in Christ is born.

LESSON 35 NOTES

_____

_____

_____

_____

_____

_____

_____

_____

_____

_____

Lesson 36
KNOWING THE MASTER

"I know him whom I have believed" (2 Timothy 1:12).

This is one of the challenging statements in the Pauline Revelation. Paul knew Jesus.

Second Corinthians 5:16: *"Wherefore we henceforth know no man after the flesh: even though we have known Christ after the flesh, yet now we know him so no more."*

Paul didn't know Jesus as Peter knew Him. John and Peter didn't know Jesus as Paul knew Him. Peter and John knew Him because of their three years' walk with Him, but they never really knew Him.

When He hung on the cross, they stood and watched Him. They watched Him until He died, but they didn't see the tragedy of His being made sin. They simply saw Him stripped naked, with blood streaming down His back and from His hands and feet. They only saw the crown of thorns piercing His brow until the blood flowed down over His face.

Their hearts were mightily stirred, and their tears no doubt flowed as they watched Him dying. They didn't, however, see Him made sin. They didn't know the awful spiritual struggle that was going on. They didn't see demons take that beautiful spirit and carry it away to the place where lost men are incarcerated. They only saw the Man.

There are three pictures of Jesus that I want you to see.

JESUS'S EARTH WALK

+ First is Jesus's earth walk, where love rules. It is love at work in the man.

+ In Matthew 4:23–24, we see Him come down out of the mountain from the temptation, and the multitude of the sick and the broken gather about Him, and He healed them.

+ We see Him, as recorded in the eighth chapter of Matthew, performing that series of miracles that stagger the heart—healing the centurion's servant with the Word, and casting out demons from many that were possessed, with the Word.

+ *"That it might be fulfilled which was spoken through Isaiah the prophet, saying, Himself took our infirmities, and bare our diseases"* (Matthew 8:17).

+ We see Him in the boat. Satan tried to overwhelm it. In the midst of the awful storm, He said quietly to the water, *"Peace, be still"* (Mark 4:39).

+ He ruled the sea. He ruled the wind.

+ We see Him turning water into wine. We see Him raise the dead Lazarus after he had been dead four days. (See John 11:17–44.)

+ In Luke 5:4–11, we see Him governing the fish of the sea.

+ He ruled every law of nature. He was the perfect Master.

+ But these are only one phase of His life, of His earth walk and teaching. No man ever spoke as He spoke. No man ever taught as He taught. Some of His sentences stand out like mountain peaks.

+ *"All things are possible to him that believeth"* (Mark 9:23).

+ *"The words that I have spoken unto you are spirit, and are life"* (John 6:63).

+ *"I came that they may have life, and may have it abundantly"* (John 10:10).

- But we remember that no man was saved by Jesus's teaching. No one ever really knew the Father through His unveiling and introducing the Father. No one received eternal life through His teaching.
- The fact is, there is almost nothing taught about the new creation. He told Nicodemus that he must be born again, but Nicodemus wasn't born again. He didn't understand it. I can see him looking mystified.
- Read John 3:3–8 and you will notice that Jesus is just stating the fact of the need of the new creation.
- It is strange that most of our hymns about Jesus are connected with His earth walk. Very few have to do with His present ministry at the right hand of the Father, or with His substitutionary work. You will find groups of hymns about the cross, but they are practically all about His physical suffering.
- If we could understand that the physical suffering of Jesus didn't touch the sin problem, that His earth walk didn't touch the sin problem, that His teaching didn't touch the sin problem, we would understand and know Him better.

THE MASTER ON THE CROSS

- This second picture is the Master on the cross. One day I saw lying in the street a little cross. I picked it up. It was a beautiful little cross with a dead Christ hanging on it. A part of the church has worshipped a dead Christ.
- The earth walk of Jesus didn't save anybody. Neither does a dead Christ hanging on the cross save anyone.
- If Jesus had gone no further than dying on the cross, no one would have ever been saved through Him. There is no new birth, no new creation, in the dead Christ.
- We have sung, "Nearer the Cross," and we have prayed that we might be nearer the cross; but the cross has no salvation in it.
- It was the place of failure, a place of death, a place where Jesus was made sin, a place where God forsook Jesus, turned His back upon Him after He had made Him sin. It was a place where Satan had apparently won a victory over the Man who had ruled him for three and a half years. So, for us to sing, "Jesus, keep me near the cross," is for us to be kept near failure and defeat.
- No, there is no salvation in a dead Christ or a suffering Christ hanging on the cross.
- Many who read this will feel shocked because they have worshipped a dead Christ. Had Jesus stopped, had He gone no further than the cross, we would never have heard from Him.
- You see, the disciples only understood what the physical senses registered, as they gathered about the cross and watched Him in His dead throes.

THE MASTER RESURRECTED, ASCENDED, AND SEATED

- The next picture of Jesus is the one that has brought life and light to the human race. It is the resurrected, ascended, and seated Christ.
- But I want you to see Him for a bit in His substitution, as unveiled to us in the Pauline Revelation.
- Write out 2 Corinthians 5:21:

_____

_____

_____

- That is the first step in that awful drama—He was made sin.

- Hebrews 9:26: *"But now once at the end of the ages hath he been manifested to put away sin by the sacrifice of himself."*

- The cross was the place where the two ages met, or where the two covenants met—the old and the new. It was the place where the sin problem was fixed—Deity becoming sin for humanity.

- Hebrews 1:3 declares, *"Who being the effulgence of his glory, and the very image of his substance, and upholding all things by the word of his power, when he had made purification of sins, sat down on the right hand of the Majesty on high."* Salvation is in the seated Christ at the *"right hand of the Majesty on high."*

- In Hebrews 10:10–15, we get another picture: *"By which will we have been sanctified through the offering of the body of Jesus Christ once for all"* (verse 10). It is a *"once for all"* mastery—a *"once for all"* substitution.

- Then in verses 11–12 it says, contrasting Jesus with the high priest in the old covenant: *"Every priest indeed standeth day by day ministering and offering oftentimes the same sacrifices, the which can never take away sins: but he, when he had offered one sacrifice for sins forever, sat down on the right hand of God."*

- It was not His earth walk; it was not suffering on the cross that made us righteous. The cross was the beginning. It was where substitution really began when God made Him sin with our sins.

  > *Surely he hath borne our griefs, and carried our sorrows; yet we did esteem him stricken, smitten of God, and afflicted. But he was wounded for our transgressions, he was bruised for our iniquities; the chastisement of our peace was upon him; and with his stripes we are healed. All we like sheep have gone astray; we have turned every one to his own way; and Jehovah hath laid on him the iniquity of us all.* (Isaiah 53:4–6)

- You see the whole drama until the time He was made sin, but you don't see sin put away. That comes after He has left His body and goes to the place where the wicked should go and will go if they reject Him. There, for seventy-two hours, or three days and three nights, He suffered until the claims of justice were fully met.

- When they were met, Satan's dominance over Him ended. I can hear God say, "It is enough. He has met the demands of justice. He has paid the penalty that the human race owed to justice for its sin."

- Hear this Scripture in Hebrews 10:12: *"But he, when he had offered one sacrifice for sins forever, sat down on the right hand of God."*

- When He had met every demand of justice, when every claim against us was met, then 1 Timothy 3:16 became a reality—He was justified in spirit. First Peter 3:18 says that He was made alive in spirit.

- Paul expressed it in Acts 13:33: *"That God hath fulfilled the same unto our children, in that he raised up Jesus; as also it is written in the second psalm, Thou art my Son, this day have I begotten thee."*

- Jesus, down there in that dark region, was made alive in spirit, was begotten of God, so that Colossians 1:18 has become a fact.

- Beginning with the fourteenth verse, we read:

  > *In whom we have our redemption, the forgiveness of our sins: who is the image of the invisible God, the firstborn of all creation; for in him were all things created, in the heavens and upon the earth, things visible and things invisible, whether thrones or dominions or principalities or powers; all things have been created through him, and unto him; and he is before all things, and in him all things consist.* (verses 14–17)

- Now notice carefully: "*And he is the head of the body, the church: who is the beginning, the **firstborn from the dead**; that in all things he might have the preeminence*" (verse 18).

- You see, there is the Creator, just as you see it in 1 John 1:4. And the One who was made sin, and that One died spiritually on the cross.

- He died twice, physically and spiritually. He was made alive twice, in spirit and in His body. His spirit was made alive and His body immortal. He was the first person that was ever born again, and the only One who has immortality now.

- When He said, "*This day have I begotten thee*" (Hebrews 5:5), that was the second birth there.

- Jesus was first born of Mary. Now He is born of God. Once He was born as a sweet, beautiful infant. The second time, He was born out of death and Satan's dominion. He has passed out of the realm of Satan into the realm of God.

- Colossians 1:13–14 perfectly illustrates it. He was translated out of the authority of darkness and death, and was translated by the new birth into the fellowship and communion with His Father.

- You see, He is the Firstborn of all creation. No one was ever born again before that time. He is the head of the church, and as soon as He was born again, He became once more the Master of Satan; He became the Master of the forces of darkness in Hell.

- Colossians 2:15 tells us that He despoiled the principalities and powers and made a show of them openly, triumphing over them.

- He was the strong One that had entered into the very throne room of Satan and bound him and tripped him of his authority.

- Hebrews 2:14: "Since then the children are sharers in the flesh and blood, he also himself in like manner partook of the same" (ROTHERHAM). In other words, the Word became flesh upon that cross that He might bring to naught him that had the authority of death, that is, the devil.

- You see, on the cross He died spiritually, a partaker of sin—not of His own volition. God laid upon His spirit our sin, and the moment He did that, Jesus's spirit became sin. Then His body became mortal. He died spiritually so His body could die physically.

- A few hours after that, physical death gained the ascendancy. His spirit left His body.

- But now all things have changed. He has become the Master of Hell. He has conquered Satan. He has stripped him of the authority that Adam gave him in the fall in the great temptation. He arose from the dead, and I arose with Him. You arose with Him.

- Then He took His own blood and carried it into the heavenly Holy of holies and sealed our redemption. Having accomplished this, He sat down at the right hand of the Majesty on High.

- Ephesians 2:5–6 says that we are seated together with Him. He is the Head of the body. We are his members. John 15:5 tells us that He is the Vine and we are the branches.

- Philippians 3:10 is Paul's marvelous prayer: "*That I may know him, and the power of his resurrection.*" For it is that ability that was manifest in His resurrection. It is that ability that is at work within us.

- Ephesians 1:19–20: "*And what the exceeding greatness of his power to us-ward who believe, according to that working of the strength of his might which he wrought in Christ, when he raised him from the dead, and made him to sit at his right hand in the heavenly places.*"

- That ability is our ability. That ability is the Spirit's, who dwells within you, and in the name that He has given us to use in our daily conflict with the enemy.

- You understand that there are two kinds of wisdom. One is the wisdom that comes from experience, of the senses. It is earthly, sometimes sensual and sometimes devilish. The other kind is the wisdom that comes from God, the kind of wisdom that Jesus exercised in His earth walk.

+ Jesus is made unto us wisdom. (See 1 Corinthians 1:30.)
+ Now that wisdom will unveil to us the sacred secrets that are hidden in the Pauline Revelation of Christ. He says, *"Unto all riches of the full assurance of understanding, that they may know the mystery of God [or the sacred secret of God], even Christ"* (Colossians 2:2).
+ Now notice the next verse: *"In whom are all the treasures of wisdom and knowledge hidden"* (verse 3).
+ With joy you can catch a glimpse of what it means to learn in a measure to know Him.

HOW MUCH DO YOU REMEMBER?

1. Contrast Paul knowing Jesus and Peter and John knowing Him.
2. What is revealed in the three pictures of Jesus?
3. Could men receive eternal life through Jesus's teaching while He walked among them?
4. What did the death of Jesus mean to the disciples?
5. What was the significance of the cross?
6. Give Scripture and contrast Jesus with the High Priest of the old covenant.
7. Why can we not see sin put away on the cross?
8. Explain Jesus's twofold death and His twofold birth.
9. Explain Ephesians 2:5–6.
10. Discuss the sources of the two kinds of wisdom.

LESSON 36 NOTES

_____

_____

_____

_____

_____

_____

_____

_____

_____

_____

_____

_____

_____

_____

_____

_____

_____

Lesson 37
THE REALITY OF THE RECLAIMED HUMAN SPIRIT

This phase of teaching has never has never been majored by our theological thinkers. It is the crux of the whole Pauline Revelation, the ultimate toward which all of God's plans move.

Man, the failure, the sin-ruled, the Satan-dominated, held in bondage by the unseen forces of spiritual darkness, is to be recreated, made a new creation, taken out of the family of Satan, and *"translated…into the kingdom of the Son of his love"* (Colossians 1:13), on legal grounds.

This is the solution of the human problem: God giving His nature, His love, to fallen man.

NEW CREATION MAN

+ He is no longer a fallen man. He is a new creation man united with Jesus Christ, the Head of the new creation. He is the *"raised together with Christ"* (Colossians 3:1) man.
+ Second Corinthians 5:17: *"Wherefore if any man is in Christ, he is a new creature: the old things are passed away; behold, they are become new."*
+ His old sin consciousness, his old fallen life, his old sin life, and his old evil habits that grow out of spiritual death, have passed away.
+ He is a new creation. He is a new being.
+ The Father has no memory of his past life. He is a newborn babe.
+ His old past life has stopped being in the mind of the Father.
+ A new creation has come into being through grace.
+ Second Corinthians 5:18: *"But all things are of God, who reconciled us to himself through Christ, and gave unto us the ministry of reconciliation."*
+ Way's translation states it beautifully:

    And of all this God is the source. He reconciled me to Himself by the mediation of Messiah; and He has assigned to me the office of this reconciliation, the Charter whereof is God was present in the Messiah reconciling to Himself the world, cancelling the record of their transgressions.

+ He has given us through Christ the ministry of reconciliation; not the ministry of condemnation that we have had for the last hundred ears, but a ministry of reconciliation.
+ We have reckoned unto men their trespasses. We have kept them "trespass-minded." We have kept them conscious of their weaknesses and failings.
+ We have preached sin instead of eternal life.
+ We have preached judgment instead of reconciliation, when God has committed unto us the "word of reconciliation."
+ We have that Word. We have that message. It is ours to give to the world.
+ We have become new creations. We have been recreated by love. Love has been imparted to our spirits.

- God is love, and God's nature is love; but God is also life, the Author of life. So, He has imparted to us His life nature, His love nature. God has imparted His nature to us, making us new creations. That nature is righteousness. It is holiness. It is reality. It is love. It has been imparted to us.

- We are ambassadors on behalf of Christ, and we are entreating the world to be reconciled to God. Why? Because *"Him who knew no sin he made to be sin on our behalf; that we might become the righteousness of God in him"* (2 Corinthians 5:21).

- God made Jesus sin to the end that He could make us righteous through the new creation.

- We have a reconciling message of love to give to the world. It is not a message of condemnation, but of reconciliation; not of judgment, but of love.

- Jesus was made sin, was judged, and suffered all that we would have suffered had we rejected Him. By our acceptance of Him we entered into all that He purchased for us.

- This message is not an appeal to human reason or sense knowledge, but the Father's appeal to our spirits.

- We ought to understand that the Father does not reveal Himself to our reasoning faculties but to our spirits. Our reasoning faculties can only apprehend the things that the five senses convey to them. Outside of that, the reasoning faculties are unfruitful.

- When our spirits are recreated, they receive eternal life.

- We can know the Father. We can enjoy fellowship with Him through His Word. We have become to utterly identified with Him, so utterly one with Him, that the "vine and the branch" is the only suitable illustration of this new and beautiful relationship.

- We are a part of the vine life. We are bearing the love fruit of the vine life. Our spirits enjoy the reality of Christ in the world.

- Our minds may not be able to grasp it; but if we let our minds be renewed by acting on the Word and meditating in it, our minds and spirits will come into sweet fellowship with each other.

- The recreated human spirit never grows old. It has received eternal life. It has become one with the Father.

- Our bodies will grow old. Our minds will grow old because they derive all their knowledge from the body.

- If our spirits can gain the ascendancy over our bodies, they will keep our minds from aging, and our bodies in a vigorous, healthy, youthful condition.

- Sense knowledge wanes with the senility of the senses.

- The senses will wear out and lose their freshness and beauty unless they are renewed by a recreated spirit.

- The development of our recreated spirits comes by meditating in the Word, acting on the Word, and letting the Word live in us and become a part of us.

SOME FACTS

- Christianity is a relationship between the Father and His family.
- It is not a religion.
- It is not having your sins forgiven.
- It is not joining the church.
- It is being made a new creation in Christ; it is being born from above.
- It is receiving the nature and life of God.
- It is being united with Christ.

RECREATION AND REMEPTION

- Romans 6:5: *"For if we have become united with him in the likeness of his death, we shall be also in the likeness of his resurrection."*

- We are united with Him in resurrection life.

- The new creation is to enjoy the dominion that Adam lost in the fall.

- In Ezekiel 36:26–27, He speaks out His heart's dream:

  > *A new heart also will I give you, and a new spirit will I put within you; and I will take away the stony heart out of your flesh, and I will give you a heart of flesh. And I will put my Spirit within you, and cause you to walk in my statutes, and ye shall keep mine ordinances, and do them.*

- Man was to have a new heart. That means that his heart was to be recreated. When the Lord speaks of the heart, He means the spirit, the real man.

- The new creation is the outstanding miracle of redemption.

- On the day of Pentecost, when the Spirit recreated one hundred and twenty in the upper room, God began the "new thing." They had more than forgiveness of sin; they had new natures; it was union of love with man; it was the new order of things.

- Second Corinthians 5:17: *"Wherefore if any man is in Christ, he is a new creature."* They are a new species.

- The expression *"new creature"* means a new thing, something unheard of before. This new man was an unknown thing just as the first Adam was an unknown being.

- This new love nature means that the old order of selfishness is ended and the new love life is begun.

- The new creation is a God-man, born of heaven. He is to be ruled by the Lord. He has been ruled by Satan.

- He is called in Hebrews 10:38, the righteous one, the God-made one. *"But my righteous one shall live by faith."*

- He is the new love man ruled by our love-Lord, Jesus. He was by nature a child of wrath. He is by the new nature, a child of God. The God who created man in the beginning is recreating man now.

- John 3:3–8 says that the recreated man is born from above:

  > *Jesus answered and said unto him, Verily, verily, I say unto thee, Except one be born anew, he cannot see the kingdom of God. Nicodemus saith unto him, How can a man be born when he is old? can he enter a second time into his mother's womb, and be born? Jesus answered, Verily, verily, I say unto thee, Except one be born of water and the Spirit, he cannot enter into the kingdom of God. That which is born of the flesh is flesh; and that which is born of the Spirit is spirit. Marvel not that I said unto thee, Ye must be born anew. The wind bloweth where it will, and thou hearest the voice thereof, but knowest not whence it cometh, and whither it goeth: so is every one that is born of the Spirit.*

- He is born of the Word and of the Spirit. Read these verses carefully and you will notice that he is recreated by the will of the Father. He is a wanted child.

- James 1:18: *"Of his own will he brought us forth by the word of truth."*

- We are recreated by the Spirit through the Word.

- First Peter 1:23: *"Having been begotten again, not of corruptible seed, but of incorruptible, through the word of God, which liveth and abideth."*

- No man recreates himself. It is purely the work of God.
- The only part we have in it is to consent to God's giving us His nature and to recognize the Lordship of the new Head of the new creation, Jesus.
- Ephesians 2:8–10:

  For by grace have ye been saved through faith; and that not of yourselves, it is the gift of God; not of works, that no man should glory. For we are his workmanship, created in Christ Jesus for good works, which God afore prepared that we should walk in them.

- When you know that you have been recreated by God Himself, you know that the work is satisfactory to the Author of the work. It gives you a real foundation for faith.
- Our chief difficulty has been the sense of unworthiness that has robbed us of faith and fellowship with the Father. This is due to our ignorance of what we are in Christ, and of what the new birth means to the Father, and may mean to us.
- Write out Ephesians 4:24:

  _____

  _____

- We are created in righteousness. We are created out of the very nature and heart of the Father; so that when He declares that we are created of righteousness and holiness, and of reality (or truth), we know that we can stand before the Father without any sense of guilt or sin.
- We know that the new creation is the righteousness of God in Christ.
- First John 5:13: *"These things have I written unto you, that ye may know that ye have eternal life, even unto you that believe on the name of the Son of God."* So, then, eternal life is received in Jesus's name.
- Romans 8:14–17 is the climax of redemption as outlined in this epistle:

  For as many as are led by the Spirit of God, these are sons of God. For ye received not the spirit of bondage again unto fear; but ye received the spirit of adoption, whereby we cry, Abba, Father. The Spirit himself beareth witness with our spirit, that we are children of God: and if children, then heirs; heirs of God, and joint-heirs with Christ

- This is the climax of redemption. This is the objective toward which God was working: to bring man into the actual relationship of a son through his partaking of God's nature, eternal life.
- Galatians 4:5–7:

  That he might redeem them that were under the law, that we might receive the adoption of sons. And because ye are sons, God sent forth the Spirit of his Son into our hearts, crying, Abba, Father. So that thou art no longer a bondservant, but a son; and if a son, then an heir through God.

- The Jews were the servants of God; we are the sons of God. First John 3:2: *"Beloved, now are we children of God."* John 1:13: *"Who were born, not of blood, nor of the will of the flesh, nor of the will of man, but of God."*
- This should forever settle the question of whether there is anything that an unsaved man can do to give to himself the new birth outside of his acceptance of Christ as his Savior and Lord.
- All of his crying, weeping, repenting, and confessing of sins has no bearing upon it whatever.

- This is hard for us to accept because we have been ruled by the teaching of the Dark Ages—the teaching of works.
- The church is under bondage today to the blend of Hinduism, Grecian philosophy, and the Christianity that we find during the Middles Ages.
- All that Luther saw was justification by faith. He has no clear conception of a new birth, of righteousness, of God as a Father, or of our place as sons and daughters of God. He saw it vaguely. He saw one truth. That one truth brought him out of bondage and gave to Germany a new civilization.
- First John 5:1: *"Whosoever believeth that Jesus is the Christ is begotten of God."*
- The fourth verse reads, *"For whatsoever is begotten of God overcometh the world: and this is the victory that hath overcome the world, even our faith."*
- The new creation is an overcomer. He is begotten of God. He is united with God. He is a partaker of God's nature.

HOW MUCH DO YOU REMEMBER?

1. Tell how recreating the spirit solves the human problem.
2. Explain 2 Corinthians 5:18.
3. What is the work of an ambassador?
4. To what part of man does God reveal Himself? How?
5. Why does the recreated human spirit never grow old?
6. Tell what being united with Him in resurrection life means to the believer.
7. Explain Ezekiel 36:26–27.
8. In recreating the human spirit, what is man's part?
9. What gives to the believer a real foundation for faith?
10. What is the objective toward which God was working in redemption?

LESSON 37 NOTES

_____

_____

_____

_____

_____

_____

_____

_____

_____

_____

_____

_____

Lesson 38
EXERCISING OURSELVES IN THE WORD

We spend a great deal of money in building gymnasiums and in training our youth and young manhood in physical exercises. Our schools, colleges, and technical institutions are for the exercising of the mind.

How little we know about exercising our spirits. The church has never realized that the spirit of man is the foundation of faith—that faith is not the product of sense knowledge begotten of reason.

You see, all the knowledge that we have has come through the senses. There is nothing creative in the senses. The senses merely receive physical facts and transmit them into mental signs.

No school of thought has ever recognized that man is a spirit, and that the fountain of all creative ability is in his spirit. We know now that no people ever became inventors or creators, great scientists, or great musicians until that nation has received eternal life, the nature of God.

THE RECREATED SPIRIT

+ That nature of God doesn't come into man's reasoning faculties. It comes into man's spirit. Man's spirit is the fountain, then, of all man's creative and inventive ability.

+ We ought to learn how to cultivate this recreated human spirit. Spiritualists and mediums have cultivated the un-recreated human spirit and turned it over to the devil to be educated, and they perform prodigious and miraculous things. The séances are spiritual, but they are never the product of the recreated human spirit. They are the product of a demon-possessed and controlled human spirit.

+ The recreated human spirit contacts divine ability and resources. It isn't only the fountain of creative energy and ability, but it is the fountain of faith. How little we have appreciated the fact that the faith that Jesus exercised and that the church has demonstrated down through the ages, is the product of the recreated human spirit.

+ You see, God is a faith God and He imparts His faith nature to man in the new creation. If man could only learn how to develop his recreated spirit, he would develop his faith capacity and faith ability. You see, faith has given birth to all the great achievements of man.

+ The great achievements of our modern man are the product of eternal life in the spirit of man. One of the amazing things is that the children of men and women who have received eternal life carry with them as a prenatal gift the divine ability, the latent ability, the creative ability of God. The sons of clergymen and of outstanding Christians have been the great leaders of all the great moral, intellectual, and spiritual forces of our nation.

+ But the recreated human spirit not only produces creative ability and faith, but it is the source of love. "Love is shed abroad in our hearts by the Holy Spirit" (see Romans 5:5). It is the fountain out of which this new kind of love springs. We have learned that natural man in the heathen state, where he hasn't contacted Christianity, has no love. He has sexual attraction, and he has the same care for his children that wild animals have for their offspring until they are able to care for themselves, but he does not love. He has no sense of relationship.

+ You remember that David didn't raise his own children. They were put out among the leaders of Israel.

+ Eternal life has been given to man. With it comes a new kind of love, and that new kind of love has affected his children. There is hardly a family of recreated people who haven't had in their ancestry men and women who had received eternal life.

- The modern divorce court unveils the utter selfishness of natural man.
- There is another thing. That recreated spirit gives birth to faith, creative energy, and love. It is the fountain out of which all wisdom comes.
- Wisdom is not the product of sense knowledge. Sense knowledge may gather and garner from experience a lot of ability and what we call natural wisdom, but the wisdom that comes down from above, the wisdom that Jesus was made to be to you (God made Him to be wisdom to us, that new kind of wisdom) is the thing that comes from the human heart. I have been long convinced that if a believer would cultivate his spirit's creative ability and wisdom ability, that he would be the most outstanding personality in his community. How we should learn to exercise ourselves along this line. Just as we have exercised ourselves physically to build up muscle, as we have exercised mentally to build up memory and store our minds with facts and data, so we now should build up our love life, build up our wisdom life, build up our creative energy.

STRENGTHENING THE SPIRIT WITH THE WORD

- How? By feeding on the Word of God. The Word is God's wisdom, God's ability, God's very life. As I feed on it, it cultivates, strengthens, and builds up my spirit. It builds faith into me. It builds God's ability into me. It builds into me every attractive thing that you saw in Jesus's life.
- Committing the Word to memory does not do it; learning the history of the books of the Bible does not do it; learning the Hebrew and the Greek words will not do it. Only one thing will do: my doing the Word, practicing it, living it in my daily life, trusting in it, acting on it. That is our secret.
- First Timothy 4:6–8:

  > If thou put the brethren in mind of these things, thou shalt be a good minister of Christ Jesus, nourished in the words of the faith, and of the good doctrine which thou hast followed until now: but refuse profane and old wives' fables. And exercise thyself unto godliness: for bodily exercise is profitable for a little; but godliness is profitable for all things, having promise of the life which now is, and of that which is to come.

- Notice that we are to be nourished in the Word. We are to nourish ourselves. We are to cultivate ourselves. We are to drink the sincere milk of the Word (see 1 Peter 2:2–3) until our spirit rules our thinking faculties. They, in turn, rule the senses.
- But notice verse 7: "But refuse profane and old wives' fables. And exercise thyself unto godliness." This is an exercise in the Word. You give yourself to the Word.
- Hebrews 4:12 (MOFFATT): "For the Logos of God is a living thing; and active and sharper than any two-edged sword, piercing even to the dividing of the threefold man: body, soul, and spirit."
- This living Word is quick to discern the thoughts and intents of the heart. You meditate in that. You see how the Word is unveiled to us in our spirits, our thinking faculties, and our body, showing the relationship, one to the other. That living Word is the thing that should direct our thinking, our meditations.
- Psalm 19:14: "Let the words of my mouth and the meditation of my heart be acceptable in thy sight, O Jehovah, my rock, and my redeemer."
- The man who controls his meditation will control his conduct and control his speech. When we learn the secret of meditating in the Word, yielding our minds over to the Word, then Psalm 104:34 becomes a reality. Our meditation will be sweet unto Him, and we will rejoice in Jehovah.

- Our spirits can be so developed, so strengthened, that we will become God-minded, Word-minded. In the morning our minds unconsciously go to Him for guidance and wisdom for the day. We have exercised ourselves in the Word until our whole being is saturated with it.

- Hebrews 5:12–14 should be carefully studied. None of us have passed beyond it: *"For when by reason of the time ye ought to be teachers, ye have need again that someone teach you the rudiments of the first principles of the oracles of God; and are become such as have need of milk, and not of solid food"* (verse 12).

- Most of the believers are faith seekers. They distrust their own faith. They are looking for someone who can pray the prayer of faith for them. They are like the ones Paul speaks of in Timothy—ever learning but never arriving. (See 2 Timothy 3:7.) They have never yet reached the place where their spirits are quiet and restful. They are having a continual combat with the adversary.

- One said to me, "I have had this combat with the adversary for thirty years. I didn't know Colossians 2:15: *'having despoiled the principalities and the powers, he made a show of them openly, triumphing over them in it.'"*

- What does this mean? It is Jesus's combat with the adversary for us before He arose from the dead. He was our substitute, and His combat with the adversary was our combat. He defeated Satan, stripped him of his authority before He arose from the dead. This victory becomes ours when we remember that the adversary that is combating us is conquered, that he is our subject instead of our master. Then we should say, "In Jesus's name, demon, you leave me," and he must go.

- Hebrews 2:14: *"Since then the children are sharers in flesh and blood, he also himself in like manner partook of the same; that through death he might bring to nought him that had the power of death, that is, the devil."*

- Notice this: that Satan was defeated, conquered, stripped of his authority; and you, by your union with Christ, have become a master of the devil. Exercise yourself in the Word, now, until that thing becomes a reality to you.

- Moffatt's translation of 1 Corinthians 2:6: *"We speak wisdom, however, among them that are full-grown; not a wisdom of this age nor of the dethroned rulers of this age."* Who are the dethroned rulers? They are demons and demon-ruled men.

- Jesus gave us a legal right to the use of His name. Write out John 14:13–14:

_____

_____

_____

- The word *"ask"* can be translated *"demand."* It is His promise to us of the use of His name in dealing with demons and disease, just as Peter used it in Acts 3:6, when he said to the man at the Beautiful Gate, *"In the name of Jesus Christ of Nazareth, walk."* Paul also used it in Acts 16:18: *"But Paul, being sore troubled, turned and said to the spirit, I charge thee in the name of Jesus Christ to come out of her. And it came out that very hour."*

- When one exercises himself in the Word until this Word becomes a reality to him, he instantly becomes the master of demons. He remembers in a crisis hour that Satan has been defeated and that Jesus gave to us the power of attorney to use His name.

- In Mark chapter 16, He said, *"In my name shall they cast out demons"* (verse 17). If you can cast out one demon, you can cast out any demon. If you can heal a disease in the name, you can heal any disease; for He said, *"They shall lay hands on the sick, and they shall recover"* (verse 18).

- You see, you become so strong in the Word that you dominate the circumstances around you. You understand that faith is not the product of sense evidences, but faith is something that grows out of your spirit that has walked in the Word, lived in the Word, and in which the Word has lived and dominated, until it becomes utterly one with the Word.

+ You remember that Jesus said, "*I am the vine; ye are the branches*" (John 15:5). There is a oneness between you and Jesus because you are a branch of the Vine. The same is true with the Word. There comes an utter oneness between you and the Word. The Word abides in you.

+ You see, that is not an intellectual thing. It is a spiritual thing. "*If ye abide in me, and my words abide in you, ask whatsoever ye will, and it shall be done unto you*" (John 15:7).

+ If you are a child of God, you do abide in Him. If that Word has found its place in your life, governing, teaching, and admonishing you in every phase of your walk, then it abides in you and you live in the Word.

+ Just as you walk in love, live love, breathe love, now you walk in the conscious authority and ability of that Word in your life. You see, it is the living Word in your lips that heals sick folks, that saves lost men, that puts courage and strength into the faint-hearted.

+ It is your consciousness of the authority of that Word in your lips. You say to yourself, "The Word of God in my lips is as effectual as it was in the lips of Peter or John, because it is the Word of my Father that I am using."

+ Hebrews 5:13: "*For every one that partaketh of milk is without experience of the word of righteousness.*" That is one that never eats anything but the first principles of their redemption. That is, they say, "Yes, I have been saved and sanctified. I have received the Holy Spirit, and I have done this and that." But they haven't grown any. They say it as a parrot repeats words it has heard.

+ But the full-grown believer has not only received eternal life, but has gone on in the study of the Word and in the practice of the Word. He has had experience in the Word that teaches about his righteousness. You know, righteousness means the ability to stand in the presence of the Father without the sense of guilt or of inferiority.

+ You are not afraid of Satan. You are not afraid of disease. You are not afraid of lack of money. You are fearless, because you have experienced the reality of the living Word in your own heart life.

+ You see, "*But solid food is for fullgrown men, even those who by reason of use have their senses exercised to discern good and evil*" (Hebrews 5:14). They have exercised themselves in the Word, and not their senses, until they have become absolutely master in their spiritual walk.

+ You remember 2 Corinthians 9:10: "*And he that supplieth seed to the sower and bread for food, shall supply and multiply your seed for sowing, and increase the fruits of your righteousness.*"

+ The sense of guilt and inferiority robs us of fruit bearing. When we recognize the integrity of the Word and enter into our inheritance of righteousness, we become fruit bearers.

+ Philippians 1:20 gives us a beautiful illustration: "*According to my earnest expectation and hope, that in nothing shall I be put to shame, but that with all boldness, as always, so now also Christ shall be magnified in my body, whether by life, or by death.*"

+ Paul wanted Christ to be magnified in his body through the things he did and said. He wanted Jesus to be magnified, made attractive, so that men would want Him. This can only come as we exercise ourselves in the Word.

HOW MUCH DO YOU REMEMBER?

1. What is the source of man's creative ability?
2. Explain how the recreated human spirit is cultivated.
3. Explain fully the products of the recreated spirit.
4. Explain 1 Timothy 4:6–8.
5. Why is it that many Christians are "faith seekers"?
6. Give Scripture, and tell why the believer need not combat the adversary.
7. Who are the dethroned rulers?
8. What authority does the child of God exercise of dethroned rulers?
9. What does "experience in the word of righteousness" mean?
10. Explain Philippians 1:20.

LESSON 38 NOTES

_____

_____

_____

_____

_____

_____

_____

_____

_____

_____

_____

_____

_____

_____

_____

_____

_____

_____

_____

_____

Lesson 39
CHRIST'S PRESENT MINISTRY FOR THE CHURCH

Christ's great substitutionary work and His work in the new creation would be of no value if He didn't take care of and protect this new creation by means of His present ministry.

JESUS'S RESURRECTION

+ Matthew 28:5–6 gives us the story of His resurrection, of the women coming to the sepulcher and seeing the angel who said, *"Fear not ye; for I know that ye seek Jesus, who hath been crucified. He is not here; for he is risen, even as he said. Come, see the place where the Lord lay."*

+ He died as Jesus. He died as a Lamb. He arose the Lord High Priest.

+ John 20 gives another little picture of His resurrection. Mary had gone to the sepulcher and found the stone rolled away. In verses 12–13, we read,

> *And she beholdeth two angels in white sitting, one at the head, and one at the feet, where the body of Jesus had lain. And they say unto her, Woman, why weepest thou? She saith unto them, Because they have taken away my Lord, and I know not where they have laid him.*

+ Then she turned around and looked behind her:

> *And beholdeth Jesus standing, and knew not that it was Jesus. Jesus saith unto her, Woman, why weepest thou? whom seekest thou? She, supposing him to be the gardener, saith unto him, Sir, if thou hast borne him hence, tell me where thou hast laid him, and I will take him away. Jesus saith unto her, Mary. She turneth herself, and saith unto him in Hebrew, Rabboni; which is to say, Teacher.* (verses 14–16)

+ She fell at His feet, but Jesus said, *"Touch me not; for I am not yet ascended unto the Father"* (verse 17). He was saying, "I must first go to the Father and carry my blood in into the Holy of holies, which must be accepted by the Supreme Court of the universe as the red seal upon the document of your redemption."

+ Hebrews 9:12–14:

> *Nor yet through the blood of goats and calves, but through his own blood, entered in once for all into the holy place, having obtained eternal redemption. For if the blood of goats and bulls, and the ashes of a heifer sprinkling them that have been defiled, sanctify unto the cleanness of the flesh: how much more shall the blood of Christ, who through the eternal Spirit offered himself without blemish unto God, cleanse your conscience from dead works to serve the living God?*

+ In Hebrews 2:17, Jesus is called the merciful and faithful High Priest in the things pertaining unto God in making propitiation for the sins of the people.

+ The first ministry at the right hand of the Father was to satisfy the claims of justice against humanity.

+ Romans 4:25 illustrates this: *"Who was delivered up for our trespasses, and was raised for our justification."*

- He was not raised until we were justified. He was not raised until the Supreme Court of the universe was satisfied.
- Now He takes His blood into the Holy of holies and puts His red seal upon that document.

JESUS'S MINISTRY AS SAVIOR

- His next ministry is that of a Savior.
- Acts 4:12: *"And in none other is there salvation: for neither is there any other name under heaven, that is given among men, wherein we must be saved."*
- He is the sinner's only Savior, but the sinner cannot reach God without a Mediator.
- Hebrews 8:6: *"But now hath he obtained a ministry the more excellent, by so much as he is also the mediator of a better covenant, which hath been enacted upon better promises."*
- This is taken with 1 Timothy 2:5: *"For there is one God, one mediator also between God and men, himself man, Christ Jesus."*
- His substitutionary work would have been of no value to the unsaved man unless Christ had become the Mediator between the unsaved and the Father.
- Job illustrates this in Job 9:33: *"There is no umpire betwixt us, that might lay his hand upon us both."*
- Job recognized the need of a Mediator. The unsaved might cry to God for a thousand years, but if there is no Mediator, there would be no hope for them. No man can approach God except through the Mediator.
- John 14:6: *"I am the way* [to the Father], *and the truth* [there is no reality outside of Him], *and the life."* That life is eternal life, the nature of God. Here is His master sentence, *"No man cometh unto the Father, but by me."*
- Man not only needs a Mediator, but after he becomes a Christian, he is living in a world dominated by Satan and needs an Intercessor, someone who will pray for him, whose prayers are always heard.
- Hebrews 7:25: *"Wherefore also he is able to save to the uttermost them that draw near unto God through him, seeing he ever liveth to make intercession for them."*
- His ministry of intercession is little appreciated by the believer. In every temptation, in every trial, and at every hard place, Jesus ever lives to pray for us. That is the reason for our victory.
- Paul says, in Philippians 4:13, *"I can do all things in him that strengtheneth me."* Strength comes through His intercession.
- First Peter 5:7: *"Casting all your anxiety upon him, because he careth for you."*
- The Father's love is manifest in the intercessory work of His Son. He is not only our High Priest, Savior, and Mediator, but whenever we sin and our fellowship is broken, we have someone at the right hand of the Father who ever remains faithful.
- First John 1:9: *"If we confess our sins, he is faithful and righteous to forgive us our sins, and to cleanse us from all unrighteousness."*
- When we lose our sense of righteousness, and the adversary has gained the ascendancy, then we make the confession of our sins and we cry for mercy. Jesus takes up our case.
- He is the righteous One. He can stand for us. When we lose our sense of righteousness, He can restore us again to our fellowship.
- Righteousness, you understand, is the ability to stand in the Father's presence without a sense of guilt or inferiority. You understand that when a believer sins, he doesn't lose his place as a son, but he loses his fellowship.

- Jesus is our family lawyer. He ever lives to watch over those for whom He died and suffered. It is one of the most wonderful things in the world to me that we have a heavenly Lawyer.

- Now you understand Hebrews 9:24. Write out this verse:

_____

_____

_____

- When the heart can remember that Jesus is there on our behalf, and that he loves us even as He loved us before He died for us, it can joyfully come with boldness. He loved us as sinners, but now we are His redeemed ones, members of His very body.

- John 15:5: _"I am the vine, ye are the branches."_

- It is the Vine caring for the wounded branch. It is the Vine that depends to utterly upon the branch for the fruitage of the world. So, He is in the presence of the Father on our behalf now.

- Now you can understand Hebrews 4:14–16:

  > _Having then a great high priest, who hath passed through the heavens, Jesus the Son of God, let us hold fast our confession. For we have not a high priest that cannot be touched with the feeling of our infirmities; but one that hath been in all points tempted like as we are, yet without sin. Let us therefore draw near with boldness unto the throne of grace, that we may receive mercy, and may find grace to help us in time of need._

- Can't you see what it means to have a High Priest, a Mediator, an Intercessor, an Advocate, and a Lover in the highest seat of authority in the universe? He ever lives to make intercession for you.

- Now He bids you to come boldly to the throne of grace. That means that you are to come into His presence with your needs. You are in the throne room, and the Father that loved you and gave His Son up for you is on the throne. The Man who loved you and gave Himself up for you is seated by His side, there to love you.

- You come boldly now because they have made you a new creation. They have made you the righteousness of God in Christ. (See 2 Corinthians 5:21.) You are now His very righteousness because you are a partaker of the divine nature. You are a very son, a very daughter, and He is your own Father.

- Can't you see what it can mean to you to come into a throne room under such conditions? There is your Advocate. There is your Savior. There is your Lord on your side.

- Can't you hear Him say, "How will He not with Him freely give you all things?" (See Romans 8:32.)

- Romans 8:31: _"What then shall we say to these things? If God is for us, who is against us?"_

- Your heart becomes quiet. You look up into His face and whisper your request. You know it is going to be granted. How your heart thrills with joy. You are making your request with thanksgiving because it is your Father who is on the throne.

- It is your Lord who is seated by His side. With that fearless confidence you make your requests—those requests that are coming in continually from men and women with sick loved ones you take with fearlessness into your Father's presence.

- There is no sense of unworthiness. You become His righteousness. Jesus is your Sponsor. You have a legal right to stand in His presence without a sense of guilt or inferiority if you are His. (See Hebrews 4:16.)

- This is His throne room. You are one of His own family.

- Now you can understand what it means to hold fast your confession. The old version gives it "profession" but the new version is better. We hold fast our confession. Your confession has been of your position in Christ, of your legal rights as a child of God, of what He is to you now as a Father, and of what Jesus is as Savior, High Priest, and Advocate. You have dared to confess that you are more than a conqueror. You have said boldly now, *"In all these things we are more than conquerors through him that loved us"* (Romans 8:37).

- You have known Romans 8:33–35: *"Who shall lay anything to the charge of God's elect? It is God that justifieth; who is he that condemneth? It is Christ Jesus that died, yea rather, that was raised from the dead, who is at the right hand of God, who also maketh intercession for us."* Then the Spirit triumphantly cries: *"Who shall separate us from the love of Christ?"* There can't be anything. Satan has no ability to do it. Circumstances can't do it; sin can't do it because we have our own Advocate, we have our own Savior, our own Intercessor. We are more than conquerors.

- But I want you to turn with me to Hebrews 7:21–22. After he has been discussing the fact of the disannulling of the old covenant and the establishing of the new covenant, he says this about Jesus: *"Thou art a priest forever; by so much also hath Jesus become the surety of a better covenant."*

- You see, here is the secret of faith. Jesus is the Surety of every word from Matthew 1 to Revelation 22.

- Here is where the heart rests with a quiet sense of security. Jesus is the Surety, the Guarantor of every word. If any Scripture should go by default, Jesus becomes responsible. He said, *"Heaven and earth shall pass away, but my words shall not pass away"* (Matthew 24:35).

- We are in the presence of absolute faithfulness. The integrity of the Scripture is based upon the throne, and the throne upon the very heart and life of the Father and the Son.

- If the Word can be broken, the throne can be overturned. That cannot be. *"No word from God is void of power [or fulfillment]"* (Luke 1:27).

- Isaiah 55:11: *"So shall my word be that goeth forth out of my mouth: it shall not return unto me void, but it shall accomplish that which I please, and it shall prosper in the thing whereto I sent it."*

- Jeremiah 1:12: *"For I watch over my word to perform it."*

- The word of the angel to Mary in Luke 1:37 verifies this: *"For no word from God shall be void of power."* There isn't anything that can void (make of none effect, or rob of its verity or strength) this living Word.

- You are depending on that Word. Jesus and Word are one. *"In the beginning was the Word"* (John 1:1). Jesus was that Word. The universe has been brought into being by the Word of God. That is the Word that we are depending on.

- You see, when you are talking about the Word you are talking about the foundation of the throne of God, the throne by which Jesus is seated.

- Jesus is the Surety of that throne, but I want you to go beyond that, and notice that Jesus is not only all that I have told you, but He is our Lord.

- Notice this wonderful sentence in 1 Corinthians 1:2: *"Unto the church of God which is at Corinth, even them that are sanctified in Christ Jesus, called to be saints, with all that call upon the name of our Lord Jesus Christ in every place, their Lord and ours."*

- We can say, "Their Lord and mine." "He is my Lord. The one who loved me and gave Himself up for me." (See Galatians 2:20.)

- Now notice this: He is my Lord here on earth in His relationship to the body, but He is my Head in heaven.

- Ephesians 1:22: *"And he put all things in subjection under his feet, and gave him to be head over all things to the church."*
- He is our heavenly Head, and the church is His body, *"the fulness of him that filleth all in all"* (verse 23).
- Colossians 1:18: *"And he is the head of the body, the church: who is the beginning, the firstborn from the dead; that in all things he might have the preeminence."*
- He is my heavenly Head. I am a part of His body. He loves me.

HOW MUCH DO YOU REMEMBER?

1. What provision has God made for the care and protection of the new creation?
2. Explain Hebrews 2:17.
3. Why was it necessary for Christ to become Mediator?
4. What is the ministry of Christ as Mediator?
5. What does Hebrews 7:25 reveal?
6. Explain what having an Advocate can mean to the believer.
7. Explain Isaiah 55:11.
8. Tell what Jesus, the Surety, means.
9. Explain 1 Corinthians 1:2.
10. In His relationship to the body, what is Jesus here on earth? In heaven?

LESSON 39 NOTES

_____

_____

_____

_____

_____

_____

_____

_____

_____

_____

_____

_____

_____

Lesson 40
WE ARE MORE THAN CONQUERORS

"Nay, in all these things we are more than conquerors through him that loved us" (Romans 8:37).

He has recapitulated all the things that can assail the believer, and He has made the believer more than a conqueror.

Few of us have realized that our combat is with the eternally defeated one. How few folks know that Satan was eternally defeated when Jesus arose from the dead, that He couldn't have risen until Satan was defeated, and that Jesus was to be the Head of an unconquerable body!

Sin consciousness had been the outstanding enemy of the believer, but there is no ground for it. If one knew that sin and sins were put away when he was born again, that there was no past that could ever confront him again, it would change his life completely. (See 2 Corinthians 5:17–27.)

Everything that he has ever been and everything that he has done was put away, his sins were remitted. His nature that has led him to sin has been changed. A new nature has taken its place. The blood has cleansed him. He is now utterly one with Christ. He is complete in Him.

Colossians 2:9–10: *"For in him dwelleth all the fulness of the Godhead bodily, and in him ye are made full, who is the head of all principality and power."*

THE FATHER'S WORK

+ That completeness is a result of the Father's own work. Ephesians 2:10: *"For we are his workmanship, created in Christ Jesus for good works."*

+ The Father couldn't create anything in His Son that wasn't perfectly well pleasing to Himself. We have been created in His Son.

+ The actual working out of that is described in 2 Corinthians 5:17–18: *"Wherefore if any man is in Christ, he is a new creature: the old things are passed away; behold, they are become new. But all things are of God, who reconciled us to himself through Christ."*

+ That new creation is a new species that stands complete and perfect in the Father's presence. This new creation is as perfect as the first creation was in the garden. The difference is that this new creation is a son, an heir of God, and a joint heir with Jesus Christ.

+ You can see what this means. It puts them over into the same class with Jesus—as conquerors.

+ Romans 8:1 was written for us, this new creation people. Write out this verse:

_____

_____

_____

+ Take also this Scripture, Romans 8:31–34:

> *What then shall we say to these things? If God is for us, who is against us? He that spared not his own Son, but delivered him up for us all, how shall he not also with him freely give us all things? Who shall lay anything to the charge of God's elect? It is God that justifieth; who is he that condemneth? It is Christ Jesus that died, yea rather, that was raised from the dead, who is at the right hand of God, who also maketh intercession for us.*

- In these four verses we have the assurance of the Father's being on our side, and that He has freely given us all things that pertain to godliness and to a life of victory in this present evil age in which we are living. He challenges anyone to lay anything to our charge. We are God's elect. God has recreated; God has justified us. God has made us what we are.

- In the thirty-fifth verse it says, *"Who shall separate us from the love of Christ?"* It can't be done. You are more than a forgiven sinner. You are a recreated son of God, a master of demons. In the mind of the Father you are utterly one with Jesus. But it doesn't end there.

- Your triumph, your victory, makes it possible for you to stand in the Father's presence just as though you were Jesus Himself.

- Do you know what is implied in that? If you can stand in the Father's presence without condemnation, you can stand in the presence of Satan or demons in any place without fear. You are Satan's master.

- 2 Corinthians 5:21: *"Him who knew no sin he made to be sin on our behalf; that we might become the righteousness of God in him."*

- We have become the righteousness of God in Christ, and by becoming the righteousness of God in Christ we have become masters of all unrighteousness. We are the masters of the forces that have made unrighteousness.

- Righteousness, here, means the ability to stand in the Father's presence without the sense of guilt or inferiority, or condemnation.

- You are superior to the forces of darkness. You are a master of everything that is evil.

- I don't know whether you are familiar with John 1:16 or not: *"For of his fullness we all received, and grace for grace."* What is that fullness? It is what Jesus is in Himself. That is what made Him what He is.

- When you received eternal life, you received the very thing that makes Jesus what He is. You received of the Father His very nature; so if you have received into your spirit that which makes God what He is, you are like Him.

- When the church recognizes this, it is going to revolutionize the whole structure.

- Jesus and Paul spoke the Father's words. That is what made Jesus omnipotent. The same omnipotence is in the Pauline Revelation for us. You can say, "I am what He says I am." He has said that you are His child, and you are what He says you are. (See 1 John 3:2.)

- Now *"in all these things we are more than conquerors"* (Romans 8:37), and we are more than conquerors through Him that loved us.

- There is no earthly power or demoniacal power that can separate us from the Father's love that was in Jesus. You are His own, and He is yours.

VICTORY CONSCIOUSNESS

- Let us go over some facts on which you can build a stable consciousness of victory. These Scriptures that we are going to use are all familiar to you.

- Colossians 1:13–14: *"Who delivered us out of the power of darkness, and translated us into the kingdom of the Son of his love; in whom we have our redemption, the forgiveness of our sins."*

- You have been delivered out of Satan's dominion by the new birth. You have been translated into the family of God by the new birth. When that thing took place, everything that pertained to the old life stopped being. Satan's dominion ended right there. Everything that Satan brought into the world by Adam's transgression has been nullified and brought under the dominating power of the new creation in Christ.

- There is a perfect redemption. When your heart knows it as you know heat and cold, Satan's dominance ends.

- Then take the next Scripture that we have given you: *"Wherefore if any man is in Christ, he is a new creature"* (2 Corinthians 5:17). Did you notice something? *"The old things are passed away."* What are the old things? They are failure, weakness, fear, a sense of unworthiness. They have stopped being.

- What are you? You are a branch of Christ. You are a part of Christ just as the branch is a part of the vine. You are a part of Christ, and Christ is God. (See John 15:5.)

- The same wonderful characteristics that were manifested in the earth walk of Jesus now can be manifested in you. All it requires is that you take your part and make your confession as boldly as Jesus made His.

- From our angle, as we look at the Master, we can see that the secret of His victory lay in His continual confession. He held fast to His confession.

- It says in 1 Timothy 6:13, speaking of Jesus: *"Who before Pontius Pilate witnessed the good confession."*

- Now your battle is directed in the twelfth verse: *"Fight the good fight of the faith, lay hold on the life eternal."*

- The good fight of faith is a battle that has been won a long time ago, in which you do nothing but acknowledge the defeat of your enemy and your own victory in Christ. The fight of faith is not a struggle on your part. It is a recognition and a confession on your part of the victory that you and Christ won over the adversary in that great substitutionary battle that took place before He arose from the dead.

- You were identified in that. You were crucified with Him. You were buried with Him. You were raised with Him. You conquered the enemy with Him.

- Now, with faith planted solidly upon this foundation, you face your enemy without fear. You dare to say, "I am the righteousness of God in Christ."

- Just as Jesus dared to say, *"I am the vine, ye are the branches"* (John 15:5); or, *"I am the light of this world"* (John 8:12); you say, "I am what He says I am." More than even that you can say, "I can do what He says I can do."

- Philippians 4:13: *"I can do all things in him who strengtheneth me."*

- You see, we are moving out of the realm of weakness into the realm of victory; and you can say, "I am more than a conqueror, for I am complete in Him who is the head of all principalities."

- Then you remember 1 John 4:4: *"Ye are of God, my little children, and have overcome them: because greater is he that is in you than he that is in the world."*

- That settles it. You are born of God, created in Christ Jesus. You are now a master. You are becoming God-inside conscious. You are learning to let Him have His place in you.

- Just as in the past we have given freedom to our feelings and have said things that at time were unseemly, now we are giving place to the One who is shedding abroad in us the very nature and life of the Father.

- We are saying to Him, "Holy Spirit, take charge of my speech, my thinking. Govern all the faculties connected with reason and teach me how to live as the man Christ Jesus lived."

- You see, you can't fail Him, for He won't fail you. You have a legal right to His ability wrapped up in that wonderful name.

- John 14:13–14: *"And whatsoever ye shall ask in my name, that will I do, that the Father may be glorified in the Son."*

- That isn't prayer. That is demanding the forces of darkness to be broken over the lives of men. You are acting in the place of the Master now. You have unsheathed the sword of the spirit, this living Word, and in your lips that living Word becomes a dominating force as it was in the lips of the Master.

- You see, you are united with Him. He is the Vine and you are a branch. You grew out of Him. You were created in Him. Don't forget your perfect union with Him.

- My heart has feasted on Romans 6:5–6:

  > For if we have become united with him in the likeness of his death, we shall be also in the likeness of his resurrection; knowing this, that our old man was crucified with him, that the body of sin might be done away, that so we should no longer be in bondage to sin.

- That new man has taken the place of the old man. There is a vital, absolute union between your spirit and the Spirit of Christ. It is as vital as the branch is vital in its union with the vine. You bear His name now, and He bears you.

- He has made you what you are, and you recognize what you are and give place to the new thing. That way, you glorify Him.

- If you demean yourself and talk about your lack, you rob Him of the glory of His finished work in you and you give place to the adversary's dominance. You must never do it. You must get used to being what you are. That may be hard with all the Christians about you magnifying weakness and failure, but you must magnify your union with Christ, your utter oneness with Him.

- You can do it. He is your very strength this day. He is your ability.

- You remember Psalm 23:1: "Jehovah is my shepherd [that is Jesus]; I shall not want."

- Now prophecy is turned into reality. I whisper, "I do not want. He kept me to live in the midst of fullness instead of in the desert place. I am drinking deeply of the water of life, the drink that satisfies. I am walking in the green pastures of His fellowship. I am enjoying the fruitage of His wonderful love life.

- You see, in all these things He and I are utterly one. I am getting to visualize myself as I really am in Him. It has been a struggle to get away from the old pictures that I had before my mind. All my early teaching was a struggle with sin that I would never get over till I died. I was to wage a battle continually day by day. Now I enter into the victory of the battle that is won in Christ."

- Someone said, "What would you do if sin had never been?" Then I saw a picture. Why, the Father acts toward me, toward us, as though we had never sinned. "Beloved, now we are the children of God" (1 John 3:2).

- And take 1 Corinthians 1:9: "God is faithful, through whom ye were called into the fellowship of his Son Jesus Christ our Lord."

- Let us put it in the first person: "My Father is faithful to me. He has called me to come and walk with His Son, to live with Him, to carry on the Son's work in His absence. He has called me to fellowship with Him."

- He is my Lord. And there is that strange expression, "God is faithful." Faithful to whom? Why, He is faithful to His Son who made it possible for me to be recreated, to become His very son. He is faithful to me as a son. He has called me as a new creation to fellowship with the Head of this new body called the church, and to fellowship with His children.

- Fellowship means eating together, bearing up under pressure together, drinking from the same cup. He has called me to drink with Jesus, to live with Jesus, to share with Jesus in the saving of lost men and the building up of the body through the Word.

- The Father acts as though sin had never been as far as I am concerned. When He recreated me, He forgot all about my past. Why, the new creation has no past. It is a "now creation."
- This is victory. There are no theories here that cast a dark shadow over the past life, but they are all wiped out. Now we are in the Beloved.

HOW MUCH DO YOU REMEMBER?

1. Explain what being a "conqueror" can mean to the believer.
2. Show the difference between God's first creation and the new man.
3. Explain John 1:16 fully.
4. On what authority can the new creation say, "I am what He says I am"?
5. Give Scripture and discuss how the believer builds a stable consciousness of victory.
6. What was the secret of Jesus's victory?
7. Explain Romans 6:5 fully.
8. How can the child of God rob Him of the glory of His finished work?
9. What is the Father's attitude toward the recreated ones?
10. What does the term, "In the Beloved" reveal?

LESSON 40 NOTES

_____

_____

_____

_____

_____

_____

_____

_____

_____

_____

_____

_____

_____

_____

_____

_____

_____

_____

ABOUT THE AUTHOR

Dr. E. W. Kenyon (1867–1948) was born in Saratoga County, New York. At age nineteen, he preached his first sermon. He pastored several churches in New England and founded the Bethel Bible Institute in Spencer, Massachusetts. (The school later became the Providence Bible Institute when it was relocated to Providence, Rhode Island.) Kenyon served as an evangelist for over twenty years. In 1931, he became a pioneer in Christian radio on the Pacific Coast with his show *Kenyon's Church of the Air*, where he earned the moniker "The Faith Builder." He also began the New Covenant Baptist Church in Seattle. In addition to his pastoral and radio ministries, Kenyon wrote extensively. Among his books are *The Blood Covenant, In His Presence, Jesus the Healer, New Creation Realities*, and *Two Kinds of Righteousness*.